SULTAN TO SULTAN

Adventures of a woman among the Masai and other Tribes of East Africa

by

May Fench Sheldon

Trotamundas Press Ltd.
The Meridian, 4 Copthall House, Station Square, Coventry
CV1 2FL, UK

"Sultan to Sultan" by May French Sheldon

First published in 1892 by Arena Press, Boston, USA

ISBN: 978-1-906393-13-7

Trotamundas Press is an international publisher specializing in travel literature written by women travellers from different countries and cultures.

Our mission is to bring back into print great travel books written by women around the world which have been forgotten. We publish in several languages.

It is our privilege to rescue those travel stories which were widely acclaimed in the past and that are still relevant nowadays to help us understand better the diversity of the countries and the world.

The travel stories also make an enjoyable reading, full of adventure and the excitement of discovery.

We are proud to help preserving the memory of all those amazing women travellers which were unjustly forgotten and hope that you will enjoy reading about their interesting experiences as much as we have enjoyed researching them.

www.trotamundaspress.com

MAY FRENCH SHELDON (1847-1936)

In the last half of the nineteenth century, Africa was still the 'dark continent,' with large areas of its territory unmapped. Tribes in many regions had not been subdued, and from their initial contacts with Arab slavers and Western explorers, they were often hostile to foreigners. Diseases against which outsiders had no immunities had been named but not cured. Roads and even trails were almost nonexistent. But these very obstacles made Africa an irresistible challenge to adventurers. Most, of course, were men, but one of the more remarkable, unconventional, and brave of these explorers was a middle-aged American woman by the name of May French Sheldon, who in 1891 planned and led an expedition to East Africa. For her it was not enough just to follow the trail of the male explorers. Her aim was to prove that women could do whatever men could do.

For her trek from the port of Mombasa, across the territories of some thirty-five tribes, up to the towering peak of Kilimanjaro, May engaged 138 porters. Thinking her at best eccentric or more likely mad, the British authorities in East Africa tried to prevent her departure. The reason they put forth merely infuriated her: they declared that East Africa was no place for a lady. That was bad enough but worse was to come. What she saw as she moved inland of the relations with the natives caused her to comment that the British and German policies were 'unnecessary, atrocious, and beyond the pale of humanity'.

May French Sheldon had her own ideas on how to express the respect she felt for the natives. For instance, in order to 'meet the men of tribal importance in their own sultanates, as a woman of breeding should meet the highest officials in any land, under any circumstances, and be civil and polite for favors granted,' she adopted a ceremonial costume which, among other things, consisted of a spangled ball gown and a voluminous blond wig.

The astonished natives renamed her Bebe Bwana, 'Woman Master,' and a delighted London press took up the title in satirical articles. But there was a seriousness to her travels. May contributed learned papers on little-known topics such as the navigation of Lake Chala, and she made some of the first ethnographic studies of African women and children. It is the latter work which today stands out as a major accomplishment. Along with her contemporary Mary Kingsley, Sheldon was among the first white people to describe Africans and African culture sympathetically.

On the basis of her first successes, May organized a second expedition to the Belgian Congo in 1894 and a third to Liberia in 1905. She went on, she explained, because exploration gave her 'very much thought, and imagination thrilled my brain with the ineffable pleasure, which I had craved, and sought for years, of being the first to visit a place undefiled by the presence of man before.'

Recognition of her pioneering studies came in 1892 in the form of election to membership in the Royal Geographical Society, then a very rare honor for a woman.

TABLE OF FULL-PAGE ILLUSTRATIONS.

TABLE OF FULL-PAGE ILLUSTRATIONS.

CHAPTER XIV.

CHAPTER XV.

CHAPTER XVI.

CHAPTER XVII.

CHAPTER XVIII.

CHAPTER XIX.

CHAPTER XX.

CHAPTER XXI.

TABLE OF CONTENTS.

CHAPTER I.

CHAPTER II.

CHAPTER III.

CHAPTER IV.

CHAPTER V.

CHAPTER VI.

CHAPTER VII.

CHAPTER VIII.

CHAPTER IX.

CHAPTER X.

CHAPTER XI.

CHAPTER XII.

CHAPTER XIII.

CHAPTER XIV.

CHAPTER XV.

CHAPTER XVI.

CHAPTER XVII.

TABLE OF TEXT ILLUSTRATIONS.

CHAPTER I.

CHAPTER II.

CHAPTER III.

CHAPTER IV.

CHAPTER V.

CHAPTER VI.

CHAPTER VII.

CHAPTER VIII.

CHAPTER IX.

CHAPTER X.

CHAPTER XI.

CHAPTER XII.

CHAPTER XIII.

CHAPTER XIV.

CHAPTER XV.

CHAPTER XVI.

CHAPTER XVII.

CHAPTER XVIII.

CHAPTER XIX.

CHAPTER XX.

CHAPTER XXI.

CHAPTER XXII.

SULTAN TO SULTAN.

CHAPTER I.

HO! FOR EAST AFRICA.

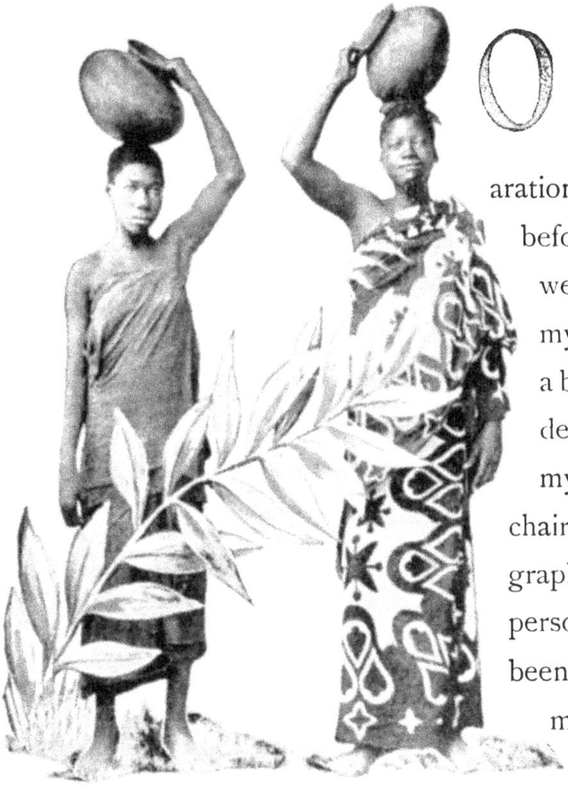

O For East Africa! possessed my brain when all the preparations possible to make before reaching Aden were completed, and a myriad of boxes and a bewilderment of nondescript packages — my tent, gun, table, chairs, pistols, photographic apparatus, and personal effects — had been sent by steamer to meet me at Naples, and for the first time I felt I was without doubt actually bound for East Africa. A hundred or more sympathetic friends and acquaintances, thronging the Charing Cross Station, albeit London was benighted in a pea-soup fog, thick, black, damp, and chilly, I was thrilled with ineffable delight. Gruesome remarks were intermingled with inspiring words of faith in my success: "Well, you have my prayers for safe return." "*If* you return alive, what a story you'll have to tell!" "Do be reasonable, and abandon this mad, useless scheme." "Brave woman, you'll accomplish all you aim to; we owe you a vote of thanks for your courage and self-sacrifice." "Be cautious, vigilant, ready for any surprise, careful of your health, and you'll win," said Surgeon T. H. Parke. And A. Bruce, the sturdy son-in-law of the great Livingstone, thrust into my hands a long-range field glass, as if to bid me be far-sighted. "Remember, nothing is accomplished without giving yourself up to the work at whatever sacrifice, and that honest failure is not defeat. We believe you will succeed." His true words were branded on my brain indelibly, and echoed through my thoughts time out of number. Around me pressed lovely girl friends, sentimental hero-worshippers, who set the

HENRY S. WELLCOME.

E. L. SHELDON.

seal of admiration upon my lips by their farewell kiss, and whispered, "*How I wish I could go with you!*" Sedate man friends looked compassionately at my husband, and involuntarily calculated that the time would be brief ere he should regret his consent, which I had flouted widely, as evidence that when he sanctioned my undertaking, it was not irrational. We were off midst cheers, pelting of flowers, and the usual half-hysterical, frantic commotion attending a departure where a friend's life seemed at stake. At last the cars were speeding away from London town, and my husband and two friends, H. S. Wellcome, Surgeon T. H. Parke, and myself were the sole occupants of the railway carriage, destined for Dover. The conversation was somewhat constrained; however, the good doctor heaped upon me a host of practical advice, the outcome of his expansive experience respecting the preservation of my own health, and the amelioration of probable sufferings from the inevitable *African fever;* as well as how to administer the contents of my extensive medical kit in behalf of my caravan. He had taken pains to write out minute directions, and so plainly that a child could follow such in fullest detail. At Dover we parted from our two friends. Arriving at Calais, we hastily counted up the luggage and met the first difficulty. The railroad officials had not prop-

SURGEON T. H. PARKE.

erly notified the manager of rolling stock of the dimensions of my Palanquin, which proved too large to get into the luggage vans. Cables were flashed back to London. We implored the officials, at our risk of damage, to place the box containing it upon a coal truck, or even to rip off the casing, all to no purpose; *red tape* prevailed to such a degree not one official on the spot had authority to make the slightest innovation. The station master waved the detested green signal flag, then came the demon screech of the unthrottled engine, and away we whisked out of the station, yelling out of the window, until beyond hearing, messages to the officials, finally to relapse in silence, and deliberate as to what should be our next move. Considering we had paid over ninety-five dollars (eighteen guineas) to register the Palanquin as personal luggage, we felt duped. Personally, I secretly thought it was rather absurd to think of trying to take the luxurious article with me, when it was next to impossible to have it transported from England to the coast of Italy after every care, forethought, and prearrangement had been devoted to make it absolutely sure that it would go on the same train with us. At every station we raided the telegraph offices, made supervisory arrangements with station masters, saw various American consuls, in the hope of more effectually engaging the attention of railroad officials. Everything was being done at both ends. Unluckily, the luggage we had with us was left in charge of a dazed servant, who sat calmly by and allowed part of it to be carried away from our train. This then had to be sent back for. Then on reaching the Italian frontier the cases containing my medicines were suspected, but fortunately I was provided with a certified inventory furnished by the Italian consul at London, so this was soon adjusted. On reaching Naples, the steamship "Madura" had not been sighted, but was expected hourly, and would not remain in

NAPLES.

port but a few hours. News also came that the Palanquin had reached Rome, and would arrive next morning; alas! in the usual course of things this would be too late for the ship, and hence, as a last resort, it would have to be taken to Brindisi, and shipped on the French Line to meet my ship at Aden. However, through the courtesy of the directors of the British East India Steamship Company, the agent was authorized to detain the steamer one day for the Palanquin.

My "white elephant" arrived, and was held in durance at the bonded warehouse. The entire day we passed going from office to office showing my passports, testifying as to who I was, and what I proposed to do, and having the cased mystery in all of its grandeur unboxed, examined, commented upon, explained; finally the next day — the ship had been

ADEN.

swinging at anchor for my benefit for twenty-four hours — the Palanquin was sent in charge of custom-house officials to be delivered personally by them upon the ship, so that it could not be tampered with ; one might have supposed it was a portable article I could pocket and surreptitiously sell to defraud the government.

The heat was torrid. Worry and our unflagging efforts had occupied our minds to the exclusion of the diresome thoughts of parting which would otherwise have made those last hours painful and melancholy. My husband accompanied me to the steamship and placed me in charge of Capt. James Avern. Striving to keep my courage up, I took snap-shots of the harbor and finally of the one whose devoted heart was aching with apprehension. The time to haul up the anchor came. Then the signal "all ashore," we parted, and the boatmen, awaiting the last passenger, pulled the oars with song, the last ineffable look was interchanged, the handkerchief that had defiantly fluttered farewell was soon saturated in tears. A resolution to acquit myself bravely occupied my thoughts as I watched the one dear to me fade from the horizon, and pondered, half oblivious to my immediate surroundings, when suddenly I became conscious that I was the cynosure of strange eyes. A firm step sounded on the deck behind me, and a voice gently said,—

CAPT. JAMES AVERN.

"So you are ho! for East Africa, madam?"

"If the steamer does not go to the bottom, yes," I snapped out with acrimony, to the amusement of the inopportune, curious interloper. Poor fellow, he had an objectionable, obtrusive nose for news, and was my constant tormentor throughout the voyage. Alas! he died after a brief fortnight's residence at Zanzibar, a victim to the indiscretion so many strangers are guilty of upon going to the tropics, which is too often fatal. Reckless exposure to the sun and violent exercise, which produces excessive heat, so intolerable to the impatient novice that the dripping clothing is inconsequently stripped off, a cold bath indulged in, which results in a sudden chill, and mischief sets in usually with gravity.

Capt. Avern, an expert seaman and an unfailing commander, as well as a man of varied experience, I found rich in expedients, and an invaluable counsellor and instructor for me upon almost all matters. My East African project was a theme of unremitting conversation. Everything was done for

STEAMSHIP "MADURA."

my personal comfort, amusement, and contentment, from the commander down to the lowest menial of the steamer's crew. There were beside myself only two first-class passengers,—men,—and soon the steamship "Madura" assumed the aspect of a private steam yacht. The captain, a most agreeable host, took apparently great delight in contributing to our individual tastes and entertainment. The "Madura" has its own history, is most famous, every timber athrill with the recollection of the tread of celebrated travellers and explorers, animated by every imaginable motive, who have trod her decks going to, or returning triumphant, or left as prey of death

THE DREDGE, SUEZ CANAL.

in Africa. The reminiscences of this vessel would comprise not only a graphic story, but give a history of startling events and tell of leaders who have acted as great discoverers and civilizers; of brave people, who knew how to be faithful to their leaders or the reverse,—a story of misguided infatuates, of honest workers, of benefactors, of selfish worldlings, of ambition's votaries, of despair's victims; yet with all, she floats on serenely, unruffled, steadfast to her course, making no visible sign of her invested greatness or reflected honors, unstained, excepting possibly the ink splashes with which I carelessly defaced her spotless decks, and for which I was more than once gently but severely reprimanded by the deck master.

Lovely mornings, bright, sparkling, clear as a crystal, with the unabashed moon hanging resplendent in the blue sky as if loitering to feel the full embrace of the uprising sun. As we passed through the Straits of Messina, in full view of the Apennine Mountains, then came Sicily and Mount Etna, the last sight of land until we reached the Egyptian coast,— a most felicitous contrast to the London fog, and conducive to mental exhilaration and physical exuberance. Just the thing to sweep the cobwebs out of one's brain and allow the mind to adjust itself to a proper focus, as well as to rest the body, and impart that order of courage belonging to physical well-being.

Then came fickle weather, the Ides of March were having a jubilee,—sunbursts, rain, even hail,—an ideal time to read, ponder, rearrange boxes, study photographic apparatus, etc.

A ship's rat established my reputation as a "brave lady." The impudent rodent explored my legs and tested my nerves! For some unknown reason, I was not in the least excited, only surprised and anxious to know how to rout the enemy. A sneeze did it! Throughout the voyage this rat was a constant visitor to me, and I became attached to the

BRIDGE BUILT BY NATIVE ENGINEERS.

little four-footed friend, nightly placing in a convenient spot a tidbit for his refreshment. He never molested me only to manifest his presence by passing his rough, coarse, hairy paw over my face. I would not consent to have a trap set to capture him.

PORT SAID JETTY.

The atmosphere was particularly clear; and although the stars were peerlessly brilliant, they seemed but few. Orion shone marvellously, and one began to mark the course of the vessel by the starry atlas. Sighting Daimetta Light, in a little over an hour we dropped anchor at Port Said, a coaling station, before entering the Suez Canal. Filled with anxiety to hear news, we all hung over the side of the vessel watching the boats pull up from shore, when a messenger brought me a cable from the gallant Capt. Nelson bidding me God-speed, and other lightning flashes from beloved friends that were like heart-throbs.

Port Said Jetty, so picturesque, seemed all too beautiful as the first impression of the strange Arabic town.

The tendency of invariably overcharging for any little article one desires to purchase impressed me with the idea that there prevails a strong Semitic strain, and unless a voyager holds out for fairness, he is sure to be the victim of extortion. During the progress of some purchases the proprietor of the quaint shop ordered a pot of Arabic coffee, served piping hot in dainty cups, thick as pea soup, but most aromatic and delicious. The Arabic quarters have a most villanous aspect; not a place one would select to promenade alone during hours the shops might be closed.

To all appearances the old gambling dens, wherein so many outrages were committed in former times, have been shut, but there is always some underhand round-the-corner avenue to gain access thereto. Nights when the mail steamers are expected, even though they arrive at two A. M., the entire town is ablaze, and every shop or, strictly speaking, bazaar is open wide to display within and without the attractive goods. Accompanied by some one who is well up in the little commercial arts and tricks, the cost of local specialties is far below English and French charges for the same articles.

Lack of confidence prevails to such an extent that even the sheiks in charge of boats, unless paid in advance by the passengers, accompany them to see that the boatmen do not filch the fees or pocket gratuities. The coaling barges stations are brilliantly lighted by cassolets, blazing with their oil or resinous beacons. Each steamship company's agent

ENTRANCE TO SUEZ CANAL.

arranges before the arrival of any steamer belonging to his particular line for the required supply of coal, and on its arrival a coal barge is moored alongside, and Egyptian coal heavers and carriers, wearing only a meagre loin-cloth and head-pad, carry the coal in baskets up a slanting plank, with such systematic regularity and rapidity they reminded me of a well-chain.

There is a total absence of women everywhere. The long, spotless, flowing white and sombre black robes of the men, their picturesque turbans and elaborate sandals, and their infinite grace while walking, make them noticeably effeminate; but there is an air of repression or secretiveness in their mien, a seeming lack of honest frankness, which forced upon me the conviction that I should much prefer to face these Arabs rather than to have them follow behind me. Egyptian and native laborers make the line of distinction between master and servants unmistakable.

If a steamer is not fitted with electric lights before being permitted to enter the Suez Canal, the requisite apparatus must be hired at a fixed sum, with an expert engineer in attendance. The canal is a marvel, especially when one considers that it was projected under the reign of Pharaoh Necho, 600 B. C., whereas De Lesseps made himself famous by renewing the original plan in an extensive way, and by this water-way between the Mediterranean and Red Seas he

BEDOUIN CHIEF.

has given a boon to the commercial world almost without parallel; reducing the distance from London to India from 11,397 miles to 7,628, thereby shortening the voyage by the Cape thirty-six days. The extreme narrowness of the canal, most of its length of ninety-nine miles, makes the traffic somewhat congested, and the nearness to the white sand banks at times painfully glaring, and the far-away mountains cut across the sky in ragged peaks, limiting the lateral horizon. The electric lights, displayed on the flotilla of steamers, lends to a night transit a weird splendor. The rule of navigation, which is strictly enforced the length of the canal, obliges steamers in sight and all following farthest away from the station, when two or more approach in opposite directions, to tie up until the other passes. This is a great trial to pilots, as it exhausts time and greatly retards progress. However, it is an absolute law, violation of which inflicts a heavy penalty upon the culprit, and is impartially applied to all. A signal from the station approached determines the right of way for all vessels.

At Ismailia we saw how the dredging machines excavated the bottom sand from the channel, carried it in a long trench and heaped it upon the banks, strengthening and increasing the levees. At this point, scarcely visible in the distance, is the chalet, built for the Empress Eugenie's reception when the inaugural functions attending the opening of the canal were celebrated. The sight provokes the thought of the downfall of an Empire, and later the downfall of a man who, at one time, was on the pinnacle of fame as an engineer. It again suggests scenes far away beyond the Biblical days, until the mind loses itself in contemplating the wondrous changes that time has wrought.

We pass an Arab camel caravan, and for the first time saw women unveiled. One woman, whom I was scanning

ARAB CAMEL CARAVAN.

through my field glasses, prior to taking a snap-shot, glared at me, and with precipitation jerked up from the banks in her arms a quaint-looking little dog, cast a defiant glance towards me, as she discovered that she was the object of my observation, and tossed the little pet upon a camel's back into a saddle made like a nest with rugs and blankets, and covered it from my *evil eye*. This act accomplished, she rushed to the water's edge and followed the course of the slowly moving steamer, imprecated and railed at me in the most vehement manner—about what?—ah! ask the Arabs who heard. This caravan was bound for the Holy Land, and a set of more villanous-appearing land sharks I never beheld. Unclean, utterly miserable, degraded beings, knowing only a migratory life, in common with their camels and their vermin, devoid of principle, eking out a questionable existence by cunning, extortion, and mendicancy. Successions of caravans of similar character occupied the foreground of the panoramic scenes; some were laden with two great, square

WATER CARAVAN.

boxes, balancing each other on either side, containing or being filled with soft, fresh water, for which the Arabs would demand from pilgrims or travellers a fabulous sum during transit across the sandy deserts en route to or from the Holy Land.

Suez presents an architectural appearance of a substantial shipping and commerical city. The background of mountain ranges breaks the monotony of its flatness, and lends a pleasing perspective.

SUEZ.

From this point the days were glorious, and the choppy sea, with white crests, truly grand. A hot sun, but sprightly fanning breezes, a steady double-awning ship, were winsome enough to make the Red Sea delightful. A greater portion of the time was employed in overhauling boxes and cases, separating and distributing in different boxes my goods for barter and personal chattel to provide in case of loss or accident. All this required an arduous amount of labor, and cost an expenditure of thought and foresight in arranging and inventorying; however, it was by far the safest plan, and I was well pleased in the end to have had the opportunity to act upon the piteous experiences of many of my predecessors in the African fields. To be stripped of all articles of barter, of food, medicine, wearing apparel, and photographic apparatus, might leave me stranded at a moment of real peril, necessity, or importance, most significant to the accomplishment of my prime object. Somehow the more I dispassionately contemplated my venture, reviewing the pros and cons, the more I was convinced that I should accomplish something worth the greatest hardships and indefatigable output of force and endeavor requisite. The voyage yielded an opportunity to acquaint myself with weak points, which had previously escaped me. I could composedly formulate vague ideas into distinct shape, and prepare for possible emergencies, and fortify my health and strength. It was like gathering one's self up to enter an arena as a combatant. In making classifications for my future work, writing out leading questions, jotting down points for anthropological and ethnological observation in order to lose no opportunity, when once in the field, of probing every topic to the heart and thrashing out the subjects thoroughly, gradually I discovered in myself a latent gift for organization. Self-amazement awaited each effort in this direction, for every diverse avenue of thought revealed fresh tributaries, until the responsibilities of my project aggrandized beyond all the limits of original conception.

NATIVE DOBE WOMAN.

After all, good work is an accretion of ideas put into effect. It is the experience of every thoughtful, earnest person in quest of knowledge in new fields where there is no precedent to follow.

The sea gradually assumed the color of a lovely turquoise green, with thousands of gleaming, glittering whitecaps, and the far-reaching horizon at the rim of the peerless, spotless blue-gray dome. Porpoises seemed scarce, although certain darting, phosphorescent streaks at night betokened their rollicking presence. Increased heat made a diminution of, and thinner clothing necessary for comfort. Mountain ranges loom up on the African and Arabian coasts; Babel-Mambed is sighted, and the Straits of Aden, called by the sailors Hell's Gate.

Aden is called Hell's Harbor; one can scarcely tell why, unless it is because of the burning sands and the treacherous coast. It was night when we dropped anchor in the Gulf of Aden. Spectacular wrecks of vessels loom up out of the water, suggestive of a fierce struggle with the elements, and as a phantom warning to those who course that way, against the high winds and insetting sea which prevail.

CHAPTER II.

ADEN TO MOMBASA.

ADEN'S ragged stone cliffs and staring, burning white sands, unrelieved by vegetation, and the low-built tropical stuccoed houses, the mosque, the Parsee temple, the English church, the hospitals, combine to make a singular but not attractive picture.

Somali boys are naked, except an excuse for a loin-cloth, and sometimes a long piece of white sheeting, which they utilize for all manner of things,—a head-wrap, a general covering when they lie down on shore or curl up in their boats, or wind about their black shiny bodies as they pull their oars, or even fasten to a pole in lieu of a sail to catch the fitful breezes. Somali men are frequently fine, hardy fellows, and move about with a native dignity which is most impressive; the few women to be seen are not as a rule fine, excepting the young queen of Somali, who rules by her beauty and overbearing tyranny one of the most desperate tribes of Africa; she is certainly fair to gaze upon. A marked difference in the shades of color of their skins provokes the query as to the cause. Well-to-do Somali men wear a leathern band passed through the centre of two valuable, large, knob-shaped pieces of amber around their necks. One purchased by me from the neck of the wearer cost ten dollars (two pounds). The same price is demanded for a new one at the shops. Others wear leather armlets, through

MOSQUE AT ADEN.

which their knives are thrust, and plain leather collars, and even long strands of beads interspersed with a few red and yellow ones to brighten up the others. Native boy divers swim out from shore and float about the anchored vessels, soliciting a coin to dive for, and utter in a comical shrill way a few pigeon English words: "Laidee, swimmee bottom littee monee." They dive and gambol in the water like porpoises. When Somali boatmen pull their oars, it is to the time of a strange, measured plaint in a falsetto tone, whereas, when they rest on their oars, drifting or tied up, they laugh and chatter incessantly in a loud voice, repeating over and over the same words, and clapping their hands on their bare thighs. As the captain's gig, with its Indian crew, pulled us to shore, the amphibious Somali boys surrounded the boat and bore us company all the way, entreating us for coin. A few whites, Arabs, Parsees, Egyptians, and Africans from every quarter of the coast and islands, Berber, Nubia, Dinkili, Galla, Karthoum, Soudan, Congo, and Somali men move about in these seaports, a motley throng, adding a quaint interest to all strangers. Once settled in a rickety two-seated cariole, drawn by a well-cared-for, fat, tiny little horse, we were driven by an old Arab who disported an abundant pale-green muslin turban surmounted by a plaited straw crown cap, a long striped kansor trailing to his feet and a bright yellow cloth sleeveless jacket braided with gold, his hands covered with rings of strange devices; he was fat, sleek, odoriferous with a blend of spices and uncleanliness, utterly indifferent to the comfort of his passengers, his sandals occupying the front seat beside him.

MASAI HEAD-DRESS.

The heat and flies and merciless glare of sun on barren landscape, to say nothing of the swirls of dust and furnace-like air, which brought whiffs of unknown odors, and the stench of camels, of donkeys, of sheep, of people, and of towns, made the outing certainly unpleasant, if a novelty. The principal street was crowded with donkeys, very tiny creatures, laden with tremendous double panniers and enormous packs travelling at a very quick pace. There were here little fawn-colored buffaloes, used as beasts of burden, as well as at Port Said; the camel seems the most reliable means of transport, and with their heavy loads awkwardly gallop at an admirable rate of speed; goats with black faces; sheep with heavy fat tails clumped upon their backs like a plume,—the result produced by cutting the fleshy part of the tail and training the clumsy appendage up at the crup, to keep it from trailing on the ground; the fleece is short and not abundant.

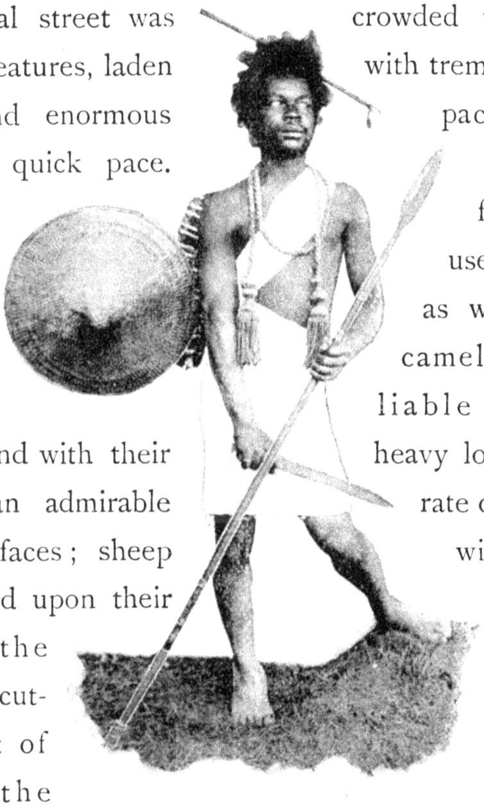

ABYSSINIAN WARRIOR.

A most extraordinary apparition of a human creature loomed upon my vision, and proved to be a woman, the first of my own sex I had beheld in the town. She presented one complete, unvaried mass of saffron color. Every tone about her was saffron; her body was tinged saffron, even to her feet in her saffron-colored sandals; her gown was saffron; her hair saffron; she wore quantities of amber beads, and promenaded the streets unveiled. This fact and her oddity incited my curiosity. I did not rest until I gleaned the reason for her pronounced jaundiced appearance. Briefly, the government regulations provide quarters for a certain debased class of women, as a sanitary protection to the soldiers there stationed, and this saffron color is enforced upon the women habitants of these quarters as an insignia of her nefarious but authorized calling.

As we were driving away from the commercial town centre towards the steep hills upon which the marvellous tanks and gardens are situated, built by the English, we passed the fort built on the steep side of the hill, which was approached by almost perpendicular stone stairways, most difficult of ascent.

The architectural formation of the tanks, or water reservoirs, is most eccentric and picturesque, quarried out of the hard granite-like stone structure of the hills, and walled up by similar cut slabs, cemented so as to make the tanks water-tight, ranged at different degrees up and about the hills in the most irregular manner. The bald rock surfaces, denuded of soil, of the declivities make the downpouring of water comparatively free from earthy particles or other débris; nevertheless every stray atom accumulated from time to time is carefully collected and removed from the basins of the tanks, and used to improve the made gardens. It was interesting to watch corps of small boys, under the direction of an Arab headman, supplied with small baskets which they carry on their heads, filled with the scant débris that they industriously collect out of the empty tanks, and

WATER TANKS, ADEN.

transported by them up ladders and stairways, to deposit upon the artificially made flower beds. Although the work certainly is not arduous, yet it showed that the children are not idle; and they were as happy as possible while at their work, full of childish nonsense, giving vent to volleys of gleeful laughter.

The water is all sold, and doled out with great economy to the purchasers; there are some private tanks, and some leased by the government to individuals or companies. Eleven months had transpired, at the time of my visit, since the last rainfall had filled the tanks, yet there was abundant water to last until the rainy season, and longer in case of drought. It is a current story that Aden has been frequently as long as five years without rain. I was surprised to see that the water showed no signs of stagnation; possibly the clever manner of cementing every crevice, and keeping the tanks free from vegetation, combined with the daily evaporation and the nightly heavy dewfall, may account for this. The almost perpendicular steps leading to the various serpentine galleries bordering the tanks were difficult to ascend and descend, for the bluff walls of the aerial narrow passages, with a narrow foot tread, and the tiny bridges with unrailed platforms, make one's head swim. I found myself involuntarily stretching out my hands into space, eager to grasp something tangible to keep me from losing my balance and being dashed below. Seeing my predicament, my clear-headed escort bade me close my eyes and rest my hands upon his shoulders whilst we slowly

SON OF THE MAHADI.

descended; this I did with ease and safety, pausing to reassure myself whenever we attained a more spacious platform. Dotted here and there, in sequestered nooks, had been planted a few acacia and other trees, vines and flowers, giving a welcome shade. Here were usually situated water wells, with quaint sweeps to uplift the water, or an old-fashioned bucket and rope. One felt inclined to peer in the deep shadows for a Rebecca. Cooing pigeons, affrighted by our presence from their resting-places, with swelled throats and ruffled feathers, uttered a strange noise and flew wildly across the open space; strange bulbous flowering plants grew out from little crevices almost devoid of soil. They appeared like wooden water-jugs, or water-skins at the base, then abruptly branched out, and without supplementary foliage blossomed into one or two waxy flowers, pink or white, which emitted a subtle, almost sickening perfume.

The prevailing drought naturally reduces the soil to a parched state of barrenness; not a fruit, nor a vegetable, nor flower grows throughout the town in the open. In the suburbs there are many very lovely villas facing the Gulf of Aden, occupied by the prosperous merchants and professional residents, where they seek respite from the heat and moil of the town, and where fishing, yachting, and sea bathing are the principal attractions and divertisements.

Driving back to town, I noticed children on the roadside making mud cakes and mud houses, whilst others engaged in a game with stones, something like draughts. Somali and pedlers of other nations circulate about the streets, offering for sale shields, *seme*, or swords, ostrich feathers single or in long tin cases, and long feather boas and little baskets; however, they always ask strangers double price, and dog the steps of those who refuse to be imposed upon, lessening the price, until they voluntarily accept what they can get from the customer.

DELIGHT OF A CORDOFAN.

Aden's market place was disgusting. Arabs and Somali venders squatting on their filthy mats, with their vegetables and fruits all about them, their bare, dirty feet indiscriminately thrust among their wares; some crouched in front of iron pans placed over a few smouldering twigs, or over smudgy oil lamps in which they cooked poor, meagre, dry ears of corn and bananas. The quality of the fruit offered for sale was wretched; bananas and apples absolutely rotten, yet they found purchasers. Wood, camel, sheep, and goat markets presented a thoroughly Oriental aspect. The wood on sale consisted of great scraggy loads of branching fagots borne on camels or mules, which would seem to be on the verge of toppling over. When the loads were sold, the camels were driven into the camel market, there to lie down or feed, whilst their drivers sprawled about, smoking, eating, or sleeping, awaiting some chance to reload and return to the country, or an opportunity to sell the animals. The live stock seemed well fed and well conditioned, as in fact do the people. I only observed a few miserable, crippled, or blind mendicants, sitting in full view at the entrance of the markets or tunnels, displaying to the very best advantage their hideous diseased bodies, covered with flies and vermin, to which they seemed insensible, emitting horrible odors, which fill with disgust the nostrils of those who might be charitably inclined.

FELLAH WATER-CARRIER.

Fellah woman water-carriers, and Arab women selling sugar-cane and corn, gave a decided local color here and there.

The tunnels, cut through the hills, connect the east and west side of the peninsula, saving considerable distance in the travel across or around the steep hills, and are fine pieces of engineering; however, so low studded, they are scarcely better than passageways. Strong, sickening odor of camels and goats passing through linger a long time after their exit. The neck of land which makes Aden a peninsula is remarkably slender, and almost obliterated when the tide is flush.

ABYSSINIAN SLAVE CHILDREN.

Many of the Arab houses are strikingly quaint, covered with a latticework of split bamboo; occasionally there is a rude attempt at exterior decoration, arabesques daubed on in the crudest red, yellow, blue, black, and green, without any attempt to blend the colors, and it produces a startling effect. The Parsee temple, the Hindoo mosque, the Christian churches, are picturesque edifices. An obscure path leading to the Parsee Tower of Silence, which is erected on the top of a steep pinnacled hill, filled me with gruesome awe. No one but a Parsee is ever permitted to visit this spot. Debarred as I was, I could not help thinking, and depicting to myself the spectacle; there on the top, an open tower serried with stone stretchers, upon which were laid the dead, exposed to the ravages of the elements, and ultimately to be devoured by filthy carnivorous birds, it seemed repulsively uncanny. Hindoo burial places were indicated by heaps of stones hardly worthy the dignity of the name Tumuli. Daubed with round red spots at the corner of the heaps of stones, fagots were planted in the ground, from which floated small red cotton flags, imparting a weird and barbaric impression on first sight. I naively queried, when seeing the flags from afar, "Are they holding an auction?" My escort bluntly responded, "Yes, a devil's auction." The Mohammed burial ground is made noticeable by the low, arched tombstones upon which are inscribed a quotation from the Koran, whereas the English "God's acre," a very unpretentious and meagrely occupied spot, had wooden and stone head and foot monuments.

Along the roads appear enclosed stone and wooden *lantrini*, for the accommodation of the people as they journey to and fro, for they have a decided delicacy, or superstition, or something else which makes them reluctant to befoul the earth on a thoroughfare.

We saw enormous fish, a species of ray, being packed on donkeys, fairly sizzling beneath the direct rays of the sun. Arabs carry with them on a journey a *charpoy*, or a portable folding bamboo latticed straight cot, as well as large square chairs, upon which they curl up to sleep, and use for stands to display their goods. Arabs, Somalis, and Indians when weary will roll themselves up in their cloths and lie down amid stones or on the hot sands, and sleep peacefully under the blazing sun at mid-day, indifferent to human comfort.

The blacks will stretch themselves out naked, with only a loin-cloth when the sun is hottest, their black skins shining and glistening as the heat causes the palm and cocoanut oil, with which they are rubbed, to ooze out at every pore. Whereas the white man avoids the direct rays of the sun when suffering from fever, the black men lose no opportunity in submitting to such as a curative agency. The primitive simplicity of these tropical people is largely due to climate; they get along with so little, and seem in admirable condition and happy as the day is long. My stay on shore did not permit me time to look into the methods of education, although I was subsequently informed, on reliable authority, that there exists a governmental supervision over the children and a compulsory educational law.

Native blacksmiths work on the roadsides, making a temporary forge wherever their work happens to be. They handle their tools with considerable adroitness. Egyptian scissors-grinders and knife-sharpeners form a very picturesque grouping.

If only the people are disposed, they can get plenty of work at Aden, for it is such a great shipping port. However, there seems to exist a great aversion to manual labor. Unless absolutely driven to do so by pressing need, the laboring classes are not possessed with an idea of bettering their position or of a thrifty provision for the future. They seem content to live and die in the circumstances and station of life to which they have been born. It is climatic as much as aught else.

THE TREACHEROUS GUIDE.

EGYPTIAN SCISSORS-GRINDERS.

After the drive we were the guests of Cowerjie Dinshaws, the celebrated wealthy Parsee merchants, whose commercial house is the rendezvous for every one coming to Aden. A delightful breakfast, with a strange and varied menu, was prepared, awaiting our arrival; and singularly enough, the host did not sit down at table with us, but said, after seating us and about to retire himself, "I trust you will do justice to our house by making yourselves at home." A Mussulman served us. He was a fat, wabbly, bow-legged, much-turbaned, and scant-begowned soul, who might have stepped out of the

Arabian Nights. Parsees wear the most delicate and sheer Indian mull garments, long and flowing to their heels, fastened with gold buttons. Their under apparel is not discernible beneath the shirt-shaped overdress. Their feet are sandalled. Indoors they wear a silk skullcap, which they surmount by

NATIVE TYPES OF PORTERS.

a strange black enamelled pot hat for outdoor wear. Some of the enterprising young men, who travel on business in other countries, adopt, when abroad, European costumes, all but the hat. Every person seemed to be well acquainted with my plan to visit East Africa, although wide of the mark as to my legitimate motive, and, naturally, had many comments to make and much gratuitous advice to give. Sir Francis de Winton, who had been stationed at Mombasa, was at Aden, awaiting the steamer for England. He considerately sent me word to prepare against rain if I was going to the interior, for it had been an unusually dry season, and it was more than likely to be followed by excessive rain. He also marvelled why I did not select the German route instead of attempting the English. Then I did not comprehend why, but it subsequently became obvious that he was cognizant of the decided opposition that awaited me on the part of a certain official in the English Company. At Aden all the current gossip and news of the world was buzzed about, as all the different lines of steamers bound for India, Ceylon, Malta, and Africa anchored in the port, and passengers have time to visit the town and exchange news.

BUSHIRI.

After making extensive supplementary purchases, I was quite content to board the steamer. My Palanquin was much admired by Messrs. Dinshaw. The senior member of the firm had an Indian one for his wife, which weighed two hundred pounds; whereas mine only weighed seventy, being made of rattan, all the metal mountings of aluminium, the linings and fittings yellow India silk, the cushions of down, and the awnings green canvas. Had it been more cumbersome, it would have been impossible to have transported it on the

SOMALI FAMILY.

heads or shoulders of men through African jungles, swamps, over mountains, and across plains.

In reviewing my purchases, arranging and familiarizing myself with what my possessions consisted in, and what their uses, and where they were, and in making triplicate inventories, I discovered myself to be a very busy individual, with an increased realization of cares and responsibility, which I was not willing to shirk, or relegate to hirelings. Undeniably the heat gradually increased, but the double ship awnings and prevailing tranquillity prevented great discomfort. When we were at table, one of the deck hands, standing out of sight, pulled a rope through the skylight by which he swung the punkah, keeping the flies from harassing us, as it put the air in gentle motion. Afternoon naps were in order, as we lolled in long chairs on deck, and the lazy languor of the tropics no amount of inherent energy could overcome. At night when I elected to write in the cabin, one of the ship's hands, usually a Malay boy, would be sent to fan me. He would scan me with curious eyes, but never say a word, nor would he leave his post unless I bade him do so. I would frequently leave the table and go to my own cabin to get some necessary article, and return in a few moments; meantime the faithful fellow would await my return. One night I left the table to retire, never thinking of my faithful comfort-maker, when, two or three hours afterwards, I chanced to open my door and found him standing fast asleep, with the fan grasped in his hand, awaiting my appearance.

One morning at the breakfast-table, where we were all convened, the chief engineer addressed the captain,—

"Captain, I don't know what we'll do about that drunken rascal; he seems to be quite beyond my control."

The captain looked up with a degree of surprise, and answered brusquely, "I'll take that in hand after breakfast."

The whole thing struck those present as being in

violation of all ship discipline, but of course none of us made any comment, and the general chatter resumed its usual frivolity until the meal was at an end. After getting settled in my long chair on deck prepared for a comfortable read, the captain, considerably flustered, followed by the chief engineer, who spoke in a low, though excited tone, rushed into his cabin and seized a rattan walking stick, and after hastily rushing half-way down the deck to the hatchway, he abruptly turned around and came towards me, looking the very picture of suppressed anger, and burst out with,—

"Mrs. Sheldon, look here a moment; I would like to show to you a living example of the ingratitude of the fellows we captains try to benefit. For example, we have on the ship a stowaway, whom I thought an honest sort of a chap when he was discovered, and he gave something of a plausible reason for his trick in trying to get a free passage, so said, 'Very well, my good fellow, we will give you employment as a stoker.' To this he consented, and went on all right for some days, but was found beastly drunk last night while on duty, and do or say what the engineer might, he has kept up his orgy until we will have to take stringent measures."

I protested that I did not care to see a drunken man, nor be a witness to any chastisement. However, the captain persisted,—

"You will do me a favor by coming with me."

So I followed him along to the hatchway, where were collected all the other passengers, the chief engineer, and several of the crew, hot and breathless, appearing as if they had had a tussle, and curled up on one side was the most dejected-looking specimen of humanity one could possibly conceive of. His limp figure was drawn up into a little heap, his head hidden from view by his arms; a large pail of water, with towels and sponges, stood hard by, and the deck all about was completely deluged with water. Upon the appearance of the captain and myself, with great excitement the engineer exclaimed,—

SOMALI QUEEN.

"There's no use, sir, I've tried everything to sober him up, he's a cure. I've thrown eight or ten pails of water over him, all to no purpose, and the men have put him on his feet a dozen times, and he has as often dropped in the helpless state you see him."

The captain exclaimed, "I'll make short work of this business"; and his cane went whistling through the air and unmercifully fell on the shoulders of the poor wretch.

Involuntarily I exclaimed, "Oh, don't, Captain! don't!"

The captain glared at me and said, "Mrs. Sheldon, I require no advice in carrying out discipline on this ship."

After this snubbing, I was about turning to leave, feeling it was an outrage to have invited me to be a spectator to such a scene. With that the captain raised his foot and kicked the powerless fellow four or five times in succession, all the while saying, "Get up! get up!" and I was tempted to return and offer one more protest in behalf of the poor wretch, when the captain's heel came down upon the man's head with a sickening thud, and the skull fairly crushed beneath the violence used.

With uncontrollable horror and indignation I screamed out to the captain, as I started to fly from the spot, "You brute! you brute! Don't ever dare to speak to me on this voyage; I shall make a report to the ship's company! You are not fit to command a vessel!"

THE QUEEN'S SLAVE WOMAN.

Convulsed with laughter, he sprang round and seized me by the arm, and all the others were simply bent double with their merriment, and to my humiliation, I saw the drunken man's head fly through the air, detached from his body, a bloodless, lifeless, *empty tomato tin!* This effigy of a man, after having served to fool all the other passengers, who had with consistent silence kept me from the knowledge of their betrayment in order to witness the effect upon me, had gulled me completely. It can well be imagined, after having left no loophole by which to escape in my crazy denunciation of the captain, what a pleasant day I had. However, some time later, when we were swinging at anchor in a certain port, and the captain had given on shipboard a dinner to the English residents, whilst the evening's enjoyment was at its height, the chief engineer put in an appearance and said with professed concern,—

CHAGA SNUFF-BOX.

"A boatman belonging to one of the gentleman guests is lying in a perilous position on the ship's rail, and I am afraid to approach him lest he rolls off into the water."

Aha, Mr. Engineer, my time had come, so I sang out in a loud tone of voice, "Mr. Engineer, had you not better take a tin-opener to rescue that man?" and he disappeared from sight. This time the laugh was on him.

At Lamu the ship's local cargo was discharged by lighters. There was a heavy tide sweeping into the narrow channel, and the rocky and sandy coast looked most treacherous.

Lamu itself was not an inviting spot from the water approaches. The scraggy, gnarled bushes in view might have been dead scrub-oak, whilst others resembled cacti.

This is the site of an English station, and at this time quite a bevy of important men connected with the English Company, who were preparing to make an official tour up country. Here, too, is stationed the original of Rider Haggard's "Captain Good." He is a noted sportsman, bird and butterfly collector, as well as treaty maker and treaty enforcer for the English Company. He still wears the storied monocle, and is most helplessly near-sighted if by any circumstance he is deprived of his ocular crutch.

Rider Haggard, during his sojourn at Lamu, made the studies for "She," and obtained the local color with which his African romances glow.

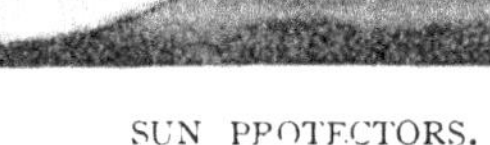
SUN PROTECTORS.

There has been found, in making some excavations from time to time, a considerable quantity of hand-painted pottery, certainly not of African origin, probably of Portuguese or other, which may have been looted or brought thither by voyagers, buried, as everything is, for safe-keeping in Africa, subsequently forgotten, or for divers reasons not reclaimed by the owners, but now excavated, to the

THE SLAVE DHOW.

bewilderment of curio collectors. The government's attention has been called to the fact that these relics were being carried out of the country, and it has prohibited further removal by the passage of a law.

Some of the native iron workers in this vicinity manufacture knives, and daggers, with ivory handles inlaid with gold and s[illegible]r that are really beautiful from an artistic point of view, although it is with great difficulty examples can be procured in an[illegible]nber, as the workers are most unreliable, and dilatory beyond the limits of patience.

The long stretch of sandy coast and narrow waterway, scarcely more than a creek, leading to the island of Seychelee and Lamu, are not in the least imposing or attractive. Seychelee has affixed to it the extraordinary tradition of being the refuge of Adam and Eve. Here, too, grows a variety of cocoanut, rare and highly valued. Its beach is strewn with bleached human skulls and bones, to mark the ghastly tale of a deadly encounter between two hostile tribes who about exterminated each other. Some time since a French sailing vessel collected a cargo of these bones for commercial purposes! So much for national utilitarianism and economy!

Very quaint dugouts dotted the harbor, equipped with long, awkward outriggers of enormous blades like sculls which balance the crafts as the natives fish. Such black fellows, swathed about with what was once white sheeting, cast about with eel-jigs, baited with pieces of quivering fresh fish. There can be no sport in hauling them so caught out of the water. These fish were a species of silver perch marked with coral stripes all over the body, whilst the gills were tinted red.

Similar style of boats put out from shore with their black-skinned native crew in quest of a silver bittin from unwary passengers who might be tempted to trust themselves to voyage with them to visit the shore.

When the captain's gig returned from delivering the mail, although not disconcerted, I was far from being pleased with a very unsatisfactory letter from Mr. George S. Mackenzie. Despite the assurances I had had in London from important men in the directorship of the Imperial British East African

Company that everything possible would be done for me, and even that they had taken the trouble to cable to their representative to use his best endeavor to procure porters for me, this gentleman evidently was neither interested in nor in sympathy with my "novel enterprise," but, to the contrary, absolutely prejudiced against it.

Like a flash I realized that without doubt he would, if he could, put a stop to the affair, believing, as he did, that my advent among the natives in the English occupation of East Africa would incur altogether too much risk upon the overburdened company. Why, I could not imagine, as I did not ask, nor had I any intention of so doing, the company to act as my sponsor, or to contribute in any substantial way to my personal undertaking beyond giving me full permission to traverse their possessions, and possibly assist

YARBON LELLI.

and advise me how to recruit a caravan. Henceforward I regarded Mr. G. S. Mackenzie as my *Obstacle*, silently bearing my chagrin, determined to quietly make my own arrangements, in so far as I could, without his knowledge or counsel, and when perfected, proceed with or without his permission, let the issue be what it might. Strange paradox, in the end matters culminated so that to this same *Obstacle* I owe a debt of gratitude. His maddening opposition developed and tried my metal, at the same time prepared me to encounter serious difficulties. I was convinced that it would be imcompatible with prudence to attempt to start interior with a caravan until the rain came. Enforced patience held in check my impetuosity, awarding me ample time to perfect and mature my mode of procedure once I should start.

GEORGE S. MACKENZIE.

From all communicated to me, it was an open secret that the Germans were carrying everything by force of arms and exercising strict military discipline, which they were enforcing with tyranny upon the natives, who were submitted to a kind of military servility they had no prior knowledge of, nor any disposition to accept. The contrast between their national ways and means of civilizing and colonizing natives and that generally maintained by the English is extremely obvious and certainly reprehensible. Throughout the German occupation of East Africa on all sides there is a tooting of horns, the rattling of guns, the salute of cannons, all that belongs to the display and announcement of military despotism and rule;

FORT BUILT BY VASCO DA GAMA, SIXTEENTH CENTURY.

whereas the English have no army, no naval force backing them to hold their sway over the natives in their occupation of East Africa, and it is but a question of time when the natives will voluntarily yield a willing homage and fealty to the English government which the Germans aim to procure, and only exact by great stringency of measures. They even conscript, from native tribes, soldiers to battle against their recreant neighbor.* The atmosphere was rife with general discontent on this score. It may possibly be that some of the statements have only a figment of truth, they may be all true. In any event it is as the down from a ripe thistle,

*Since this went to press, have been received the rumors of English disturbances at Witu and Uganda.

and was flying about in the air on all sides. My ears were filled with the unpleasant statement that for divers reasons, in harmony with the arbitrary policy of the Germans' reign and rule, they would not permit any alien Europeans to traverse their East African occupation. Alas! these rumors have a mysterious "they" that no one can give individuality, or name, or place to, and this "they," during my sojourn in East Africa, I discovered had no recognized parentage, no local habitation or home, but was a bastard, double-headed monster, most ubiquitous and slippery, and not above the most petty spites and jealousies. Every one who felt uncertain as to the origin of an assertion dodged behind "they said." I had to be patient until the good time arrived when occasion was given to test the veracity of the distracting hearsays, and discovered them as a whole distorted, and too often worthless.

The picturesque Fort of Mombasa, built in the sixteenth century by Vasco da Gama, loomed in sight.

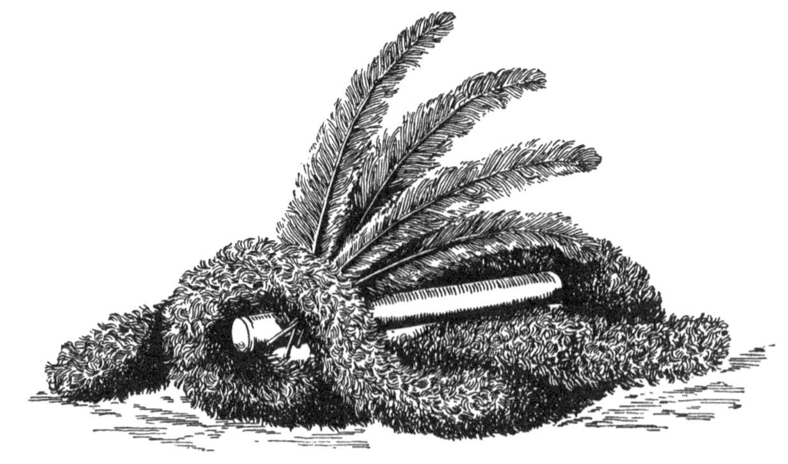

CHAPTER III.

MOMBASA TO ZANZIBAR.

WE approached Mombasa in the sparkling rays of a tropical sun. It seemed most strange and unlike any harbor I had ever seen. It was very difficult to navigate, not being properly marked by buoys, but in a most idiotic way the pilot must steer in line of a pole no thicker than a bean stalk to get a course between two pillars no larger than a good-sized oar planted on shore. The channel is at best narrow and interspersed with sand bars, consequently nearly every steamer going into this port runs aground.

There was a great commotion; all the everybodies and nobodies, white and black, hallooing, gesticulating in an excited manner, while rushing along the shore, leaping from rock to rock, the natives, of course, in such a majority that the white men appeared most conspicuous. The old Portu-

COCOANUT PLANTATION, MOMBASA.

guese fort and the low native huts, thatched with cocoanut leaves, and huddled together, were more interesting than attractive places of abode. Certain landmarks are conspicuous. At last the Imperial British East Africa Co.'s agent, the ship's agent, and all the usual crowd which throng an incoming steamer in these ports, pushed off in boats and came on board; and one who for the moment, in the absence of Mr. G. S. Mackenzie, was the representative of the I. B. E. A. Co.'s interest, came on board to see me, and commenced a long harangue about the impossibility of the company's officers procuring for me even *one porter* for my inland journey; and in the course of his conversation he revealed to me the one prevailing fact that my Obstacle, Mr. G. S. Mackenzie, did not approve of my presence, and denounced my undertaking. Then followed a long dissertation as to the popular idea of my insane undertaking. This courteous, much-hampered envoy appeared completely cut up when I calmly inquired,—

"What do the officers of the I. B. E. A. Co. suppose I want of them, that I am not prepared to get without their assistance? I require no financial aid, and I have already obtained permission from those in authority in England to pass through the English territory."

He looked perfectly abashed for a moment, then graciously put himself at my disposal in so far as lay in his power as a gentleman, although as an officer he was utterly powerless to act.

Many of the posts occupied by white men in the English and German possessions are too insignificant to be deemed desirable, unless through some concealed or some ulterior end or aim they are sought as a matter of personal eccentricity. It can be imagined that a man of activities, who enjoys freedom, and possesses a natural propensity for leadership, should desire to break away from the narrow, cloying environments of civilized society, with all of its set rules, conventionalities, shams, and cant, for just such a life as one might find in Africa. Had I visited East Africa to

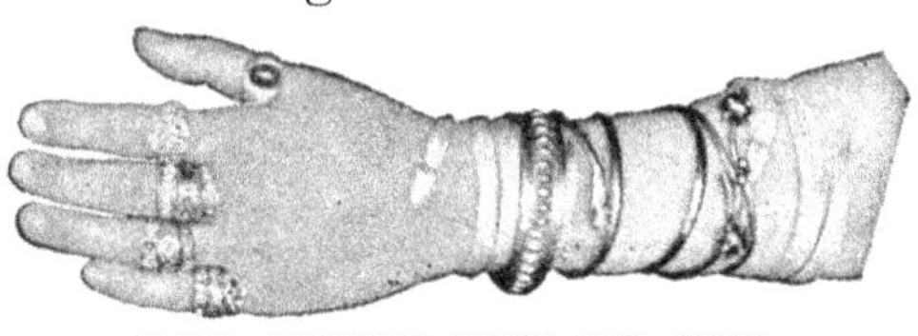

HAND SHOWING RINGS FOR GIFTS.

study the anthropology and ethnology of the white man, instead of the native races, I have no doubt the research would have afforded novel results. However, my curiosity became keener and keener to study the native Africans, and I was most eager to get fairly at my work. All the volunteered advice and hints proffered on all sides I was quite prepared to accept as stock in trade, which might redound, by judicious application, to my ultimate success. In such a country as Africa one must have physical force, health, and endurance, as well as strong mentality, in order to get and hold control over the natives, in order to command with the power to govern one's porters. Better mysterious silence when one is in doubt, than awkward indecision or a display of blunders and a confession of deficient knowledge. It is not a country for half-tones or vacillation, at least not while the natives are in their present state of civilization. The fact was, it was feared that the consequences of a woman's leading a caravan might throw the natives into a frenzy, bring difficulties about which would involve the I. B. E. A. Co. in trouble and expense to come to my rescue.

The Frere Town mission people came to take me to the lovely spot which overlooks the entire Bay of Mombasa, on which is erected their mission houses. The native crew were dressed in the usual length of unbleached body-cloth, bordered with a red stripe and a loose woven shirt. The gentleman who escorted me quite agreed with me that it would be a mistake to replace the natives' present style of dress

ARAB QUARTERS, MOMBASA.

by European fashions, and yet he confessed it would be most difficult to check the tendency, as the home societies were all the time sending out made-up articles of clothing, especially for the girls and women, that were totally unsuitable for their position or the climate; and the good creatures, zealously devoted to the propagation of the gospel among the heathen, were constantly making requests that the converts in the mission should be clothed with Christian decency. He frankly averred that no one could possibly know without living in the climate, studying the necessities of it, and looking into the habits of the people, how utterly preposterous are these modern innovations. However, he made an exception in the case of the best educated native men who were teachers, saying that "European clothing seemed to set well upon them."

After landing I was taken up to what was called the Ladies' House, Bishop Hannington's old residence, and here was

DATE PALM.

cordially received and entertained by the ladies of the mission, shown about their institution, allowed to inspect the work taught to the girls, visited the school, and was presented to the leading man in the work, Mr. Binns. Having been told that Mr. Mackenzie had incidentally said that Mr. Binns's opinion of my expedition might be considered with gravity, my desire was to convince Mr. Binns of the plausibility of my plans. He perfectly agreed with me that success would attend my efforts, if I set to work properly. After explaining my aim to mingle much with the native women and children, I asked, in order to facilitate the work, if he could supply me with woman interpreters. Such a thing had never been thought of, nor ever before required, and he evinced great astonishment and was decidedly disconcerted when I persisted, saying, "Certainly, in an old-established mission like this, there must be among the pupils women or girls capable of interpreting." Finally he imparted, in an evasive way, his opinion that the mission girls would have a disinclination to go on *safari* (journey), and mix with the rest of the caravan, besides they would not expect to carry even their own budget; furthermore, that their education was directed towards making them teachers in behalf of the mission, and not to acquire money in secular service. This revealed to me the utter impracticability of their methods of religious training. Such educational discipline must necessarily undermine their self-reliance and leave the imprint of irresponsibility upon the native pupils. The woman missionary workers happily are not so much swayed by supercilious sentiments, and with an amount of practical common-sense seem to realize that all natives rescued from slavery by the mission have not by nature the aptitude which makes them eligible for teachers.

SOUDANESE WARRIORS.

These women are trying to introduce simple, useful industries, such as Zanzibar mat braiding, and have taken contracts from a commercial house for stringing barter beads, besides teaching them to sew. The boys are mainly instructed in Arabic, Ki-Swahali, and English; which fits them as porters and interpreters, but so inefficiently that the mission boys are the horror of most caravans, and they apply the precepts of their religious training as a cloak for all their shortcomings. If a lamp is broken by one of them, or anything is lost, or a misdemeanor committed, when taxed as to who did it, with naïve sacrilege, not knowing what it means, it is common to hear them exclaim, "Jesus did it." And, if reprimanded, they reiterate with some degree of logic, "Dio Bwana, Jesus did it. Jesus died to save sinners — me mission boy — Jesus did it." This does not represent an isolated circumstance, but accords with the experience of numerous travellers.

Since my visit to East Africa, Rev. Dr. Stewart, celebrated as the founder of the Livingstone mission, assisted by Dr. Moffat (Livingstone's nephew), through the instrumentality of half a dozen Scotch philanthropists, has established, about two hundred and fifty miles from the east coast, an industrial mission on the most practical lines. He aims to teach the natives some craft or avocation, according to the trend of their minds and physical capabilities, which will fit them to fill the existing demands, or those which may be created, of the country, and not such as will have no outlet. It is but just to declare in favor of the medical men who go out to uncivilized lands, either under secular or religious auspices, that they are truly the most devoted, abnegating adjuncts to class or church, and if so disposed, can exercise the most beneficial influence towards the amelioration and

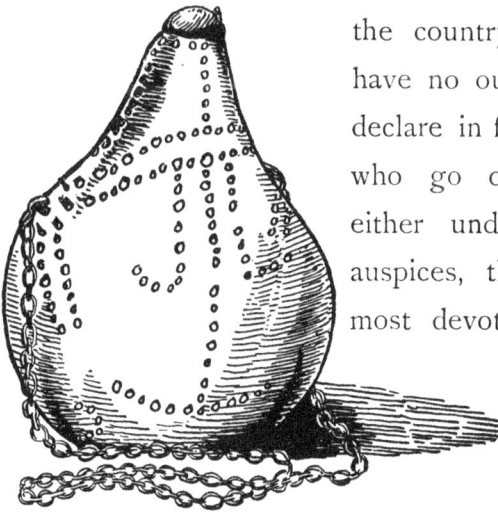

SNUFF-BOX, STUDDED SILVER, METAL CHAIN, WA-CHAGA.

progress of the natives. The women and girls are clothed in white cotton dresses, made like a chemise, bedecked with a Turkey-red stripe around the skirt, low neck and short sleeves. Most of them have their ear lobes distended to an accepted size by a painful method of introducing graduated plugs; then they wear as an ornament leaves of young palms coiled very tightly and trimmed so as to display the white veining that runs through the centre of the leaf, which makes a spiral and looks very pretty. Some of the grander natives disport fine brass ear ornaments. They are permitted to wear their bead necklaces and bracelets. The girls who have not their hair shaven tight to their head coiffure it in an elaborate and intricate fashion. It is impossible to comprehend how they can braid it in such an endless variety of patterns, so

ARAB WOMAN SELLING BANANAS TO PORTER.

neatly and closely to their heads, in tiny flat plaits, each strand pressing close against the scalp at every turn, and not in long pendent strands. All of the girls and women are splendid boat-women, and manœuvre their ugly, heavy, awkward canoes with a skill equal to the boat-men. They eat squatting on the ground or at a long table with their wooden or metal basins before them filled with porridge, which they gather up with their fingers and roll into a ball and stuff into their mouths in the most piggish way. Not only does this habit obtain with the children, but adults eat in the same manner. It seems to afford an unfavorable commentary on the methods of education employed. Their dormitories are of the rudest kind,—a long shanty or room, where a certain number of girls and women are alloted a long trestled couch, the spaces divided for each occupant by mats; but there is no attempt to provide that order of privacy which develops the refinement of civilized decency. As a rule they eat one meal daily, when they stuff themselves to disgusting repletion. Whenever they

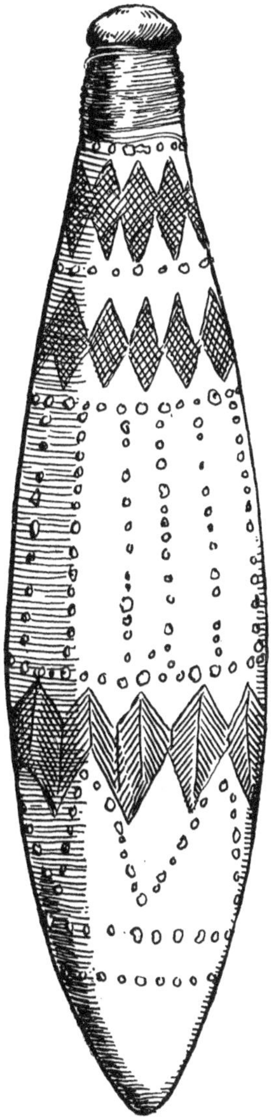

GOURD SNUFF-BOX, STUDDED SILVER AND CARVED PATTERNS, WA-CHAGA.

can get fruit they munch it at all times, and drink to their detriment fermented cocoanut milk, called *tembo*, upon which they frequently become intoxicated. This does not so often occur in the mission as in the freer life outside. The bread, alike for the whites and blacks, is raised with tembo yeast. The mission people, being convinced that it creates an appetite for drink, try to supply for their own followers, as well as those in the vicinity, bread raised with other yeast. The women pound the corn and millet in stone and wooden mortars, with a clumsy wooden or stone pestle. Mothers bear their babes suspended in a cloth upon their backs whilst pounding the grain, without evincing any fatigue. I asked one woman why she did not put the little one down whilst at work. She looked puzzled for a moment, then smiled, and pointed to an ant hill, thrust her fingers into her mouth and caressingly touched her baby.

ARAB BLIND BEGGAR.

Inspired by a secondary thought, she swayed her body in a rocking manner and crooned out, "La-la." Her first pantomime simply indicated that she feared her babe might be eaten by the voracious ants; the second, that the monotonous rocking motion whilst she pounded the grain put her infant to sleep. Soon as the children are weaned, they are placed in a special house, to which is attached a circular cemented playground, where they are daily amused, cared for, and taught by a native woman until able to attend the schools. The maternal wisdom displayed by the lady missionaries in the employment of a native mother teacher is beyond question, for she could know at once the little one's ailments and administer some simple native medicine; she could learn better than a white woman its little grievances and soothe them. Then, too, she is infinitely better adapted to understand what would best amuse the little ones. The custom should be emulated.

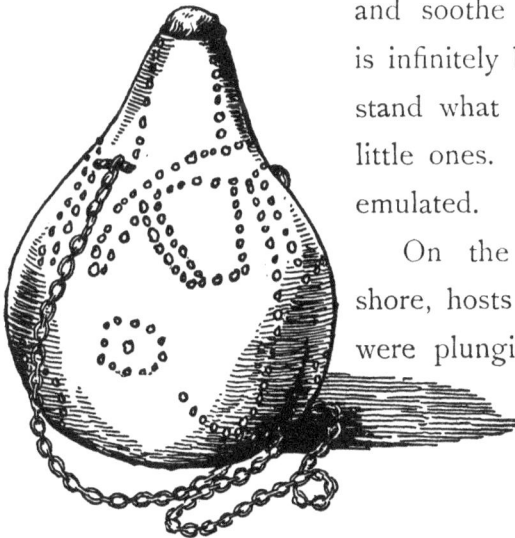

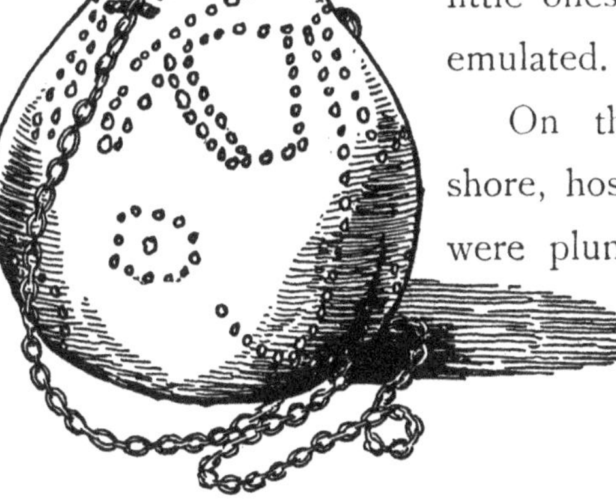
SNUFF-BOX, STUDDED SILVER, METAL CHAIN, WA-CAHGA.

On the Mombasa wharf and shore, hosts of nude boys and girls were plunging into the water from the framework of a pier over seventy feet high, giving vent to hilarious shouts of delight and vying with

RESCUED SLAVE GIRLS, VARIOUS TRIBES.

each other. They dive feet down, and are most expert swimmers. Respecting the amphibious traits of the natives in Africa, an English officer exploits the fiction that some antecedent of the African race was crowded off the ark and had to swim or drown.

Noticeable on the shore were women and boys of the Wanyki tribe, presenting the most extraordinary distortion of the abdomen, which they esteem a great beauty. The abdomen is bulging and rotund and like a lesser dome upon a larger dome; the umbilicus has been distended by artificial inflation during infancy to the size of a tennis ball. I was permitted to witness the abnormal operation. Many of the women wear kilted skirts of common dark blue muslin, seldom over a foot long. Such a jumble of white men and total absence of white women can hardly be conceived of; no man seemed to be in the place that he was fitted to occupy, yet he had signed a three years' iron-bound contract. Some of these men were refined and highly educated, from the great centres of the world; fired by ambition, stimulated by a desire to enlarge their horizon, they had sought these openings, scarcely realizing the deprivations incumbent upon their posts and the monotony thereof. Others were volunteers from the humblest ranks of life. Unfortunately there are no white women, apart from the few woman missionaries; hence these men are thrown promiscuously together and too much upon their own resources, and the customary habit of taking "pegs"—brandy and soda or whiskey—in the course of time, in too many instances, enervates alike the constitution and character, although many of the men become so inured to the habit they never are the slightest bit maudlin. Of those gentlemen whom I met on the coast and elsewhere in

ABYSSINIAN SLAVE GIRL.

East Africa, I must proclaim that, with few exceptions, they acquitted themselves in a most manly way, and extended to me upon every occasion offered the greatest courtesy. It was touching to witness their efforts to entertain me under trying conditions, so devoid of outside resources, far away from marts, and how they ransacked their meagre stores to get little delicacies, and how earnestly they hunted to bring in a bit of choice game. They were to a man on their best behavior, and put their best foot forward in extending the amenities refinement prompted. They did all they could for my comfort and convenience. Men never could have been more charming nor more circumspect in their deportment. Occasionally, when as my guests on *safari*, they would accompany me for a day or so, their good-natured acceptance of my leadership and willingness to accede to my arbitrary rule of camp, and order of march, proved them to be well-bred men and admirable disciplinarians. To these gentlemen, none of them I regret to say of my own nationality, I desire to make public acknowledgment of heartfelt appreciation.

There were the usual friction and dissension belonging to occupants of newly defined posts in a new enterprise, with the tendency to revolt against conditions. In due course, with experience gained by the directors as well as the men, these crossgrained things will modify themselves.

I went on shore to visit the quaint old fort, which is a superb ruin, and has a fine outlook toward the sea, and gives one a bird's-eye view of Mombasa, with the native huts huddled

NATIVE WARRIORS.

as close together as possible, with their quaint cocoanut roof thatchings. Here I had pointed out to me my first line of march away from the English settlement that I should take if I went away from the coast. The fort was occupied by Capt. Rogers, who commands a troop of sepoys loaned by the government to the British East African Company. In the fort quarters there were some Arabs stationed, who disported magnificent studded cutlasses and belts, as valuable as they are beautiful. They are worn thrust into the belt in front. Leaving the fort, my attention was called to the superbly carved doors and lintels, which are evidently of Portuguese and Persian origin, forming the entrances to tumble-down buildings. The streets were quaint, circuitous passage-ways. The ivory custom house possessed considerable interest to me, as the bids were given and accepted by a Parsee commissioner, in order to appraise the value of the tusks, and assess duties. A scribe cut little Arabic designs upon each tusk valued and passed.

SOMALI WARRIORS.

An excursion was arranged, to my delight, to take me over the seven miles and a half temporarily laid of the Victoria Nyanza Railroad, mooted as the greatest of all benefactions for East Africa when once completed.

I was greatly chagrined to be informed that there was not to be hired a single porter at Mombasa; so, after meeting and discussing my open plans with my Obstacle, whom I finally succeeded, by diligent argument, in convincing that, despite his intense prejudice to my proposed undertaking, at least I very decidedly had considered its magnitude, the personal risk involved, and the immense liability incurred, he seemingly became my advocate, and so far consented to my application for permission to go through English territory as to say, "If you can form a caravan at Zanzibar, I will put no barriers in your way." I mistrusted it might be a genteel evasion on his part to checkmate me, and yet avert the disagreeableness of out-and-out opposition. With propitiatory gallantry he even proffered for my use when, *if* I should return from Zanzibar, his fine, airy bungalow at Kilandini, a suburb of Mombasa; although unfurnished, he urged it would be a cool and airy place of refuge, much better than to camp in the open, although I was quite prepared to do that if necessary. In passing, I would say my Obstacle had advanced the objection to me that Mombasa was an unfit place for a lady, because there were no hotel accommodations.

EAR STRETCHER WORN BY MISSIONARY GIRLS, MOMBASA.

So by this gentleman's recommendation, with all my goods and chattels, which I had largely increased by additions in the different ports, I betook myself to Zanzibar on the "Madura," full of apprehension, but determined to turn over every stone before admitting I was frustrated, and try what skill I had at recruiting and organizing a caravan.

CHAPTER IV.

FORMING MY CARAVAN.

FORMING my caravan — how to do it, and how long it would take me — monopolized my entire thoughts, to the exclusion of all others, in the short voyage to Zanzibar. Notwithstanding that practical obstacles had arisen, and rebuffs whistled like small shot on all sides, I never quaked even secretly beneath a vague forecast of defeat.

Alas! at Zanzibar I found that my world-renowned reputation of mad woman had preceded me, to my prejudice. In America, England, Aden, and Mombasa, and now here, I had to listen to and confront as best I could public censure. The bare idea that a woman should be foolhardy or ignorant enough to dare to enter Africa from the east coast and attempt to penetrate interior as far as the Kilimanjaro district of the late Masai raids, at a time when great disturbances had been provoked by the Germans and a revolt was brewing, and essaying thus to do as the sole leader and commander of her own caravan, — the thing was preposterous, and the woman boldly denounced as *mad*, *mad*, principally because there was no precedent for such a venture; it was a thorough innovation of accepted proprieties. It never had been done, never even suggested, hence it must be impossible, or at least utterly impracticable, and certainly outside a woman's province.

MOMBASA FROM ENGLISH POINT.

Zanzibaris porters could never be induced to go into a district terrorized over by bloodthirsty, buccaneering Masai on *safari* (journey) led solely by a woman. Any woman with such intentions, whoever she might be, must take no offence when set down as a reckless fool. The movement ought to be first scoffed, then, if necessary, obstructed, and finally, if need be, prohibited by the authorities. Despite her intrepidity, or her attributes for leadership, or her ability to spurn hardships as she might dangers, she must be irrational in attempting such a hazardous undertaking, and doubtless would gladly abandon not only an ambitious but impractical and suicidal plan when once she was properly informed of the dangers, and convinced of the uncontrollable odds against her. Having listened to these same sort of protests and persuasions until my ears were dulled to their unsavory repetitions,—aye, in truth, I think I knew the formula of every objection by rote and rule, and could ring the changes as deftly as my opponents,—did these gentlemen know that my empire of folly was not ostracized, and that I had received over two thousand applications from both men and women, as a rule accredited with unusual sense, occupying almost every rank in life, and the majority of them professional and scientific men, entreating me to allow them to accompany my free and independent expedition?

The most insuperable difficulty urged upon me was the fact that there were no porters to be had, even at Zanzibar, so many caravans had been equipped for the Germans as well as for the I. B. E. A. Co., and for some private expeditions that had combined to drain the country of available porters.

After much persuasion, Mr. Boustead, one of a firm for equipping caravans, agreed to constitute himself my agent, if I so desired, and endeavor to obtain fifty men to go with me to the interior, without any masculine European to aid me. This, however, he did in a very discouraging way.

"If it were a feasible scheme, even then there are not fifty men to be had," he urged. "Besides, Zanzibaris would not

M. FRENCH-SHELDON. BÉBÉ BWANA.

consent to go in such a small number into hostile Masai land, and certainly not without being properly armed."

I protested, urged, argued, and finally got him to consent to *try*. I wanted to start from Mombasa within a fortnight; hence he must work sharp to collect the men and to provide the necessary supplies. My urgency for speed was met in a dubious manner. He would try, but he had no hope he should succeed. Then cropped up another vital reason for delay.

There was no water in the interior, and would be none until the rains. Very well, then, I would wait until there was rain, if he would set to work about the caravan, in order that I should not be detained when the auspicious time came. That very day the rain fell in torrents.

I asked him if influence with the Sultan would aid him in any way.

"Certainly it would."

So I proceeded to use my diplomatic passport, and, through the courtesy of American Consul-General Ropes at Zanzibar, arranged for an early audience with the Sultan. There were certain difficulties here again to be encountered. It was unusual for his Highness to

* SULTAN OF ZANZIBAR.

receive a lady, but, in consideration of Consul-General Ropes's persuasive arguments in my behalf,—that I was the first lady to attempt to lead a caravan that history had ever known, and various flattering claims he made for my personal importance,—a message came to say the next day at four he would receive me, but I must come alone, conducted to his Highness by two dragomen, who would attend me from the consul's residence to the palace. As I walked through the narrow, dirty apologies for streets, sandwiched between these two marked dragomen, with all the black people gazing at me as they deferentially drew aside to let me pass, and squatted on their heels in lieu of bowing, the thought came flashing into my brain that even these wretched blacks, in their debasement, imagined the very worst thing possible about the white woman, and I felt choked with self-indignation that a freeborn American woman should have sought the opportunity to conspicuously place herself in such a questionable position; then the absolutism of my one determination asserted itself, and the humiliation was from thence a mere detail, albeit keen and uncomfortable.

Arriving at the palace, which is a most unpretentious structure, I was conducted up a flight of long stairs and was met by the Sultan on the landing. The few words of salutation in Ki-Swahali I had mastered came tripping off my tongue in response to the Sultan's *jambos*, obsequious smiles, and bows of welcome. After these ceremonious preliminaries were over, one of the dragomen was commanded by the Sultan to act as interpreter. The walls of the large, showy saloon were hung with red panels embellished with quotations from the Koran in embossed gilt characters; great showy crystal chandeliers hung from the ceiling; tables

WHITE IVORY.

of beautiful inlaid workmanship were ranged through the centre of the room, and tall-backed gilt chairs with crimson satin cushions were arranged in a stilted fashion throughout the long saloon. The floor had a crimson velvet carpet with such thick pile the tread of feet became noiseless.

Once seated at one of the tables, feeling flushed by the curious scrutiny of all the attendants who hovered about, I was gratified when the Sultan ordered a particularly staring oleaginous creature to serve coffee. This I drank with relish; but no sooner was my cup partially empty than there was a quick succession of various sorts of sherbets paraded for my refreshment; truly they were marvellous concoctions of all colors, beginning with brown, closely followed by red, green, and white syrup-like fluids in the daintiest glasses imaginable; but, with suspicion, I avoided the strange, spicy, honeyed beverages; only touching the rim of each glass with my forefinger, then, out of courtesy, pressing my finger to my lips in sign of satiety, to excuse my declining such choice nectars.

Subsequent to these delicate civilities, the Sultan explained, with evident embarrassment, that it was not his custom to *ceremoniously* receive ladies, nevertheless he was quite desirous to be of service to me in every possible way. This was my chance to tell him of my proposed expedition to Kilimanjaro and Masai land. Pulling his *joho* (long loose embroidered coat) around him, exposing his bare feet encased in sandals, he expressed regret that I should desire to go to such a dangerous, wild section of Africa, and wished I might be dissuaded.

"Is not Zanzibar charming? Why not linger here as the friend of the Sultan?"

"No, not dissuaded," I firmly rejoined: "however, his Majesty could make it far easier and safer for me, if he felt inclined."

Again he wrapped his splendid gold-embroidered *joho* about him with a certain majesty and said imperiously, "Command us and it shall be done."

Explaining the difficulties my agent experienced in procuring porters, I urged that he would aid me by having all slaves volunteering speedily sworn in on the following Saturday; and when masters interfered with their slaves, or middlemen objected, to declare himself my friend, and command it otherwise.

SULTAN'S THREE HENCHMEN.

"It shall be done."

He ordered his band to play some special pieces in my honor, which, as usual, wound up the performance by the national anthem, an explosive *pot-pourri*. When I was on the point of leaving, after drenching me with otter of rose, he invited me, with great effusiveness, to return on the following Friday with a woman interpreter, to visit his harem; he also placed a carriage at my disposal during the entire time I remained in port,—I will not mar the lustre of his gallantry by describing the Sultan's vehicles and horses, — and he offered to take out his war ship "Glasgow" for my pleasure. This war ship, by the by, it is satirically said, was presented to the Sultan by a celebrated shipbuilder for the paltry sum of $200,-000 (£40,000).

WOMAN OF THE HAREM.

Friday's arrangements, owing to the difficulties of procuring a woman interpreter, either from the mission people or through my agents, seemed to be unavoidably cancelled when I received a message from the Sultan summoning me to come, as he had himself secured the services of a woman interpreter. So I went, and received a most friendly reception. Through locked and barred doors I was conducted from one of the palaces — there are three in a row — to the other; and finally reaching a large saloon, the place where the interpreter was dismissed, that was in wild disorder, like the show-room of a barbaric merchant prince, — a dazzling variety and array of valuable gifts, curios, all sorts of purchasable splendors heaped incongruously one upon another upon tables, on the floor, and nothing showing to any advantage, the only impression given was of quantity and enormous value.

The Sultan's eldest daughter was brought in by a black woman slave, attended by two little black slave boys.

With a flash of pride the Sultan exclaimed, "See how a Sultan dresses his daughter! Look well, and tell to other Europeans how splendid are her jewels." The heavy gold anklets worn by this little child, but five years of age, impeded her moving with any freedom. Her crown, studded with jewels, must have pained her tender brow; and the gorgeous as well as curious necklaces suspended one upon another to the number of a dozen, and numerous bracelets and finger rings, certainly must have been burdensome. The Sultan's lament is that he is unfortunate in having three daughters and no sons. He was curious to know if I had children, and when the negative response was conveyed to him, he asked boldly, "Has your husband many wives?" He smiled in a cynical way.

WOMAN OF THE HAREM.

"Certainly not," I retorted with some contempt, vexed by his effrontery.

At this juncture a heavy embroidered portière was drawn aside by two Malay eunuchs, whose tongues were cut out to limit their power of disclosing secrets, and there appeared a haughty woman, gorgeously attired. Possessed with all the imperious disdain of an empress, she approached me, and rudely threw out her hand to me, at the same time ungraciously darting a glance of outraged feeling upon me. This then was the Sultana! Poor woman, did she presume I was another usurper of her legitimate place? Only a few moments expired when she was ushered out by two gross, horrid, greasy eunuchs, and the portière was drawn over the closing door. Within ten minutes after her Highness's exit, through another door entered in Indian file woman after woman of the Sultan's harem, to a number most amazing. Each one in turn approached me, extending her hand. To the first, who was a fine, frank-looking creature, I arose to respond to her greeting, when the Sultan waved me down,—

"Do not trouble yourself for them. There are too many, all alike, and not worth it."

Some of these poor, degraded concubines were sad-eyed and full of sorrow, others seemed defiant and triumphant, and yet others looked envious. Comparing the vast difference in the costliness and quantity of their jewels and dresses, it flashed across my mind that these distinctions were marks of favoritism. Each and every one of these royal concubines, at the command of the Sultan, bathed my right foot in rose-water, and in recognition of my superiority and evidence of their humility, each gave me one of her jewelled rings. The sum total was one hundred and forty-two.

بسم الله الرحمن الرحيم

من علي بن سعيد

الى كافة من يراه وبعد فهذه الحرمة الامريكانية هي من المحبين

معنا ومتوجهة الى اطراف كلمنجارو وانا المرجو كل من يصادفها او تحل معه يقابلها

بالمراعاة والحشمة التامة ويمنع كل من يتعرض عليها لانها من المودين لنا ليعلم

الواقف والسلام

١٣٠٨

١٧ شعبان

رقم بامر خادمه عبد العزيز بن محمد

SULTAN'S PASSPORT.

TRANSLATION OF SULTAN'S LETTER.

In the name of God the merciful, the compassionate.

FROM ALI BIN SA'ID.

To all who may see it, and to proceed: This respected American lady is one of those arriving here and travelling into the region of Kilimanjaro; and I command that every one who meets her, or with whom she puts up, shall receive her with absolute regard and attention, and shall restrain any one who interferes with her; for she is one of those who are much esteemed by us. This is for the information of those whom she may meet. And peace be with you.

Written on the seventeenth of the month Sha'ban, in the year 1308 4 (March 2, 1891).

By the order of

ABDAL AZIZ BIN MOHAMMED.

The Sultan, after showing me about through the private rooms, as he professed he had never previously shown any one, queried what I thought of it all. With true American frankness, I declared it atrocious. He said he would gladly renounce his harem, "But I should lose my Arab constituency."

Most cautious man as this Sultan is respecting signing papers, always suspicious of some governmental policy that will involve him, he offered to *visé* my passport. This I declined, desirous that he should give me a special letter to any Arab caravans I might encounter on my route up country. This he did. He also gave me his autographed photograph; and I had the Sultan's word he would always be more than pleased to serve me in any possible way as his friend. His gifts were most lavish; a pair of Muscat dogs, and four Muscat donkeys, which policy dictated it was best to decline. Saturday my men were sworn in without the usual difficulty, and when the steamship "Madura" sailed out of port I had the satisfaction of knowing that in six days the so-called impossible had been accomplished, and by *a woman*. Eight of my people were on the ship. My headman of headmen, Hamidi, one of the best known and most reliable of Zanzibaris, had come to pledge to me perfect faithfulness. I had started out with the idea of having plenty of women as porters, and to have a native woman interpreter. I saw only one native woman who could in any way fill the requirements of the latter post, and my conscience would not allow me to employ her, much as I desired, as she had started for the mission a children's school, which would have come to a standstill if she was taken away. As a slave, when a child, she had been rescued from her cruel captivity and befriended by the mission people, educated and supported by them during her helpless childhood; although she had been in other employ since, until the school was inaugurated, she scrupulously owned that the mission had a first claim upon her services,—a sentiment in which I accorded.

ARAB LETTER-WRITER.

We steamed back to Mombasa. There, for the first time, my freight and luggage, which were far from being modest, were disembarked, for I had taken everything with me to Zanzibar in case I should be compelled to go to Kilimanjaro through German territory, via Bagamoyo or Pangania.

Malignant fever was raging at Zanzibar, and a general

panic possessed nearly every European resident. Clinical thermometers flourished, and a friend's or an acquaintance's temperature was a theme for open discussion on the highways and byways. It was and is the universal practice during an epidemic for every one to test his or her own temperature several times daily. A friend meets a friend; the daily bulletin of their respective temperatures is discussed. "My temperature is 102, what is yours?" "Mine is 103, and I'm going to get a chance to go on board of one of the war ships." "Poor So-and-So's temperature was 107 this morning, they have him in an ice bath. He'll pass in his chips!" This habit is one of the most ridiculous and pernicious, rendering many a person liable to fever, and should be tabooed.

ARABIAN MUSICIAN.

Zanzibar to a stranger presents the guise of a pest-ridden

SUGAR-CANE SELLER.

land. No sewerage, and all the filth pitched into the sea to ebb and flow with the tides, polluting the atmosphere and stinking in one's nostrils. The streets are narrow, crooked, and dirty. Bazaars are everywhere, and bedecked with all sorts of articles. I took great delight in watching an Arab family at table, also an Arab woman selling sugar-cane. Oranges of the most luscious variety and sweet limes and mangoes were extremely cheap and plenty. There are two very good clubs, and nothing else but dinner parties and a montonous drive of seven miles for recreation. A Sunday spent with a friend at his *shamba* (country place) is always enjoyable. There are never but a very few white women, the wives or relations of the consuls. When a war ship or a steamer is in port, the residents are permitted an opportunity to go on board, and the commanders frequently inaugurate a series of little dinners or luncheons; but at best the outlook is very circumscribed, and a man's ambition must, in the end, be downed. Girl water-carriers made a pretty picture going in bevies to and from the wells, carrying their hammered copper, brass, and earthen pots upon their heads; one girl always supplied with a long-handled ladle, the dipper part made of a calabash.

Upon return to Mombasa, Mr. Mackenzie, no longer my Obstacle, but my converted friend, with kind courtesy tendered me the use of his large, airy, two-storied bungalow, most picturesquely surrounded at Kilindini, during my sojourn, while awaiting the balance of my caravan.

The scenery and lovely climate made the nine days of my tarriance well worth remembering. The principal men associated with the different departments of the I. B. E. A. Co. called upon me. One can but be amazed at the kind of men that have taken up their work so far away from all that civilization means to men of education and ability. There are but few counterfeits of houses. Every one must live in a structure of four corrugated zinc walls, with a *makota* (cocoanut leaf) plaited thatching placed over a zinc roof. Most of the dwellings are constructed right upon the ground, and the best of them have only a cemented floor and outsheds. There is a slanting makota-pent forming the covering to a rude veranda, beneath which it is the custom to lie and sit during the hot noonday, as well as during moments of leisure, where long chairs are ever in view, and dripping calabashes of water hanging to cool where the air freely circulates.

DERVISH MUSICIAN.

MOMBASA.

There are no luxuries, not even proper comforts in this new country, where young men have rushed with the love of adventure and the hope of making a mark for themselves and achieving a future. Somehow there seems to be a fascination enshrining adventurous Africa for fine, energetic men who are fired with ambition. Alas! I greatly fear all is not as they pictured it in their far-away homes. There is no royal road in this new El Dorado. Ability, steadfast work, patience, abnegation, and time are the only stepping stones.

One week after leaving Zanzibar my entire caravan arrived at Mombasa, and in the late afternoon, with songs of salutation and general yells resounding through the *shamba* of Kilindini bungalow, there came ninety-five porters, *askari*, palanquin bearers, headmen, and interpreters, making my little army of Zanzibaris up to the goodly number of one hundred and three. Seventy of these men were to be armed with guns. The balance carried knives. It was only under this condition porters could be induced to go into the Masai country. They camped as they could until Monday, when all my loads would be delivered from the dhow. I gave the porters one and all a general address as to my requirements from them, and what to expect if they were unfaithful. To all I said they replied, "Dio" (yes), and "Inshallah" (God willing). The same shuffling irresponsibility as with whites.

HARBOR OF ZANZIBAR. SULTAN'S PALACE.

بسم الله الرحمن الرحيم

الى كافة من يراه من العرب والسواحلية الذين هم يسافرون

في البر وبعد الذي اعرفكم من طرف هذه الانجليزي من اعز الناس
عندنا وهي صاحبتي وانا افرح غاية الفرح وانا احب كل
احدا الى عارضها في سفرها يكون يعمل لها حشمة عظيمة هي وجميع
القفيلة الذي معها في سفرها والى اردت شي من المساعدة
يساعدوها بقدر مقدرتكم وكذا الكل ان كان احدا جاب لنا
خط من عندها وذكرت لنا ان فلان بن فلان افعل لها احسان
جميل نحن نوخذ منه الخط المذكور بالحشمة التامة في حمالة
وكذا الكل الى كان احدا افعل شي من الضعف في سفرها يكون
لديه معلوما انه افعل ضعف كثير امع اهل انكليز من يستحق
الاذى التام معنا في حمالة والسلام في ٢٤ شعبان ١٣٠٨

من جرج مكنزي كبير شركة الانكليز

Geo. S. Mackenzie,
Mombasa
4th April 91

TRANSLATION.

To all Arabs and Swahilis travelling in the interior: This is to inform you that this lady, to whom I have given this letter, is my friend, and I wish every one who meets her caravan to be kind to herself and her porters, and to do everything to help her *safari.* Any one who does this, and brings a letter from her to say she is pleased with what has been done for her, will receive thanks on arrival at Mombasa. Should any one interfere with her caravan, annoy her in any way, and do any act of disrespect to her, will be considered to have offended the company, and will be treated and punished accordingly.

(Signed) GEORGE S. MACKENZIE.

MOMBASA, 4th April, 1891.

In my caravan I found I had men who had been with several great explorers, and with some of the big game hunters who had memorialized Chaga land as the Hunters' Paradise. I looked with amazement over all these strange black and every shade of brown faces, with much brutality imprinted thereupon, and marvelled if I should always be able to control them and make them subservient to my commands. After a moment's contemplation I felt somehow that I should, and would not have hesitated to have started at once with the lot as they stood, for a three years' journey The work in providing the right and infinite variety of beads and wire and cloths for barter to procure food for all this body of men, for no longer a period even than three months, was a great anxiety, and, when properly done, I had more loads than men, and was forced to telegraph to my agent to get for me thirty more porters and have them follow me to Taveta. When they, with the headman and two soldiers (*askari*), arrived, I had one hundred and thirty-eight men. Usually many desert, for they receive so much of their wages in advance; in this instance, three months'. However,

BLACK IVORY.

the Fates were in my favor, for, upon calling the roll, there were only a few who had remained at Zanzibar, and these were replaced by volunteers.

When Monday came, and the guns, which were brought to me by a chain gang, were distributed, Mr. Mackenzie harangued the people, telling them if they deserted and were found by him or his agents, they should be condemned to serve a year in the chain gang. The Sultan had promised any miscreant far worse punishment,—to cut their throats if black-listed. Then there was a heavy penalty put upon the whole caravan, and for that matter upon me too, respecting the firearms. No one could sell, or lose, or break his gun without a fine of about forty dollars, — double the value of the gun when new. All this, I was assured, was in my behalf, and doubtless proved a great protection to me, although I could not refrain from expressing temporary indignation at what seemed extortion. So, gathering up all the loads, carefully numbered, embarking my Palanquin and all the people in a large dhow, and some in smaller boats, the I. B. E. A.'s steam launch, for a given sum of rupees towed us across to Railroad Point, and from there we were really to make the first start the next morning.

CHAPTER V.

THE FIRST MARCH.

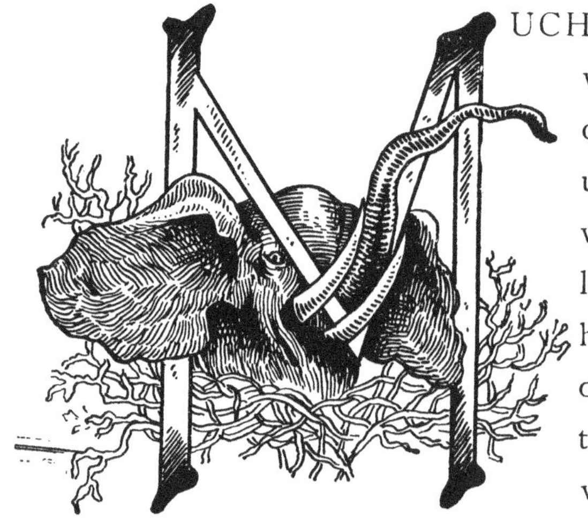

UCH-COVETED rain, with its heralded season of benefits, propitiated us, and the entire caravan was athrill with delight, knowing how the hardships and fatigues of the *safari* (journey) they had enlisted for would be ameliorated now that they could anticipate plenty of water.

Having put out from Kilidini at a late hour, although our point of landing was a short distance above and across the narrow stream, in consequence of the weight of loads, the throng of people, and the swift current, we reached Railroad Point, after considerable delay, too near night to make any progress on our journey. Persuaded by the officers of the I. B. E. A. Co. stationed here, I consented with pleasure to remain over night as the guest of my friend, Mr. C. Macdonnell Lemmi, who most graciously vacated his premises for my personal accommodation, whereas my men camped in the adjacent open. If so inclined, my friend could have boasted of being the possessor of the most tasteful dwelling thereabouts. Instead of giving way to the uninviting barrenness and uncongeniality of his surroundings, he had with self-respect exerted himself to make the best of conditions in his endeavor to maintain a semblance of his inbred home refinement. The interior of his tiny corrugated abode was daintily hung with bright trade cottons, and photographs were grouped about on the walls and tables; his toilet articles were arrayed in such a fashion as to betray his fondness for elegance; the floor was covered with pretty Zanzibar mats, upon which were spread lion and leopard skins, and over the chair backs were draped bits of bright cotton stuffs; a large

JOSEFE AND NATIVES.

ARABS RESTING.

Milan plush rug answered for a bedspread. Everything, without being costly, was most decorative, and presented a vivid contrast to the heedless don't-care manner most men permit themselves to lapse into when isolated from home ties. Some way it was ineffably touching to witness these evidences of this great stalwart man's clinging to the artistic conventions of his far-away Italian home life. He was one of the "wise men" who, according to Shakespeare, "make every port a happy haven," and never made a display of his disappointments when his dreams were discounted by stern reality, but, to the contrary, tried to infuse fact with fancy. Denied the refined companionship of white women for a long time, this man was most charmed to have the fleeting opportunity to converse with me; and I have thought, since my return, if for no other result than the undisguised pleasure afforded to lone, forlorn white men I encountered in East Africa, by my presence and society, my expedition would, even so, not have been made in vain.

The Indian bullocks and their drivers interested me very much. These expensive, handsome little animals had been imported to send to Victoria Nyanza, but during the wait were employed on the railroad construction works. However, they were finally shipped as accessories to Capt. Rodgers, and his troop of *sepoy soldiers* loaned by the government to I. B. E. A. Co. in his expedition to Witu. A camel caravan had gone up country a few weeks prior to my appearance, and bad news came back to the effect that the camels were coming to grief and dying. This portion of Africa does not conduce to the use of camels for transportation. Donkeys die off very speedily, and horses are impossible; therefore there remains no relief to the poor Zanzibar porters, nor immunity for the natives from slavery until a railroad is constructed.

POMBE CUPS.

Unfortunately, the recent rain had washed out the temporary roadbed of the railroad and undermined the rails so that they were not safe to drive the heavy engine over; therefore the seven miles I had anticipated to have conveyed my caravan by rail was now impossible.

During the evening and night some straggling porters came into camp, reducing the list of deserters materially. My friend kindly gave me a lesson in roll calling, as well as how to quickly inspect loads, count the rifles, and set my tents. For the last time everything was overhauled.

When it is recognized that a caravan going into the interior or up country in Africa is like a migratory community, and must be provisioned and armed for the entire expedition, take sufficient goods for barter to insure immunity from hunger, and be enabled to give tribute to purchase from the natives a right of way (*hongo*), if required, as well as a variety of presents for the natives one wishes to negotiate with, and that it is essential to provide for necessities and all likely emergencies during periods of health as well as during sickness, that precaution must be taken against tropical heat as well as against the bitter cold trade winds, which at certain seasons blow up during the afternoon or night, and for dry as well as for rainy weather, living as one must in the open, the incongruity and variety of an African outfit is beyond conception of any one who has not had experience therewith. Not only must one prepare against the elements, but against ferocious wild beasts, as well as the invidious attacks of creatures no larger than white ants, which are perfect vandals in the way they carry out their work of rapid destruction upon all wooden objects. Precious or valuable articles must be kept, to insure them against damage, in air-tight and water-tight tin cases; the coils of metal wire

BUFFALO BULL.

(*senengé*) are sacked in round packages; the beads (*shanga*) are carried in boxes or canvas sacking; the cloth in long bales, covered with *makota* (cocoanut) matting; the rice in strange, trumpet-shaped bags; the provisions in boxes; pots, pans, and kettles upon poles exposed to view, and a certain

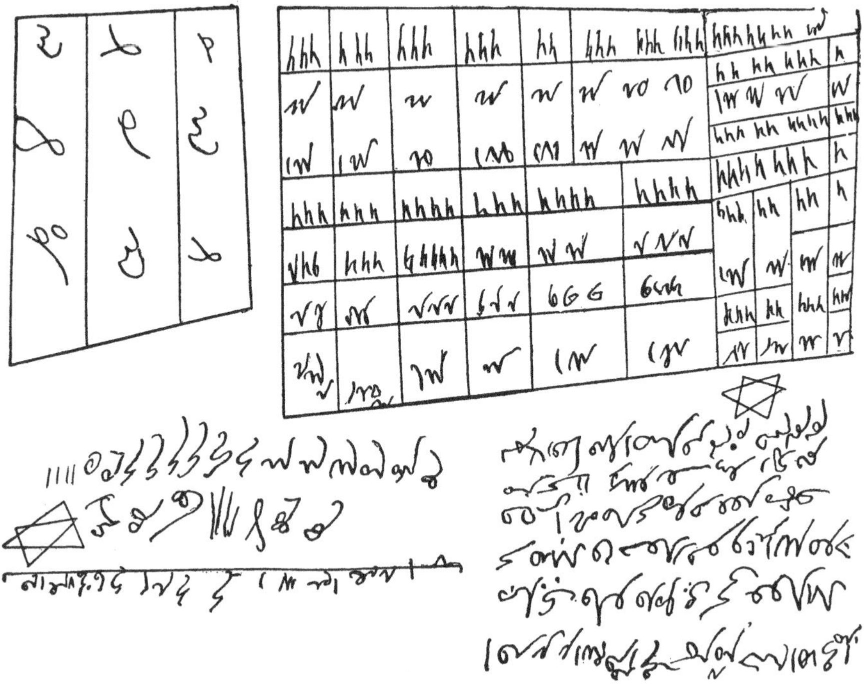

MASAI FLAG OF TRUCE.

number of iron pots, in which the porters and men cook; calabashes with water, tents and poles, chairs, folding tables, large waterproof canvases enveloping cork ground beds; large pieces of waterproof cloth, the ground cloth with which the tent is carpeted to keep the damp from rising from the earth; boxes of candles, soap, cartridges in boxes, matches, flints and steel, cotton waste to clean the guns, cocoanut oil, kerosene in large square tin cans, when emptied used for water cans, or bartered to the natives; coffee in sacks; lanterns, by night swung on poles, carried by a porter, with a light load; water bottles; photographic apparatus and instruments for observation; tools; medicine cases; large tin buckets for water; bath tub, hammock for the sick, and all manner of trifling accessories, and luxuries, and endless et ceteras. Then come the men's mats, upon which they sleep; the cloth, of which they make their little tents, used as a turban (*vitumba*) during the day to ease up their loads from their heads, and kept by them to the last as a means of barter with natives.

In the selection of the beads, the quality and size of the metal wires, the cloths, the silks and velvets, gold-lace, and other presents which one takes for chiefs, of all kinds and sizes, the most valued among which will be British soldier coats, flaunting red, with gaudy gold-lace and plenty of brass buttons; European hats, and red umbrellas, tooting horns, music boxes, clocks, matches, razors, knives, bells, rings, bracelets, metal belts and jewelled weapons, needles, sewing

KHARTOUM NEGRO.

thread, pins, fishhooks, tops, kites, dolls, picture books, clay pipes, tobacco, snuff, tea, sugar, silverware, china cups, knives, spoons and forks, paint boxes, mirrors, sewing machines, tools.

Needless to say, great thought and attention are required, and one must profit by the experience of other travellers in order to avoid falling into mistakes which it is impossible to rectify after once leaving the coast, if indeed one can rectify them at the coast. All of these loads must be weighed, numbered, and allotted to the men and rearranged, or as they say in Africa, *tangenezed*, from time to time, as one journeys on, according as articles are taken from different packages, in order to fairly distribute the work upon all of the porters throughout the caravan; then, too, as illness always ensues after one has been out on *safari* a few days, the sick must be relieved of the burden of full loads, if not, indeed, relieved altogether, and they themselves carried in hammocks. This unloading, *tangenezing*, as it were, as one proceeds, is both advantageous and necessary. Almost daily can be gauged the depletion of supplies, and extravagance checked; it also affords an opportunity to detect pilfering, and discover if loads have been discarded, sometimes in time to recover them.

One possessed of a spark of humanity will not leave a sick man by the roadside to die of starvation, and even become, alive or dead, food for the vultures and prowling animals; hence, if the afflicted is too ill to walk, two of his com-

WHIRLING DERVISHES SEEN AT ZANZIBAR.

panions are obliged to be relieved of their loads and carry him; in order to do this the contents of these loads must be distributed to the other porters. They have no objections to carrying a *mzunga* (white man), but they very much object to carrying a fellow *pagazi* (porter).

However, I found it an admirable method to quietly say to an objecting porter, "Look here, my man, to-morrow you may be ill, and if you object to carry your companion to-day, who will then be willing to carry you when you are stricken? We will leave you to your fate, the prey to the wild beasts! Come, come, fall in line!"

This usually ended all grumbling; for the dissenter, seeing there was no chance to shirk, would assume his part of the burden. The end was accomplished; he did his duty, although too often with ill grace.

NATIVE SOLDIER.

The method of dealing out rice, which is carried for *posho* or rations during the first eight or nine days from the coast in bulk of sixty pounds in a *kanda*,—a long and narrow matting bag, broadest at the bottom,—is somewhat peculiar. A brass measure, like a straight tumbler, called a *kababa*, which should legitimately bear upon it the offiical imprint of the Sultan, resembling the figure "8," holding about a pint of rice, is the accepted dole; but in lieu of this, the headman of headmen will deal out the portions by putting his two hands together and allowing the grain to rest within so that none of it falls over when he shakes his hands. The amount given to the men varies according to the rank of each man.

Porters, carrying the heavy loads, are paid the least and receive the smallest *posho;* the headmen, who are paid the largest price and never carry even their own mats, receive four to five times the amount of food or allowance, and their wages are in proportion larger. However, I was obliged to submit to the usage of the country, believing it must have virtue from its time-honored existence.

The small quantity of food that each man eats daily would seem hardly to suffice for the maintenance of his strength, but they as a whole are comparatively hearty and, as a rule, thrive when on *safari*, and if treated fairly, seldom are sullen or murmur, unless it is very cold; then they begin to ask for meat, and for more cloth, as they huddle, utterly miserable, with teeth chattering, round their fires in the open, sometimes the rain pelting furiously down upon their half-naked bodies.

NATIVE SOLDIER.

During a noonday halt or a few minutes' rest to catch breath after a stiffish climb, it is very amusing to see the porters making cigarettes, or extract from their turbans, where they were placed for safety and convenience, little pipes, draw a few whiffs, then pass them on to their less fortunate comrades, and in five or ten minutes be ready and content to start again, apparently thoroughly refreshed, if not docile and obedient to the demand of their *bwana* (master).

They carry water in calabashes until they get in the mooted vicinity of pools or streams, when they hastily empty them, averse to carry the additional weight. This frequently causes great distress among the men, for water too often fails, or is unfit to drink in well-known localities; then their rashness becomes obvious, too late to remedy, yet they never profit by experience.

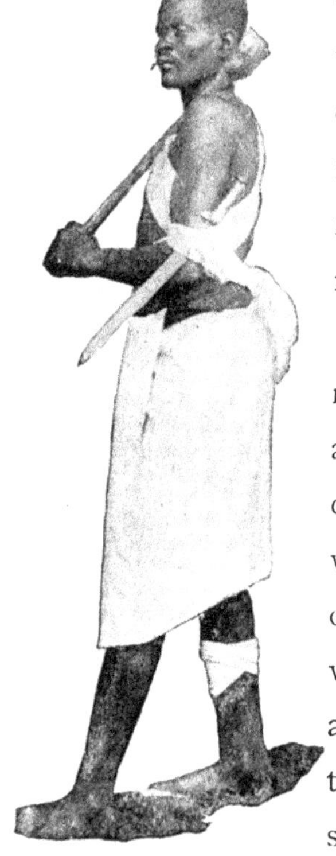
NATIVE SOLDIER.

When a difficult journey is being made and the men are fagged, there is always one man near the head of the caravan who starts up in a loud voice a song of encouragement; the drift of it is that they are paid for work and that they must be faithful, and when the journey is finished or the day is done, they may rest and sing, dance and eat, and all this for their brave *bwana*. Then they have songs of emulation, which are directed, with caressing policy, toward their leader, the *bwana;* the rhythm is very quaint, and the terminal chorus resembles a hunter's call, with a succession of long-drawn sounds. As far as I could ascertain, these sounds did not represent articulations, but were a species of rally whoops and yells, as well as a tone pledge of acquiescence in a crude way very much esembling Tyrolean trills.

Swahali porters, collectively called Zanzibaris, natives of almost every different African province, reveal their nativity by the manner in which they naturally carry their loads. A Zanzibari proper never carries a load on his shoulders, and his head seems provided with a thickness of scalp for his accustomed duty; just as the Wa-mawenzi have a muscular development on their shoulders in consequence of their habit of carrying loads upon them; and if on *safari* there is to be taken a palanquin or a hammock, which requires the services of two or more bearers, the leader should always aim to provide himself with Wa-mawenzi *pagazi*, otherwise he will be made very uncomfortable, thrust upon the heads of the others, swinging mid-air in a crazy way. The Zanzibaris carry their loads sometimes balanced with their hands extended overhead, on either side of the load, but with their bodies and heads perfectly erect, never looking at the immediate footpath,

NATIVE WATER-CARRIERS.

avoiding with deftness the overhanging branches or side projections. They put one foot directly in line of the other, without turning the toes out, making a very narrow tread.

This is a most difficult way for a European to walk, and I experienced great awkwardness in trying to stride from side to side of paths that we followed, or across the tiny water beds of mountain rills, because it was impossible to walk without stumbling, or stepping on my own heels, in a four-inch track.

SMALL GAME.

They universally carry long stout staffs, cut by the way in an adjacent bosk, which they thrust ahead of them, and bear upon when ascending or descending mountains, and employ to sound streams when fording, in order to find and avoid water-holes. The staff at night serves as one of the props on which they stretch their tent cloth.

MASAI SPEAR.

The Wa-mawenzi thrust a pole through the cords of their packs which they stick in the earth and prop against a tree to support them, and never place the loads on the ground when on the march.

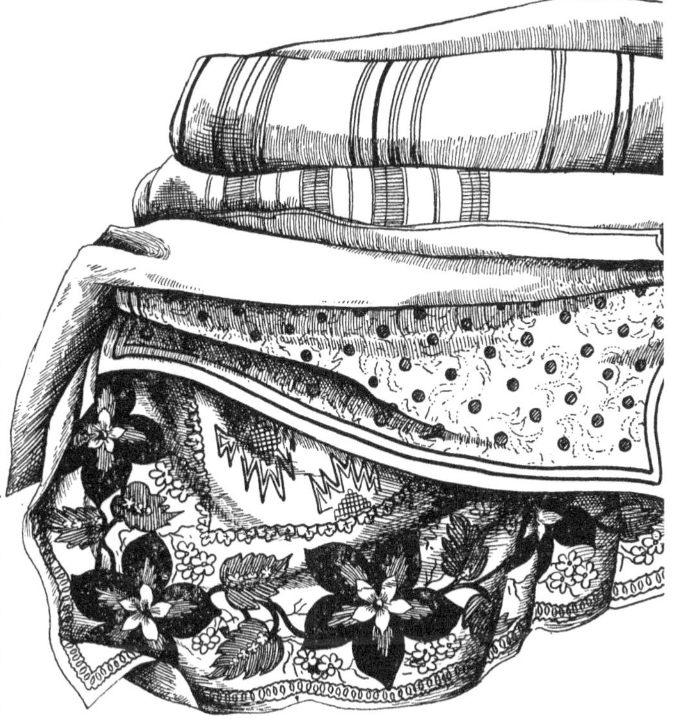

TRADE CLOTHS.

Frequently, when the roads are very muddy and slippery, the mud, being of a sticky clay consistency, adheres to their feet, and accumulates all the particles of grass and stones until they are obliged to stop and scrape it off, the weight becomes such a great hindrance to their progress. The tenacity of this mud and its depth at times, in consequence of the prevailing rains, caused me great personal difficulty. I was obliged to have one of my porters, with his bayonet, excavate places for me to thrust my toes, in order that I could walk upright instead of going on all fours or falling backward.

The refracted heat and glare, which most travellers complain bitterly of, reflected from the red and white sand, I was fortunate in being spared, as the season was auspicious and vegetation very abundant. But even the blaze of the sun, as it bursts suddenly from behind lugubrious clouds, will affect the eyes of one unused to it, and bring about serious affection of the vision. By using colored glasses with side pro-

POMBE CUPS.

tectors, this is easily mitigated. When approaching the natives I was always obliged to remove my goggles; for they were terrified whenever they caught sight of them, and would run away, screaming in fright.

This calls to mind an incident which occurred on the plains of Taro. After having thoughtlessly kept my goggles on, and the natives had experienced the usual scare, I endeavored to coax them back, trying to amuse them by showing them some pictures, which they did not comprehend, and finally started my music box to play. This delighted them so that they forgot all about the spectacles, which I had in the mean while cautiously removed.

When a large throng of natives was about me, feeling thirsty, I ate an orange, and the idea popped into my head that one of the pranks of my childhood might amuse them. So I cut a quarter section of the orange skin into points in imitation of teeth, and pressed them over my own teeth, operating them by opening and closing my mouth. This delighted the natives beyond expression, and an old chief besought me for the coveted sham; in his delight at procuring the trophy, he started off in great haste, soon returning with the blood streaming from his mouth, and a great splendid tooth, which he had just extracted, as a gift to me. He sat down when I had inspected it, and commenced to puncture a hole through it in order that I might string it round my neck as a charm against hunger.

GOURD WATER BOTTLE.

He indicated this to me by saying, "Chukula," which

means "food," and then touching his stomach with his hands, took the tooth and pressed it over his stomach, saying, "A-i-e, la-la," which meant that hunger would sleep.

Their gestures are so very significant that any one who pays heed must understand what they desire to indicate, without being able to comprehend a single word of their language. I have thought, since returning from Africa, that a clever and thoroughly good-natured pantomimist might be able to reach the intelligence of the natives more effectually than any other person.

A native desiring to tell me he had plenty of bananas on his plantation, which he was eager I should visit, took a bunch of bananas, put it down in front of me, pulled several of the bananas off, surrounded me by placing one after the other in a circular row, then lifted up the bunch and placed it successively beside each one of the distributed bananas. The whole thing revealed so clearly what he meant, that when my interpreter interrogated him on the point, it corroborated my idea; for it transpired that he owned a plantation which he averred

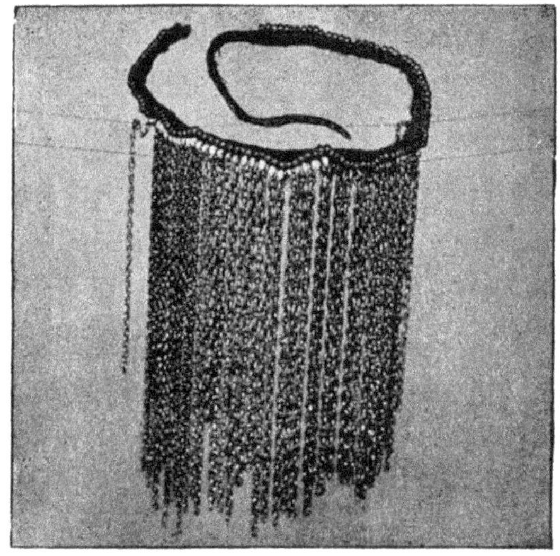

BRASS CHAIN NECKLACE.

was fruitful enough to provide the whole caravan; and as my porters wanted the fruit and he wanted to barter it for their beads and cloth, a bargain was at once struck.

Many of their antics in their sign language are not only grotesque, but childish. I was remarking to an elder in a certain tribe upon the fact that I saw very few deformed people, and none lame, when a native doubled himself up in a sitting posture and commenced to hop before me. When he concluded this little performance and again stood erect, he pointed with his tongue to his village, and made me understand that in it there was a man in this condition, and he wanted some *dawa*, or medicine, for him. This was verified when I accompanied him to his village. He took me forthwith to a hut where a lame man sat upon a long wooden framework which he used for his bed as well as his work-table, — a cripple from some accident which had occurred in his early youth; however, he was so useful to his people, even as a boy, — he is a clever craftsman now, — that he had not died young; like true Spartans, these natives adhere to the idea that if nature has frowned upon a human being, it is their duty to see that he does not eke out a life of misery or dependence.

Whatever they may resort to I am not able to state, but it is an exceptional thing to find adult cripples in Africa. This idea may also explain the fact that there are no decrepit old people; but as they do not allow even outside tribes to know of the deaths that occur among them, I think it would be very difficult to trace the time and method used to put away those who promise to be either imbecile or helpless. If a woman gives birth to twins, one of these significantly dies; if an animal has twins, not only are the twins slaughtered, but the mother is slaughtered also, for her prolificness is regarded as an omen of bad luck. There is something more subtle than I could discover actuating them in these seemingly senseless deeds, based undoubtedly upon some long-abiding superstition. I was informed of several cases of women being killed who had been considered traitors by taking lovers in a tribe hostile to their own, to whom they confessed having revealed the secrets of their own people. Without loss of time they were summarily killed, in accordance with an arbitrary law among themselves. A Masai woman of considerable importance, trusted as a purveyor between her own and hostile tribes, was discovered false to her tribal allegiance, having formed a liason with an enemy. She was thrown, so goes the story, with her abundant adornments of metal coils incasing her legs, arms, and neck, into a smelting furnace to be consumed by fierce flames. Her forty or fifty pounds of metal ornaments in due time melted into a mass.

EAR ORNAMENT MADE OF WART HOG TUSKS.

Little chunks of iron alloyed with copper and brass, displaying tiny glints of colored glass, all fused together and reputed to be of the unfortunate woman's worldly splendors, are given to or forced upon an enemy as a token of bad luck. Surreptitiously, at my solicitation, my headman procured for me a bit of the stigmatized metal. Men who are traitors are punished with more rigor, and with an idea of spectacular example. The man is tied to a tree, and all the men in the tribe will come and stick him with their knives, at first just enough to make the blood flow; then these stabs are given with increasing violence until the knives enter deep into the flesh, and the culprit quivers from head to foot in supreme agony; never, however, uttering a sound, but stoically enduring the punishment as his life ebbs out. His body is then allowed to remain the prey of rapacious vultures and hyenas, until there is nothing but a few bones and the ropes left.

The name of the traitor is never mentioned, and should one of his children — if he have any — bear his tabooed name, the child receives a new name; and in speaking of this man, his widow or family say, "He who has gone to the black world," evidencing that they have an idea of purgatory or of the more enlightened, dogmatic, fiery regions.

CHAPTER VI.

FIRST ALARM. EXCITABLE PORTERS.

SIMAMA! simama! Bébé! (Stop! stop! lady!) suddenly yelled my *askari*, "Masai! Masai!" This was certainly a trying moment. The porters at once launched forth into a voluble, rapid gibberish, out of which I could barely distinguish here and there a word I could comprehend.

But "Masai! Masai!" predominated, and every man was pointing to certain vague objects far away in advance on our line of march, and manifested unfeigned alarm and fear. The result was wild confusion, which I realized would lead on to a decided panic, if not promptly checked.

My field glasses revealed the cause to be the presence of several almost nude natives armed only with bows and arrows, and carrying a few calabashes and water-skins, who were dodging through the long grass and thick undergrowth in a coy, timid fashion, far from indicating hostility or aggressiveness.

Quickly halting my men, I proceeded to meet these natives, accompanied by an interpreter and two *askari*, who carried our Masai flag of truce and my little American mascot. Seeing us advance without fear or threats, they squatted abjectly upon the ground, their long bows and arrows planted straight up and down in front of them, their startled countenances, with eyes opened wide in amazement, speechless to see such a strange apparition of a *mzunga* (white man) as I presented.

WAIT-A-BIT TREE.

To remove their lurking apprehension as to our actual intention, I gave them several name rings, and Josefe imparted to them the elaborated statement that Bébé was a white queen of limitless power coming to make friends with them and to bring them many beautiful tokens of peace. To all of which they quizzically ejaculated, "A-i-e! a-i-e!" more amazed than before. Finally among themselves they talked in a subdued tone, casting inquisitive glances at me, evidently studying my attire, and christened me "Bébé Bwana"

BRASS BEADS.

(woman master); a *sobriquet* that was spontaneously and universally bestowed upon me as a satisfactory and all-sufficient appellation by all natives whom I met in East Africa; and this too with a certain directness and aptness that surprised me, not only in this title, but respecting the full meaning of all of their nouns. Sometimes they were no other than adjectival substantives in their cogent expressiveness of a like thing and kind combined.

These natives were stray sellers of calabashes, and *gee*, a substitute for butter made from goat's milk, strong smelling and rancid flavored, yet prized highly by natives and Zanzibaris and even white men on *safari*. They had meandered three days away from their settlement of Teita, in hopes to dispose of their produce and wares. They maintain themselves by their bows and arrows and the wild fruits found on all sides, carrying a small supply of maize, sugar-cane, and bananas, and sleeping under the shadow of the trees. As fine, fearless children of either forest, plain, or mountain, these specimens could not be regarded as types.

After the scare had subsided and we had resumed our march, meditating over the alarm exhibited by my valiant little army on such slight provocation, I could not but expe-

LUNCHEON IN THE OPEN.

rience a qualm of insecurity, and for the first time fully realized the terror the African bogy-man — the Masai — struck to the Zanzibaris heart. It was too late to repent, there was no chance for me to abandon the venture I had so confidently embarked upon, if I had so desired; therefore with a more serious sense of personal responsibility, and an awakening to the necessary requirement of self-government, in order to hold indubitable sway over my men, I bent my every thought, with more absolute determination to accomplish my aims at every sacrifice apart from relinquishment of personal dignity, and by the enforcement of discipline and exaction of duty and obedience by any means short of inhumanity.

Bravery and fearlessness have nothing akin to recklessness or heedless disregard of consequences. This statement is made in the full consciousness of the fact that during moments of sudden emergency, action must be taken without tardy deliberation at the time. However, previous training and consideration of possible peril, and general adaptation of ways and means, with a cool, well-balanced head, nerve, and tact, stand in the gap as a bulwark of power and unfaltering wisdom.

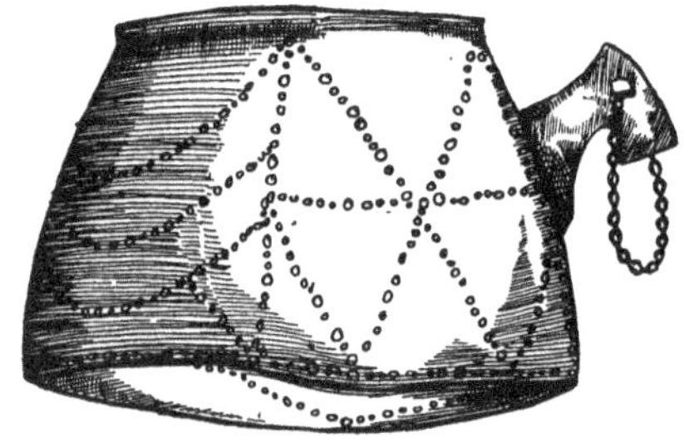

INLAID WOODEN BOWL.

My constant study was to know my porters, to learn their personal characteristics, and to put each man at his best. The tax upon my judgment was great, for these untutored fellows are creatures of ungovernable passion. If one porter calls another "a goat," like a flash the affronted man whips out his knife and makes a vicious lunge at the gross insulter; unless authorized interference puts a stop to these accessions of murderous passion, the result is likely to be a tragedy. Nothing is so effectual as the time-honored stick, the *kibosh*. I have been much maligned, and accused of ruthlessly flogging the *natives!* I do not feel called upon to explain on this score, yet will state the facts, so as to prevent misunderstanding in the minds of truth seekers.

One day a porter in anger stabbed one of his comrades through and through his body, imperilling his life. He was flogged.

Another porter violently pitched upon and brutally hurled to the ground the daughter of a chief, for no greater offence than that she persistently offered some sweet corn for sale, after he had ordered her to quit the encampment, which, by the way, was occupying the grounds of the native market place. This act came very near embroiling me with the natives. The man was flogged.

WOODEN POT.

Another hot-headed porter, maddened out of his reason, if he ever had any, wrested a rifle from a comrade's hands and shot at the headman, who had enraged him by assigning to him a load he objected to carry, missing his victim by a hair's breadth. He was flogged.

In glancing over my black list and counting the men who were flogged during my entire *safari*, the actual number does not exceed, in fact does not attain, the fingers of my two hands.

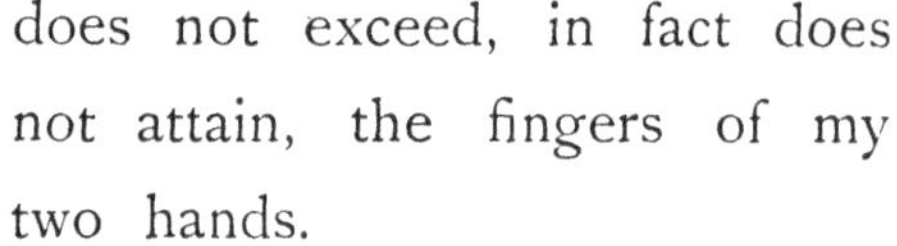

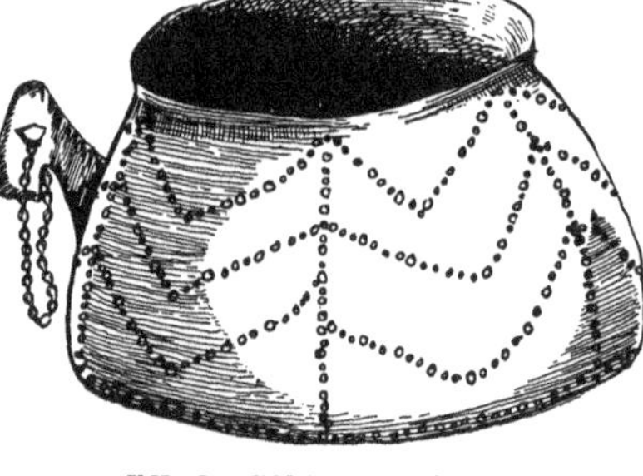

INLAID WOODEN BOWL.

Starting out on my expedition, I fondly nursed the idea that the porters could be governed by kindness and moral suasion, and that the discipline so necessary to their own individual safety, as well as the safety of the expedition, could be consistently maintained without resorting to the usual punishment with the stick. This cherished belief was soon modified by actual experience. I found that discipline could only be maintained by chastising serious offenders in the accepted way,—a method familiar to them and approved by the sentiments of their comrades. Coaxing arguments and persuasive talks were disregarded and sneeringly laughed at, probably the more so because *I, their leader*, was a woman. As time wore on, they found that I was always at the head of my caravan, and if there was any danger to be encountered that they could rely upon me; soon they were imbued with confidence and respect. They found, also, that wilful offenders would suffer just punishment, that orders must be obeyed without demur, that no idle threats were used, that promises were cautiously given but religiously kept, that yes meant yes, and no, no; that if any of them fell ill, I personally attended them daily, setting their broken bones, dressing their wounds or administering needed medicines, and having them carried when disabled.

The result was that I soon obtained complete control over every man. I do not think I could have succeeded in this if I had not most unwillingly changed my lifelong ideas about whipping. An appeal to physical force has always seemed to me to be brutal, and degrading alike to victim and administrator. However, circumstances alter cases. A caravan on *safari* as a travelling community must have order and laws of its own for the safety of the whole; it must, in itself, form a body politic to enforce these laws and assist in the preservation of order and discipline.

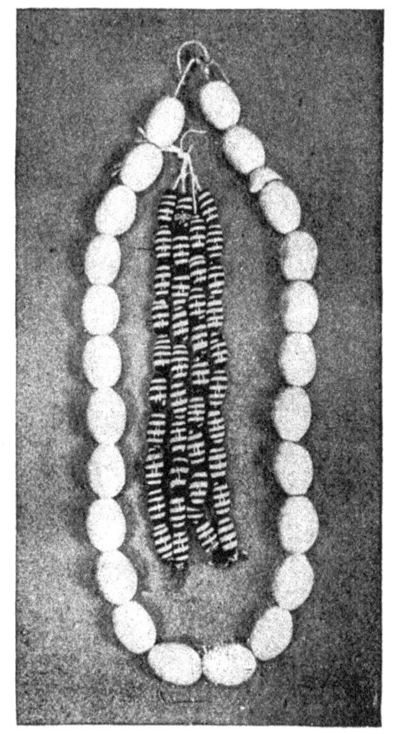

EGG-SHAPED BEADS.

The only thing when a man has committed an offence, and his punishment has been agreed upon by having his fault submitted to a jury of five or six of his comrades, is to have the headman execute it promptly, and if the culprit shows signs of atonement, never to permit him to be nagged or twitted; instead, to accept his good behavior for all it would seem to indicate. Other methods of punishment are particularly cruel, and disable the men.

There is, without exaggeration, more real good than intended evil in the Zanzibaris, if they are properly and judiciously treated. They have patience, obedience, devotion, and above all, pride.

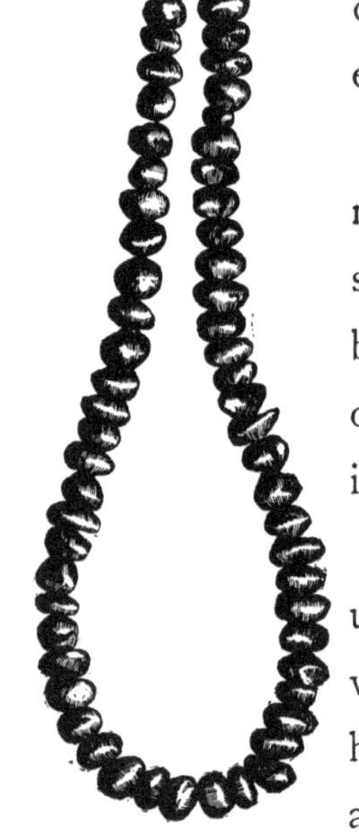
DAWA BEADS.

A circumstance revealing the pride animating them to excel each other and win some meed of praise may be best illustrated by the following story connected with one of my porters, known as the "strong man" in the caravan: —

Among the baggage was a long tin uniform case, which, because of its weight, was a double load; I fully expected to have had it carried between two men, but after a few marches this plan was found to be exceedingly awkward, owing to the steep, rugged country we traversed, so, with discontent, the porters put down the load upon the ground after a difficult day's march. My attention was drawn to them by the confusion that ensued. Getting at the true inwardness of the commotion, I called all the porters together, and stepped before them to try my art in soothing their fretted tempers.

"Here is a box which is a double load; I have heard a great deal concerning the renown of a strong *pagazi* in this caravan. Now, where is that strong *pagazi?* A man who earns double money and double *posho*, because he does the work of two men?"

JEWELLED SWORD GIVEN SULTAN MANDARA.

There was a decided rustle, then a jostling and parting at the back of the throng of porters, and forcing his way through there came forward a tall, stalwart fellow, with a beaming face, his smiling open mouth revealing his glittering teeth. He stood out conspicuously apart from the others, and announced proudly, "Bébé, I am that strong man." Then whirling himself like a spinning top round on his heels to display his muscular superiority, he stretched out both his arms, clinched his fists and forcibly drew them tightly up to show off his pronounced biceps, saying, "Bébé, command me."

Indicating the box with my staff to him, he salaamed, and grasped the handle of the great tin box, and with one single swing lifted it clean and unfalteringly from the ground on to his, I presume, thick head, balanced it there, and walked off triumphantly, sending a song of defiance and rally to the other porters, who gave vent to their adulations by slapping their naked thighs, by nods, and a general hubbub such as only a Zanzibari caravan can make.

This same porter had as tremendous a voice as he had a body, and was always talking garrulously, and roaring out in thunderous tones when we were on the march; and as he had naturally taken his post, as a man of entitled honor, in close proximity to my ears, frequently I thought he would drive me distracted. No sooner was one story finished than this inexhaustible narrator commenced another, and no comrade dared interrupt or gainsay him. One day, when my nerves were particularly rasped by his continual loud-voiced chatter, I summoned him during the noon-day halt to my presence.

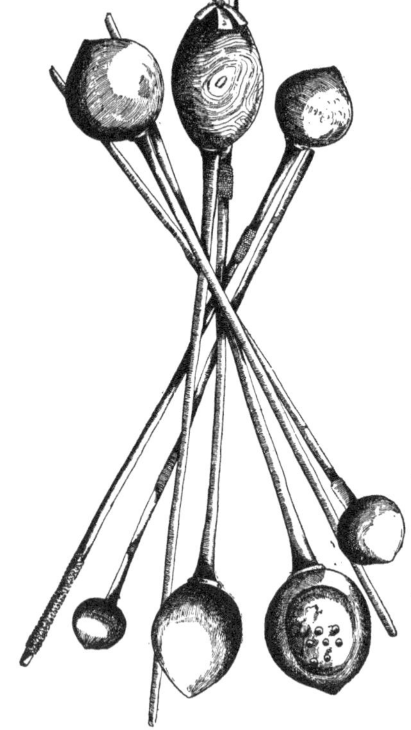

KNOB KERRY STICKS.

"Kara, you are a very fine fellow; you do your work well; you are always thoughtful of Bébé; you bring me beautiful grasses and flowers; no fire is so bright as the one you build for me; nevertheless I cannot have you screaming as you do behind my ears, and if it continues I shall be obliged to order you to the rear."

He made me profuse, emphatic promises to correct his

error, saying, as he again struck his breast with his sledge-hammer fist, "Bébé Bwana, you see I am so big in the lungs, and my voice is as big as I am strong."

To this I quite agreed, assuring him, whereas, I did not wish to diminish his strength, I did care to silence his lusty voice. That day things went on very peacefully. There was not the slightest occasion to complain of my Samson, and, in good truth, during the entire day he took it upon himself to cry out indignantly, "Kallela," to silence his fellow-porters in the rear when they, forgetful of my wishes, began to talk in a loud tone of voice. At night I called him up to me and complimented him on his effort to be quiet, telling him how well he had pleased me.

MY GUN. FIRST GUN CASE MADE BY NATIVES.

With a burst of enthusiasm he exclaimed, "Ah, Bébé Bwana, I am so happy! because I have sweat prickles from my marrow all day trying to be quiet."

The quaintness of the remark and the knowledge of the

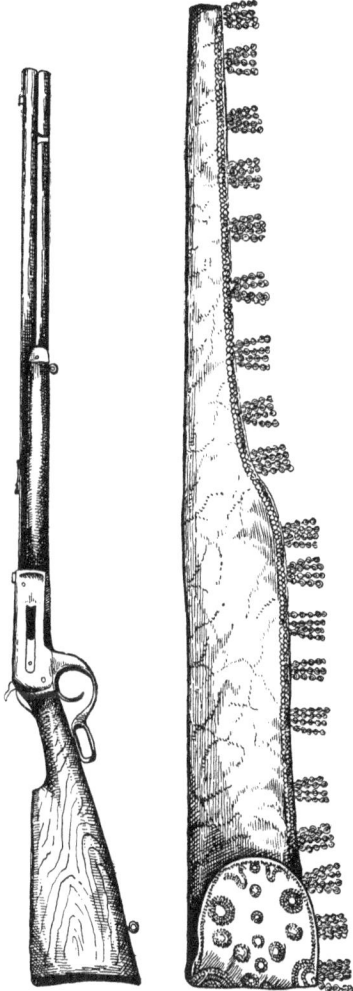

severity with which the prickly heat attacks these men, sufficed for me, and caused me to think him not inept in simile.

This same man was a great gormand, and the preparation of the food in the little knot of men with whom he messed was a work of art, and almost a work of devotion. He tasted the pot, when the chicken stew with vegetables of various kinds had reached the point when it required to be seasoned, and if the flavor was not up to the mark, he carefully added the deficient condiments. Before eating he always bathed himself and put on his spotless, clean *kanzu*, a long, white garment like a nightdress, fancifully stitched or embroidered about the neck; and if there was something particularly dainty, according to his idea, a choice portion of it was brought with great flourish to my tent, and ceremoniously proffered to me. He was always the first to establish his own tent and get everything shipshape and comfortable at the time of our encampment; and when his day's work was done, he would change his attire, and seemed to enjoy with sensuous delight the comfort with which he had so deftly surrounded himself. Unfortunately, poor Kara, whilst trudging up the foothills of Kilimanjaro, was sunstruck; he was not only incapacitated from carrying a load, but was in a serious plight for some days; yet he would not surrender his place of

HEADMAN.

honor, or give the load to one of his companions, but, with great fortitude, struggled beneath it until I personally observed his flagging condition, and was compelled to authoritatively interfere. I had him come to me, apart from the others, and told him he must surrender his load, and possibly be carried himself until we reached a proper resting

NATIVE KNIVES.

place, and his acute agony should yield to medication. He protested with great vehemence, exclaiming,—

"What! I, the strong man of every *safari* I have ever undertaken, give up my chosen load to one of those goats? Oh, no!"

Then I said, "Kara, my good fellow, I will tell you what I will do. Your box is known as the heavy load. Come, now, I will empty it, and you will only have the weight of the box on your head—just seventeen pounds—and no man in the caravan will know but what you are still carrying your heavy weight."

This artifice delighted him, and he fairly howled in barbaric glee when I dismissed him, to think he was going to get the best of his comrades by this subterfuge, yet maintain inviolable his prestige. So it was that Kara, the proud porter, carried, with comparative ease, during the period of his indisposition, for seven days, the empty box, no one in the caravan, not even my headmen, knowing that I had extracted its contents, and had, unsuspected, distributed the same among other loads without perceptible increase of weight.

KARA, STRONG MAN.

As Kara recovered his strength, he voluntarily sought me and suggested that the legitimate contents of his box might be replaced, saying he was feeling so well and strong and full of life that if he did not have a heavy weight upon his head as a sort of safety valve, he should fly from the top of one of the mountains and be dashed to atoms, so he needed the load to hold him down and exhaust his superfluous force.

Inadvertently I was just in the act of putting my foot upon an ants' nest, concealed from my sight by overgrowing grass, when, like a whirlwind, something suddenly grasped me about the waist, lifting me up from the ground, and seemed to dart on the wings of the air, away beyond on the open plain, when I was as suddenly dropped, and then discovered my captor to have been Kara, my strong man, as he prostrated himself, his face pressed close on the ground in the dust, pleading pathetically, "*Bébé Bwana; siafu! siafu!*" (ants, ants;) so it was that this ever-watchful porter, seeing me unwittingly about to step upon the vicious ants, himself knowing from sad experience what a terror they are to man and beast, had dropped his load and, unceremoniously seizing me, had carried me beyond the danger. In narrating this and similar incidents I must aver that these half-civilized porters, although deficient in many advantages that modern education brings, are far from being devoid of the highest chivalry.

NATIVE BANANA KNIFE, UNPOLISHED.

Apropos of these ants, they attack human beings in great droves, and have frequently been known to compel every man in an encampment to turn out, in the middle of the night, and seek refuge at some distance away from the original camp; it is no uncommon thing to hear the men grumbling and growling at night, followed by the flapping of their mats, when trying to shake off these invasive insects. Their bite is painful, and poisonous to some people. They have periods of migration, when they make long journeys in vast armies, devastating a tract of country by cropping a noticeable swath where they have traversed. The other ants, which build the strange red-sand structures, looking like broken battlements on the top of a palace or bastion, are perhaps more interesting to study. Then come the termites, or white ants, which seem bent on destruction; not only do they attack splendid forest trees at the roots and work up, devouring as they proceed the body of the trees, leaving nothing but the outer bark, in perfect semblance of solidity, but which will topple over and fall into fragments at the slightest push, they will also attack the foundations of any wooden structure, however massive; frequently wooden boxes that are put upon the ground for one night will be simply riddled by them, leaving only a mere veneering of the wood itself, however solid, which crumbles into dust when touched.

Travellers and inhabitants of Africa find these destructive creatures a great pest, and the wooden mountings of many fine instruments, to the sorrow of explorers, are totally destroyed without warning. The native woman invariably carries her infant slung upon her back in hides or cloth while at work pounding corn or millet, or when tilling the soil, fearful of allowing the child to remain on the ground lest it become a prey to the ants.

Mosquitoes and stinging flies infest Africa in vast swarms

PLODDING THROUGH AN AFRICAN BOULEVARD.

during particular seasons, especially towards and on the coast. One of the essential articles for comfort in personal outfit is a large, sound mosquito net, and large squares of gauze or netting to wear over the sun hat, and enclose snugly the head and neck; otherwise the flies dart into the traveller's eyes, which is even more painful than their sting.

WOODEN POT.

Then, too, the flesh-burrowing jiggers and grass ticks cause much distress; the jiggers usually burrow under the toe and finger nails, whereas the ticks work head first into the flesh, and breed therein in a prodigious manner if not dug out. Every one caught by the porters is cut in two. The poor, faithful fox terriers which adopted me from Taveta until they reached Moschi were simply besieged with these pests, and out of sheer mercy every day I would pick and dig their tormentors out of their flesh. The dogs' ears and groins were the favorite spots of attack. The poor little animals would be maddened in their helplessness to free themselves. I was told of several fine dogs having been made blind, and finally succumbing, pestered to death by ticks, and carelessly neglected by those who were caring for them in their masters' absence.

Old camping grounds are to be consistently avoided, as they are more than likely to be infested with jiggers, ticks, lice, and a nameless host of other vermin.

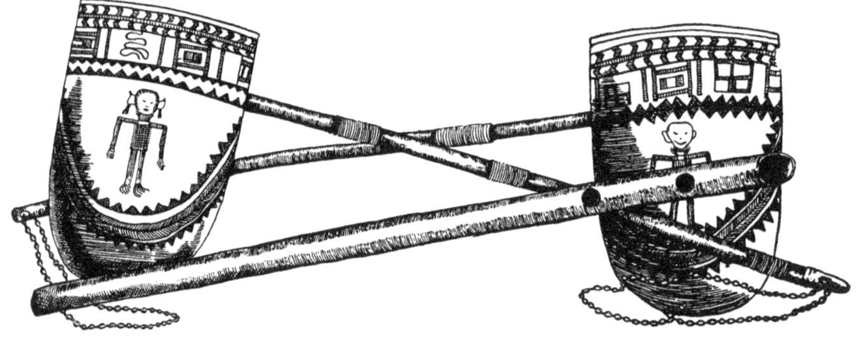

POMBE CUPS AND PAN PIPE.

A singular thing occurs respecting the animals and color of the sand; the tones all seem to marry one with the other; and when you chance to see a number of *hartebeest*, or deer, against one of these ant structures,— for such they are,— you cannot distinguish between the two until you see some movement on the part of the animals; and so it is with most of the creeping things, especially the mantis, the "praying mantis," which appear like the bark and twigs of trees, and like moving leaves which they so illusively simulate; even the butterflies look like winged flowers, and will, by some strange attraction, settle on flowers their own counterfeits in color and variegated condition, and when they rise and take wing, disturbed by some passing thing, the first impression to the vision is that a mysterious phantom breeze has blown the petals of the flower off the parent stem. The variety and gorgeousness of these butterflies are beyond description, but the choicest species, according to collectors, are the white,

TWIN MEAL POTS.

mottled with brilliant crimson spots, bright blue, pale green, yellow, and violet.

Pink locusts, clapping their wings and harshly chirping, swarmed in millions over our heads like a floating cloud all through one morning.

Another noticeable thing in the physical aspect was the prevalence of all shades of heliotrope, violet, and purple in the flowers; and whereas pink would prevail in England or temperate zones, this tropical East African nature seemed to be more fashionable, and dispense with the old-time beauties for some new diversity in the floral world. Clematis is very profuse, and a species of white, pink, and crimson magnolia, with great waxen buds and enormous fragrant flowers, with large, thick, smooth leaves; rhododendrons are gorgeous; balsams, narcissus, buttercups, asters, and poppies star the grass-lands, and milkweed galore and gladiolus, wild heliotrope, geranium, and orchids of the rarest, but no roses, not even a sweetbrier, to greet the eye. Every shady nook is a superb fernery of every variety. Maidenhair fern trails and twines to the top of high trees in a prodigal manner.

We constantly met myriads of land turtles of rather a small variety, and the porters would never pass one without taking their staves and turning it over on its back; and many of the shells that were brought to me for inspection bore upon their carapace Arabic characters, showing that some previous traveller or porter in a caravan had captured the little thing and carved a device upon its back, whether as a message to other caravans or merely out of personal amusement I am unable to say, for the natural tracings of the mottles of the shell and the characters were so intermingled that it was

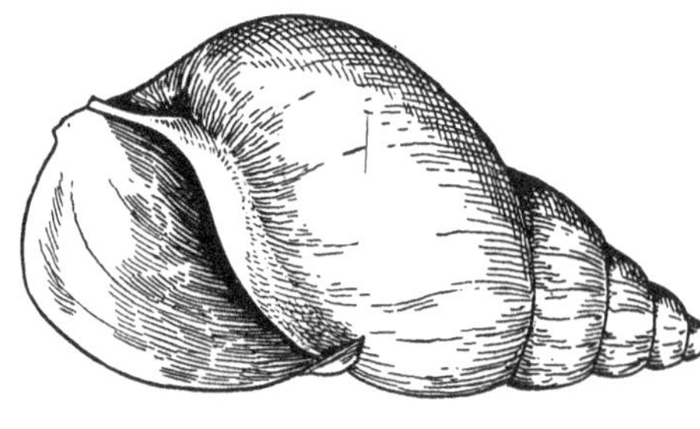

HELICES.

impossible to separate one from the other. I picked up from Teita throughout my entire journey, on the foothills of Kilimanjaro and even so high up as Kimangelia, beautiful pure white and delicate brown and buff helices, some very small and others enormous.

FRENCH–SHELDON RINGS.

Unwilling to travel among these natives without leaving some evidence of my presence, I had taken the precaution to have several thousand rings, on which were engraved my name, and to every native with whom I personally came in contact in the course of time I presented one of these souvenirs; they were also most useful to tie round a package of letters or send as an earnest, affixed to a seal, to a mission station, or when I required to send a messenger to a sultan whose country I desired to pass through or had already traversed. These little souvenirs became heralded from native to native, and tribe to tribe, and I was always asked for a *pété jini*, which meant a "name ring." Whilst fitting rings upon their fingers I was enabled to observe how small as a rule their hands were, and out of upwards of five hundred clay impressions on paper I took of feet and hands of natives of various tribes, it was exceptional to find a very large hand or foot.

CHAPTER VII.

WA-NYIKA AND WA-DURUMA.

THE tract of plain skirting the Shimba or Lion Mountains, where meander vagrant Wa-Nyika and Wa-Duruma, spread out before us as we started exactly at five o'clock at sun up, with rain-laden clouds overhead rapidly coalescing into dense, ominous masses, was certainly most uninviting and well entitled to its name of the wilderness. Everywhere the tropical vegetation seemed to offer a bristling protest to intrusion, — euphorbias, mimosa, acacia, wait-a-bits, cacti, and nettles of endless variety; the most lovely foliage to my sorrow I too often found hispid by a nap of infinitesimal needle-points; the very grasses were spiked and saw or blade edged, tearing, pricking, and gashing alike the flesh and garb, causing no end of discomfort, if not actual pain.

Suddenly a great cackling of poultry was heard, which answered well as a sounded tocsin to announce the appearance of a party of unseemly Wa-Nyika who were issuing from the woodlands to engage in trade with the *mzunga* caravan they had heard was coming. A pariah dog flew at me, and to ward off his attack I lifted my Alpine stock, and

POMBE CUPS.

at the same time discharged a pistol over his head. The dismayed natives were thrown into a wild state, and angrily rushed forward, flourishing their bows and arrows in a threatening manner, when my alert *askari* pointed his gun at them, shouting, "Stop! speak! salaam Bébé." When they discovered they were in the presence of a white woman, in consternation they kept ejaculating, "*Jambo! Jambo! Bébé mzunga?*" (How do you do, lady white man?) and dropped down upon the ground in a squatting position, staring me quite out of countenance, now and then chatted among themselves as though marvelling what it meant. Soon they queried the porters to know if there was a *bwana mzunga* (a white man-leader) of the *safari*. When the negative response was given, their amazement did not abate; indeed, they were thrown into a deeper quandary and exclaimed, "*Aie! Aie!*

Aie!" as they wagged their heads and riveted their eyes with fixity upon me, forgetting their feathered, fluttering, squawking merchandise, which, tethered to walking poles, had been heedlessly pitched upon the ground when they had rushed upon me. Then surged around me women and children, with equal amazement and more audacity than evinced by the men. They curiously commented upon my color, hair, hat, costume, shoes, gloves, crooked staff, and pistols; and in glee yclept, the latter, *m'toto bunduki* (baby guns). Language with all these tribes has a full-fraught meaning, making clear the thing they desire to communicate. Phrase harlequinade with its quips and pranks and abstrusely involved sense is reserved for enlightened supereducated races; barring their quaint poetic similes, — and these too are marvels of expletives, — the natives aptly short cut word and sense.

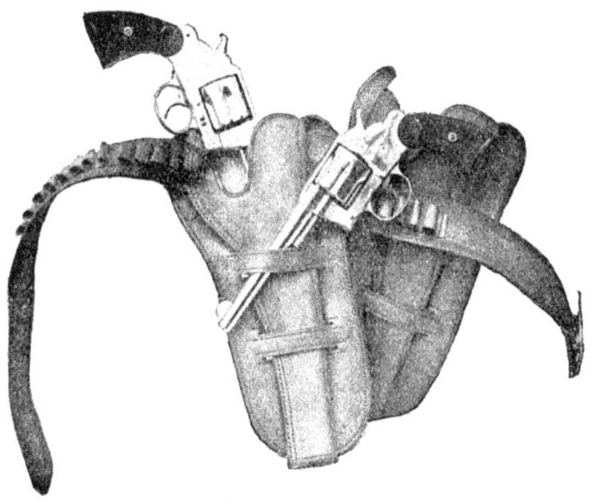

M'TOTO BUNDUKI.
(BABY GUNS.)

So these grovelling, intimidated, unclean creatures were the men of the wilderness! Their bodies tattooed indiscriminately without significance, and smeared with umber-colored clay and rancid grease, emitting an odor far from

EGYPTIAN MUSICIAN.

agreeable to civilized nostrils. Their teeth filed and discolored, hair bushy and rather animated.

The men, when not naked, wore a bit of hide about them, or a filthy fragment of cloth; whereas the married women disported a miserable blue calico kilted skirt, reaching half-way from their waist to their knees, and some indifferent beads and rough wire necklets and bracelets.

Trade was sharp for a brief time, and the general hubbub of the porters and angry protests of the natives squabbling over the chickens became deafening; the natives grew uproarious when a burly porter would cut a chicken from its tether and put down, in exchange, a string of red beads called *sem-sem*, and cry out "*Buss*," finished as a *finale* to the transaction, which was not satisfactory to the crafty, avaricious native. It always ended in the porter being compelled to relinquish the poor, thin *ku-ku* (chicken), and commence a new deal. At first these proceedings interested me exceedingly, but in the end I was obliged to take a firm stand to escape being fleeced beyond reason by the extortion of my long-sought ideal primitives, and found a magic in that same word *buss* that ended all dickering and disputes. Fives seemed to be the span of enumeration, and they use as an abacus, sticks, and in trade place one down, cry out *moja* (one), and follow it up with another and another, *pili*, *tatu*, *une*, *tano* (two, three, four, five); gather them up and go over the same again, if the trade exceeds five. And when they want to enumerate one half, a stick is broken in two; then they are thrown into a dilemma by possessing two half-sticks instead of one whole one. One hand doubled up stands also for five, two hands for ten, when sticks are not convenient.

If two bunches of bananas or other produce are offered

WOMEN OF THE HAREM.

for barter at the same price, the simple native will not sell both together, but one at a time. Exacting the fee agreed upon, he hands over the article and closes the sale by saying *buss*, which the purchaser repeats, then goes through the same detailed performance again. Should a dispute arise, as it generally does, between customer and trader, the latter will dog the former and by degrees accept the proffered stipend, after which a host of his tribe, finding the market price broken, will solicit barter on the same diminished terms. Yet the tenacity with which they hold fast to their first price, until they must own defeat or conform to a lesser offer, is admirable. Leaders of expeditions narrate, with striking unanimity, instances where their barter and the native's products have been placed in full view on the camp grounds for mutual consideration, and the natives could not be induced for days and days to yield, until time and patience failed, and an order was given by the leader to gather up the barter, and even then often the natives would permit the *mzunga* to depart without budging from their original demands. Extortion seems a latent trait with all African tribes; this properly directed in connection with their trading propensities may in good time result in converting them to thrifty commercial peoples, and in uplifting them beyond dependence upon philanthropic indulgence and helpless subserviency.

Wa-Duruma kept sneaking out from their thorn-hedged seclusions all day as we proceeded on our march, and presented a strange appearance, some few with their wool bleached yellow with unslacked lime, which is found hereabouts, and bushed out like Somali men, into which were thrust porcupine quills and short lengths of reeds and fish-bones.

Their ear ornaments consisted mainly of tiger and other

animals' teeth, and striped quills of vulture's feathers with a tiny tuft of feather at the end. A few slender strings of blue beads, a goatskin anklet, a meagre strip of clay-stained, coarse cotton cloth tied over their shoulders hanging scarcely to their hips, constituted their dress. Hardship and thriftlessness, if not poverty, seemed written on their lineaments. They suffer so from famine that they gladly sell themselves into bondage. This brings me to the statement that many Wa-shenzie, — which is an African equivalent for backwoodsmen, — when once enslaved and taken to the coast, are unwilling to be liberated, and have no desire to return to their former haunts or lives. A master must provide food and shelter for his slaves when they are not hired out. Then the slaves are obliged to give half, if not all, of their earnings to their master. A peculiar African institution is that of slaves owning slaves, and in my caravan there were men, not in my employ, but the slaves of some of my porters, who

EGYPTIAN COURIERS.

were themselves slaves, and were taken on *safari* to relieve their slave masters of their packs, and to do odd jobs for the headmen and others, remunerated by a mere stipend given to their owners, or remnants of food that would otherwise be thrown away. They seemed merry and contented to lead the nomadic life of a *safari* in companionship of the regular porters.

When not living in the open, they huddle with their families and their goats in dome-shaped huts no better than pig-pens, very low, made of branches and sticks plastered over with mud and dung, entered by a tiny aperture on hands and knees; the interior filthy and stifling with the dense smoke from an ever-smouldering fire, without a vent for its escape or for ventilation. They practise polygamy when they can; sell their female children and wives to the Masai or Arab traders; are a wretched, ill-favored people, debased even in the eyes of other African natives,

NATIVE GOSSIPS.

living not so far from the coast as to deter them from going thither, yet in their indolence preferring to skulk about, getting a precarious livelihood as they may. Their worship is fetich. As a whole, they have nothing to recommend them. They are stunted in growth, unhealthy in appearance, victims to skin affections, and look thoroughly degenerated and are of low-grade mentality.

My feet began to blister, and the men showed evidences of lameness from the same cause. To overcome the prevailing distress I issued an order to give to each man a certain allowance of carbolized grease to apply daily to his feet. This would naturally make ruinous inroads upon my stock of unguents, and it was necessary at the outset to think from what source to replenish. All goat and sheep and beef fat from thenceforth was understood to belong to me, no matter from where or by whom procured, and my bountiful *mafuta* (grease) supply was the unfailing comfort of every one in my caravan to the finish of my *safari*.

We passed several pairs of comparatively good sandals, discarded or lost by others who had travelled the same way. I fully expected to see my porters make a grab for them. To my surprise, not one man even touched them. It appears that some porters have a foot disease which is dreaded so intensely, in consequence of its infectious nature, that they one and all avoid any sandals not their own. When a goat, sheep, cow, or game is slaughtered, the porters beg for pieces of the raw hides, out of which they roughly cut soles

LOADS FOR FOUR PORTERS.

which they strap to their feet with a leather thong, and wear occasionally when traversing stony roads, and swing from their gun-stocks when not in use.

When we camped for the night we were obliged to form a hedge of thorn-bushes and circle the encampment with huge bonfires to keep the wild beasts from attacking us. It was terrifying to hear the continuous roar of lions resounding on all sides, and the scurrying feet of panting jackals, and to see the glare of hyenas' eyes in the darkness of the umbrageous surroundings. A sense of abject helplessness momentarily possessed me, vanquished by a courage that had only been dormant.

Orders were issued to have the camp doubly guarded and the men well armed and allotted extra ammunition. My gun and pistols were my close companions during a sleepless night. I felt I should have at least thirty-one chances before reloading if attacked. The night was particularly black and the growling, rumbling thunder was in unison with the mundane horrors. Day dispersed the impending storm-clouds, as well as silenced the nocturnal voices. The experience was beneficial, insomuch as the happy, safe *dénouement* dissipated all future cause for a similar scare during the entire *safari*. Unfortunately I had no Wa-shenzie hunters, and the majority of my men knew nothing about the use of firearms except

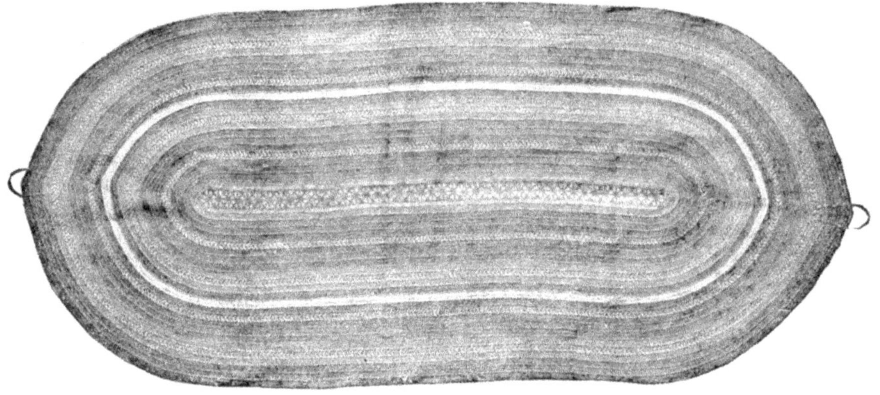

GRASS MAT FOR PORTER'S BED.

what had been drilled into them since enlisting for my expedition, and were clumsy at best. Nothing contributed more to my personal comfort than the numbers of lamps scattered about, four always outside of my tent, and the huge fires my *askari* (sentinels) kept up nightly.

Daily, hourly, I may aver the uniqueness of my position grew upon me; in truth, the farther away from touch with the coast we journeyed the more my personal responsibility and cares and anxieties, for nameless reasons, increased. A chronic insomnia gained upon me at such a pace I scarcely ever slept over two hours out of twenty-four; this, too, without a sequel of ill effects upon my health, although every nerve was strained to its highest tension. Walking conduced to my general well-being, and I am constrained to admit proved invaluable, with other rational hygienic observances, in giving me an entire immunity from fever. I never drank water that had not been first boiled and filtered, refrained from all stimulants excepting coffee, indulged daily in hot-water baths, cautiously avoided the sun's rays upon my head and spine, put on an additional garment when hottest, if not on the move; changed wet clothing as soon as convenient. A small bathing tent proved of the greatest use and comfort; it was always set just outside of the back flap of my tent, in close proximity, so I could step from one to the other with ease and privacy. Not least in sanitary consideration was my Palanquin, in which I slept, elevated at least two and a half feet from the ground, above the strata of miasmatic mists. One of my black women had a natural gift of massage; and whenever we

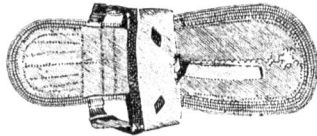

SANDAL.

TOP OF SANDAL.

paused for a noonday's rest, I made a habit of standing or moving about to avoid stiffness; and Suzani always came, despite her own fatigues, and if the seclusion of the trees or bushes was opportune, otherwise she called one of the other women, who would plank herself back towards me in front of me, and spread out her body-cloth to screen me; then Suzani rubbed me as a jockey might have rubbed a favorite horse between races. Abdullah, my civilian cook, likewise proved an excellent accessory to my migrating establishment. He was also a capital interpreter, not only of words, but alack! of my goods and chattels. Many and many a chicken was carried off by the hyenas that by natural assimilation was translated into his well-conditioned self.

POMBE CUP.

For general convenience I was provided with a huge waterproof, padlocked *dobe*, or wash-bag, into which was stuffed, protected and separated in lesser bags, immediately necessary articles, for example, a change of costume, extra shoes, toilet articles, and a small supply of soap, matches, candles, flint and steel, coffee, biscuits, as well as a small quantity of barter articles, and close at hand, as another pack, a cork ground bed. Through this precaution,

WOODEN PIPE.

an emergency retarding the bearers of my tent or special loads never left me in the lurch for ordinary comforts and essentials.

Every night or morning my women washed every travel-soiled article, snatching the opportunity to dry them as they could on the bushes or guys of my tent. When a dress or other articles of wearing apparel became useless through shrinkage or damage, they were carefully washed and placed in a load of utility oddments to await a time when they were worth their weight in gold for bandages, or to repair other garments. Every article of my clothing was light, durable, and as dainty as possible; in fact, everything had been done to minimize weight, in order to maximize quantity, in every department of my personal effects and caravan supplies. There were men scattered throughout the caravan who could turn a hand at almost every trade, or do a bit of jobbery, and even barbers and "leeches" were to be found when wanted; and I had taken a large supply of tools and articles to meet almost every conceivable demand,—rope, canvas, nails, sail needles, and great hanks of linen thread, as well as considerable aluminium wire, solder, and irons.

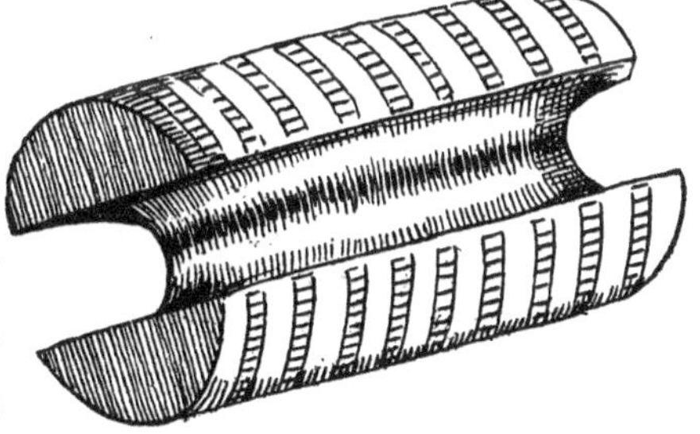

WOODEN EAR STRETCHER.

The indigenous products of the country offered all that could be desired in the way of fibrous plants and trees, and all the timber we could possibly require. A saponaceous shrub from which the natives and Zanzibaris cut their tooth-sticks was very prolific. One of the porter's attendants would be sent to cut an armful of this wood and distribute it right and left until his supply would be exhausted.

CAPT. WM. E. STAIRS, R. E.

*Capt. Wm. E. Stairs, carefully prepared the subjoined rules for camp making for me, supplementing them with a score of practical counsel, invaluable as the thoughtful outcome of his vast experience as an officer of famous repute in African exploration, for which I shall ever be grateful.

* Since the above went to press, the direful news of Capt. W. E. Stairs's death near Zambezi has made all solemnly grieve who knew the loyal, gallant, high-spirited soldier, the refined gentleman, and unselfish, lovable friend. His untimely death is an irreparable loss. M. F. S.

Although I found it expedient to deviate from the letter in some of the minutiæ, as he would have advised had he been on the field cognizant of the situation. His watchword, "Discipline for yourself and for your subordinates," was never forgotten. In proof of his own acceptance of this axiom was his trite expression, "Never question a duty to be executed, *do it* quickly and leave it accomplished behind you, or face it like a Briton *a l'outrance.*

NATIVE WOODEN BASIN.

HINTS FOR CAMPS, ETC., AS REGARDS DEFENCE.

I. Choose commanding position, one not near long grass or bush, if hostile natives are about.

II. Beware of long, dry grass near camp; natives may set fire to it and burn you out. So clear a space round your goods of twenty to thirty yards diameter.

III. Cover up your goods with tarpaulins, and place sentries, and as a general order let this be the rallying point in the night or when danger appears imminent.

IV. Place sentries (black) in groups of not less than three men each at exit and ingress of camp, seventy yards from centre, and in great danger, groups to right and left.

V. In an attack on camp at night the first notice will be some arrows falling in the camp. At once order silence, smother down the fires, as the natives invariably fire at these in hopes of hitting men lying about them, and rally near the centre pile of goods, and store of ammunition; then send out some of your most reliable men, *but you* yourself keep in camp and direct matters.

VI. Never move a step in Africa without two or three attendants with rifles. Make this a maxim, for one day it may save your life; and remember there are maniacs in Africa as well as elsewhere.

VII. Your column organize as follows: * first, your riflemen, without loads; then the carriers, then a small force under a chief in rear, and for this pick your very best man.

VIII. Insist on your personal baggage, tents, and blankets being near your person, and always up in front, otherwise you may arrive in camp and your things be hours behind.

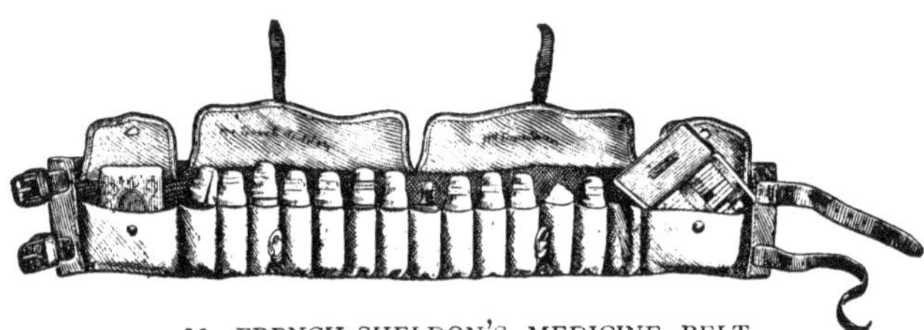

M. FRENCH-SHELDON'S MEDICINE BELT.

IX. Number every bale, box, load, or bundle, and enter in a book against the name of its carrier, and endeavor to give same loads to same men each day.

X. Fall the men in each morning, call the roll, and give out their loads in person. This keeps up the discipline and prevents favoritism, as the best black chief will give his friends light loads if left to himself.

XI. Always try to keep near you quinine, carbonate of ammonia, and one or two other standard medicines.

XII. Natives as a rule prefer day to night for attack; a night march may often put you out of a difficulty.

XIII. Go slowly at first, with frequent halts till the men and women get strong; allow as many women as possible to accompany you, as it shows peaceful intentions.†

* This was impossible, as my loaded porters carried rifles.

† The few women in my caravan were a decided detriment, and caused me unceasing anxiety and chagrin.

XIV. Do all the palavering yourself if possible. Swahali will carry you far along your journey.

XV. You as a woman possess many points that no man would have in dealing with Africans. You therefore should find an *entrée* easy anywhere.

General principle of a camp in danger:—

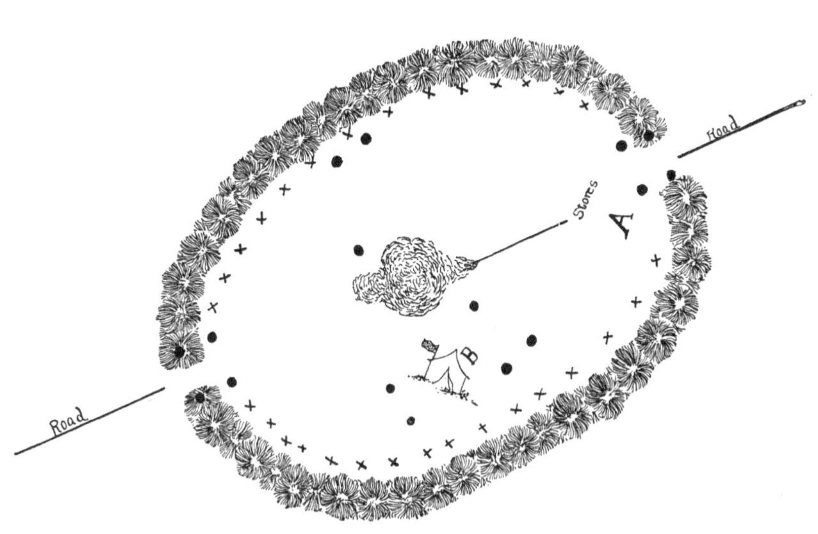

: : Sentries.

A. Stores and rallying point.

B. Tent.

XXX. Men sleeping.

Never put your tent on the edge of the camp, and always have trusty ones sleeping near you.

When no immediate danger is apprehended, the sentries should be *outside* the camp, fifty yards, which is about bow-shot.

In conclusion, I feel sure that your invaluable tact and perception will pull you through much that a man would fail at.

In danger or in safety, do not forget to have always in camp some watchers, or sentries, with their rifles handy.

You can never be safe till this is done, and the men know what to do in an emergency.

Yours sincerely,

W. E. Stairs.

To Mrs. French-Sheldon.

CHAPTER VIII.

REVOLT AND DEATH.

PLAINS of Taro stretched out in vast, sloping, sandy lengths, defined by the clusters of hills on either side, and an isolated sand mound now and again looming up like a dome without apparent connection with the hills. An occasional length of thorny vines and trees, gray, spectre-like, gaunt, gnarled, bare of leaves but clad in cruel repellent thorns, were made more conspicuous by the luxurious wide-spreading branches of a baobab, or a mango, interspersed with brilliant flowers, prolific, delicate ferns, and marvellous cacti.

The rain had imparted an agreeable, smiling freshness to nature, veiling the burning red sands and tufted stubble with a generous verdure, which spared us all much discomfort. This portion of the route, however, is generally conceded to be full of hardships, especially as the porters are scarcely broken in to their work, and their feet are soft and easily burnt. In making such a detour as the wait-a-bits and other natural obstacles provokingly compel in Africa, lengthening the journey to a given point at times immeasurably, my men became surly, evincing symptoms of insubordination. Suddenly the leaders wheeled around, halted the line of porters following, pitched their loads in wild disorder upon the ground, saying Bébé did not know the road, and refused to budge, and as the porters in the rear kept coming up they were incited to manifest the same spirit. The minor headmen made futile attempts to rally the men, and beat about in a lusty manner with their *kibosh*, all to no effect. Hamidi, my factotum, was in the rear, far away; and Josefe, my interpreter, was simply guyed and scoffed at for every order he issued from me. Then or never I realized I must demonstrate to these mutinous, half-savage men that I would be obeyed, and that discipline should be enforced at any cost. Only for one instant in perplexity I paused, a vulture flew overhead, I drew my pistols and sent a bullet whizzing after it, and brought it surely down at my feet, to the astonishment of the revolting men.

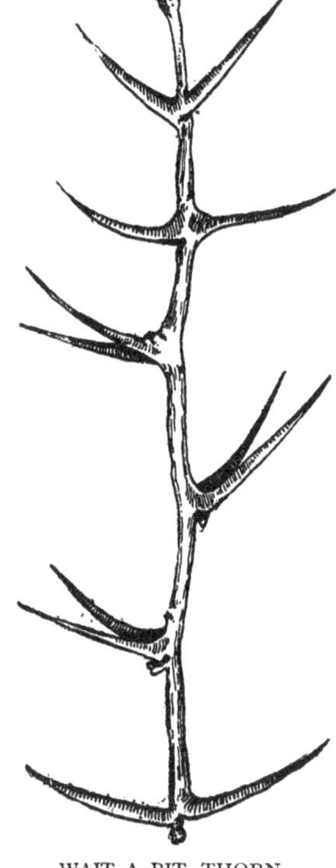
WAIT-A-BIT THORN.

With both pistols cocked, suddenly I became eloquent in the smattering of the Swahali which I knew, without interpreter, inspired with fearlessness and strength I started through the centre of the rebellious throng, pointing first one, then the other pistol in quick succession at the heads of the men, threatening, and fully prepared, determined, and justified to shoot the first dissenter.

As with unflinching, angry eyes fixed upon them, I exclaimed, "Get up! take your load! One! two! th——!" and before the three was pronounced the man addressed was on his feet, grasping his discarded load. After half a dozen men were thus warned, and the entire throng revealed uneasiness and were stirring, I turned upon them and said, "Every man who is not on his feet with his load on his head, when I have counted three, I will shoot!" They knew I would, and knew I had been empowered to do so by the Sultan of Zanzibar.

RACONTA BEADS.

Then I had no fear; now I marvel how ever I had the temerity to take such extreme measures.

NATIVE WOODEN COMBS.

I halted my caravan, and through the pelting rain, attended by Josefe and two *askari*, retraced my steps to meet Hamidi, who had been delayed by the accidental disablement of two porters, who were being slowly carried. He returned with me, and the men were harangued in such plain language there could be no future misunderstanding. The two ringleaders were flogged, order restored, and that march resumed.

This was the first and last revolt during my *safari*, and if it had not been promptly and fearlessly quelled, my life would not have been safe, and the entire caravan would have been in constant danger from similar outbreaks.

MEDICINE BOX.

Although it rained daily, many well-known pools, or *ziwi*, were filled with mud and slime, and the porters would drink the loathsome fluid, heedless of resultant illness. On the hill of Taro are famous water-holes, or small cisterns, which irregularly honeycomb masses of flat rocks, called *ungurunga*. These are remarkable natural formations, cupped into and channelling a short distance beneath the surface of granite-like rocks. Many theories are offered to explain their existence. Some suggest that they have been carefully enlarged by the hands of the wild men from time to time, when they have traversed the plains. Slight

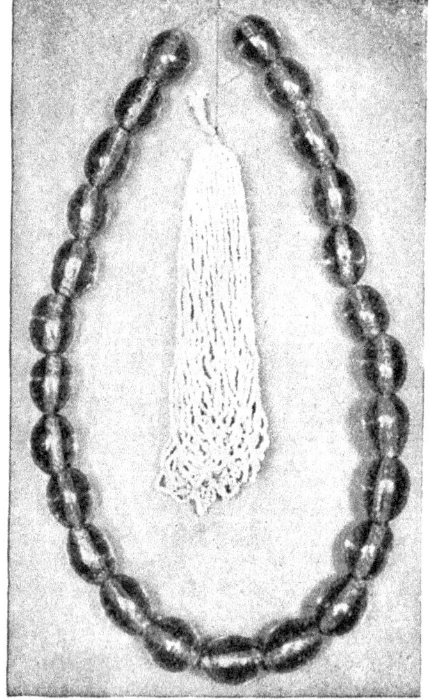

TRADE BEADS.

depressions in a soft portion of the rocks, where water was observed to accumulate, have been scooped out by travellers, and increased by the decomposition of decayed vegetation. Many of the holes are mere pockets; whereas others I discovered were connected beneath the surface of the rock, some two to four feet in diameter and ten to twelve feet deep.

Here every *kibuyu* or calabash or bottle or kerosene tin was filled, to meet the requirements of one of the most difficult marches through an up-hill country.

METAL NECKLACES FOR GIFTS.

As we were about to move on, I observed a tree covered with what seemed to be yellow blossoms, so thickly set that the color of the bark from root, branch to top could not be discerned. Casting my eyes up, and lost in wonder, my Masai interpreter, who was something of an African cicerone, pushed forward, and tossed his turban into the tree. The yellow rose on wings, and proved to be the tiniest birds imaginable, in size between a humming-bird and an ordinary butterfly. Not one twitter, only the rustle and whir of thousands of wings, as the yellow gradually coalesced into an airy cloud overhead, and was gently wafted far away out of sight.

Useless to narrate day by day the routine and detail of marching, or to make much ado about hardships and trials, which were the consistent outcome of such a journey. We met only a few straggling natives. Fever began to be manifest among the men. Warburgh's solution was promptly and lavishly administered; their feet and legs swelled, and great gaping ulcers appeared. These were most miraculously healed, through a simple treatment. First, the ulcers were washed out, and the cavity was filled with powder iodoform; then bandaged with a strip of antiseptic gauze, over which was tightly tied a piece of goat's or sheep's hide, and left without redressing for several days, when the ulcer would have healed and present a wholesome surface. This simplified and minimized the medical labors which were incumbent upon me. The swelled and blistered feet were relieved by hot water when available, and constant use of grease, which I provided in almost limitless quantities.

With considerable horror I discovered that two of my men were afflicted with a malady simulating, if not actually, leprosy. They were kept isolated as much as possible, to await developments, and in a few days when the toes on the foot of one man dropped off, and

MASAI LONG SPEAR.

the other case became an aggravated form of leprosy, there was nothing left for me to do but arrange to provide for them and leave them with some kind natives, until they could join a coast-bound Arab caravan, or by degrees work back to Zanzibar.

Every man in the caravan who had not had smallpox, or had not been recently vaccinated, I vaccinated, and strangely not one man was disabled thereby, although every case "took"; this may be attributed to the excellency and purity of the vaccine and certain hygienic laws I unremittingly persisted in having the men observe.

KAUZU WORN BY HEADMAN.

When encamped the temporary invalids were assigned the duty of camp scavengers, swept with besoms of their own make-up all the litter, and burned all rubbish, and it was forbidden that any one should in any way befoul the camp or its immediate vicinity.

The nights were made hideous with the roars, howls, grunts, chatter, yappings, and croakings of wild beasts and frogs, crickets and cicadæ. Our camp was always surrounded by a thick thorn hedge, and camp-fires blazed on all sides. Through the interstices of the hedge could be seen the red glaring eyes of the prowlers, and when the animals became too intrusive, a random shot sent them helter-skelter to a safe distance.

We intercepted a caravan, and I sent a package of letters

to the coast, sealed and tied, with a name ring affixed. There was a thrill of delight in being able to communicate with the world of civilization through this means of mail carriers not included in any zone system.

COPPER BEAD KIBOSHO NECKLACE.

After marching during a perfect hurricane, with the rain pelting and soaking us, the van of the caravan led as ever by me, we arrived at the camping ground at the foot of Mungu to await the weary stragglers. As filthy and disgusting a spot as can be imagined, infested with vermin and cluttered with all manner of discarded rubbish, provision tins, bits of garments, old sandals, rinds of fruit, the chewed pith of sugar-cane, bones, fragments of rope, broken bottles, and ash heaps. The storm increased with such violence there was no choice; the camp must be made there, until we could get a supply of water from the quenchless well at the top of the mountain. Two thousand feet of rocks to scale by the footsore and weary men, and jackals and lions in hazardous proximity. Every one was irritable and fractious, their din grew unbearable, when suddenly the storm abated and the sun burst out dazzling, shedding a good-night radiance over all. Good-nature was restored, the men began to sing, and each one eagerly performed his task; those detailed to bring water started swiftly with their utensils and their guns up the steep mountain to the well, in order to return before the sun should vanish and night set in. A warning charge was given to a young porter not to tarry, and above all not to wander away from the others, knowing full well he might be enticed by the sight of the wild pepper and berries that there abound.

WOODEN MEAL DISH.

Awaiting the return of porters sent for water and watching the laggards of the rear come into camp, my attention was attracted by seeing upon the arms of a Wa-Duruma woman a curious pair of pink and white bead armlets. I tried to purchase them from her. She waxed very angry at the mere suggestion, her eyes flashed indignantly as she gathered herself up on her feet, and placed her back against a tree as if to defy me.

"No! Bébé Bwana, no! no! no! My man has gone to Chaga land, and these he placed on my arms to prove my faithfulness to him. They were his marriage gifts to me. No! no! no! I will not!"

Nor could she be induced to part with her bridal bawbles, although I made her tempting offers of cloth and beads she much coveted. However, her protest and sentimental indignation were worth tenfold the value of the armlets as a revelation of character; and yet these natives are reputed by white men to possess no idea of nor disposition to faithfulness in their marital relations. They may be inconstant, but they are faithful in a way.

SWEET GRASS BEAD NECKLACE.

Night fell; the moonless darkness was so intense it seemed palpable. Every man was in camp but one. The roll was called. Alas! no answer came to "Ferusa bin Sura," the boy who went with the others to bring water. Every man was questioned concerning him. Yes, they had filled their vessels all together; he was there with them, and they had all started down together; no one had noticed that he loitered, although the wild pepper was plenty and they all had gathered some as

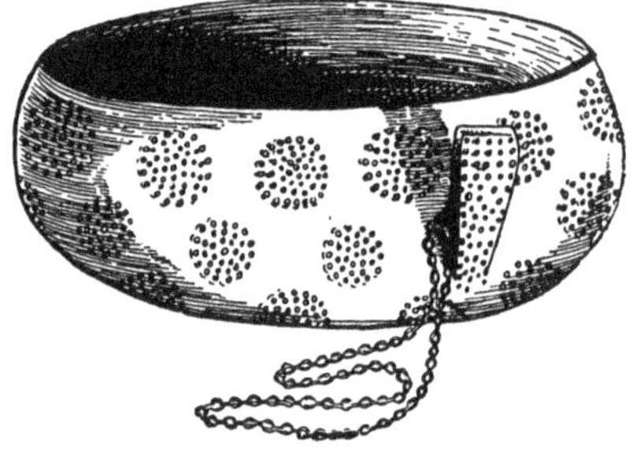

BEAD-INLAID BOWL.

they came leaping down the rugged mountain, but driven by hunger, fatigue, and the fear that night might overtake them, they had not tarried.

Hamidi organized a search party with torches and guns to search for Ferusa bin Sura. Kerosene cans were opened and great bonfires made. The relief party shouted, yelled, and sung. A protest resounded on all sides from the wild beasts. Presently an unearthly shriek overrode all other noise; my heart fairly choked me in its agonized plunges and curdled my blood, for I realized that poor Ferusa was being devoured by the lions. Nothing could now restrain me. With a well-armed body guard and torches I made them conduct me up the mountain path and fire volley after volley, trying to frighten the animals; all to no purpose. We finally discovered that he had fallen into a gully, and there had been pounced upon by lions he had disturbed. Nothing was left but to retreat, and in the morning search for his remains. We found a bone or two, and the water pail ominously marked with my name. Sometimes in the night my memory

NATIVE DISH MADE OF ONE PIECE OF WOOD.

vividly brings back those ear-splitting shrieks, and the whole scene, with its spectacular horrors, parades through my brain. This was the only human creature I left dead in Africa; although later on I had an attendant so violently ill with fever, so mad in delirium, forcing upon me great personal solicitude and requiring hourly vigilance on my part, and a total surrender of all other special attendants to the invalid's care, in order to prevent another tragedy. The caravan ambulance of this one invalid required the service of eighteen during four fifths of my *safari*, but reached home comparatively well.

SPIRAL METAL NECKLACE. NATIVE WORK.

During the day I visited some villages we passed, where there was scarcely any sign of habitation; the huts wide open, the fires burning, completely deserted, with the exception of a few old men and women lolling about; for every one else had gone to work on the *shambas*, or plantations, which the auspicious rains had made fertile, or had followed those who did work in order to secure to themselves companionship. But when the sun was about to set, surging from all directions came the natives, the women bearing upon their heads long loads of grass or wood, happy and joyful as if the day had just begun and they were anticipating some fête, rather than having just finished their labor and returning home for rest and refreshment.

NATIVES COMING TO SEE BÉBÉ BWANA.

Methods of working the plantations seem rather hard upon the women, because the few tools they use are without handles, and the Zanzibar hoe is a bastard pick and hoe combined, something like an adze.

WOODEN SPOON.

The shortness of the metal haft, which is projected from the tool itself, compels the women to bend almost double as they break up the ground.

Fortunately the rare fertility of the soil lessens the necessity of much work of this kind. They cut the grain with curved knives sharpened on the inner edge,

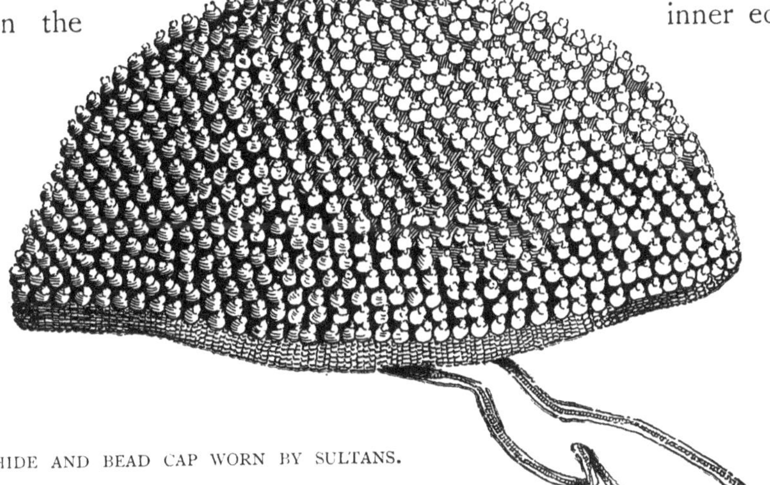

HIDE AND BEAD CAP WORN BY SULTANS.

something like a modified sickle, as well as with long straight knives looking like dirks. The curved knives are principally used for cutting banana stalks and grass. The women resort to a rather singular artifice in case the bunch of bananas they essay to cut happens to be very heavy; they manage to stand up directly beneath it upon a stone or log, and by throwing their heads back and a peculiar curving of the spine, manœuvre until they make platforms of their necks and breasts, upon which they ease up the heavy bunch, while they reach overhead to the extreme limit of their arms, grasp and hack it off by a sweeping motion of their curved knives; and I have seen a woman supporting a bunch of such ponderous weight that when it was liberated from its parent stem she would fairly reel backward, stagger a moment to recover herself, and with difficulty keep from dropping her precious burden until she was able to place it carefully on the ground. Finally she would, with regathered force, firmly lift it on her head and walk away with her burden, displaying the lightness and agility of a gazelle. The women never seem to shirk carrying a load, however heavy it may be, if they can once manage to get it settled and balanced upon their heads.

CHAPTER IX.

DEPRAVED WA-TEITA.

DIFFICULTIES and hardships were steadily in the ascendency from the moment we left the sycamores at Maungu, and struck the steppes to the west. The mountains of Ndara, presenting their rugged gneiss wall, stand out boldly, and beyond the mountains of Teita hazy like a half-tone. Nature became more erratic, vegetation more varied; the breccia rocks were full of bits of glittering quartz and mica, thorns and angular branches made phantom-like profiles, grasses of a height exceeding ten feet hid the glaring red sand, and brilliant odoriferous flowers attracted swarms of honey bees. Our march in the broiling sun, up the rising ground, fatigued us considerably. Unfortunately, my advance *askari*, whose business it was to lop off the intrusive branches and vines to make a way for me, allowed a branch of a thorn-tree to escape his grasp, which flew back and struck me in the left eye, leaving a thorn thrust in my

TEITA HUT.

eyeball. Such agony I never previously experienced, and the attendant horror that, in removing the thorn, the eye might possibly be destroyed, disquieted me to the degree when all knowledge of expedients was vanished for a time.

Terror reigned supreme over every member of the caravan, and the poor unhappy culprit supplicated me for mercy, fearful that the penalty for his fault would be nothing short of death. Although sorry for myself because of the seriousness of the accident, there was certainly no wrath in my heart for him. A singular coincidence occurred which I feel justified in narrating, as it impressed the Zanzibaris as to the actuality of the superhuman powers they heretofore had supposed were enthralled in my being. The same *askari* met with a similar accident to his left eye thirty-six hours after my misfortune, and gradually his eye ran out, so that when we reached the coast, at the finish of the *safari*, the empty socket tortured my conscience, knowing that he believed it was a retribution I had called down upon him. He was a Roman Catholic convert, and during the remainder of the *safari*, after his own injury, he addressed orisons first to God, then to me. He fully accepted his affliction from the beginning as a righteous punishment I had called down upon him, and nothing could eradicate this idea from his mind. He would pathetically and without cant say, "Bébé is merciful, kind, and good; a *bwana* would have shot me."

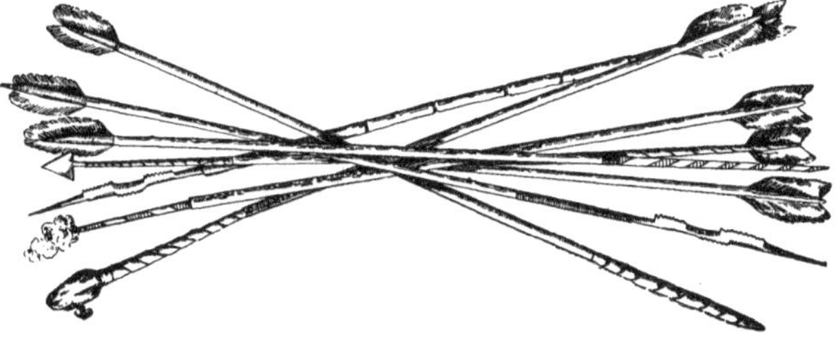

POISONED ARROWS.

After the shock had abated, my eye was bandaged, and on we marched. One does not stop for an eye or a limb or a life in Africa; one is ever impelled to proceed, *per augusta ad augusta*. With one eye I saw more than I can ever hope to recount of the grandeur of Kilimanjaro, and am repaid tenfold for all I suffered in Africa by the possession of the confidence and friendship bestowed upon me by the African primitives.

At the foot of the Ndara Mountain we halted just below the Sagalia mission station, at least six hundred feet above. This camping ground, so well known to all caravans traversing that region, contains a number of uninviting straw and banana-leaf thatched sheds, filthy with the indescribable *débris* of many caravans, and giving out a strong odor of chickens, goats, cattle, and, at this particular time, also of camels, for the I. B. E. A. caravan taking camels up country had only a few days before passed that way. Some of the tired porters hastily put down their loads, and threw themselves upon the litter, heedless of the filth and stench, in their eagerness to avail themselves of the dubious shelter. A pool of water fed from the mountain rills, if not indeed from a living wellspring, a dark, dank home for wriggling, loathsome creatures, silently rested beneath outspreading sycamore and baobab trees. Here the men scrambled and threw themselves flat on the ground, plunged their heads into the water and drank until they had quenched their inordinate thirst.

NATIVE METAL RINGS AND GOATSKIN BROTHERHOOD RINGS.

In quick response to our signal shots the natives discharged two rifles, and men, women, and children, the young and the old, began to swarm down the rugged escarpment with amazing precipitation, bearing on their heads all sorts of salable green stuff, and chickens, eggs, butter, *gee*, milk curds, honey, and what other articles of barter their meagre stock in hand warranted.

A great hubbub ensued, to which the porters largely contributed, as there would be a mutual recognition of an old acquaintance. Mr. Wray, the former resident of the Sagalia mission, also the agent of Ibea, had resigned their posts in consequence of the dissatisfaction manifested by the natives in a series of unbearable persecution. Their absence deprived me of an opportunity I had largely counted upon whereby to obtain some interesting data.

SNUFF-BOX.

Whilst the men of the caravan were bartering, cooking, bathing, and filling their calabashes, attended by Josefe and three *askari*, I climbed over six hundred feet up to the top of the hill to take a bird's-eye view of the surrounding country and visit the people.

Depravity seems to be an eminent characteristic of natives in easy touch to coast traders and caravan traffic. The Wa-Teita, especially that branch of the tribe known as the Wa-Sagalia, who inhabit this portion of the mountain in the province of Teita, situated as it is at the four corners of caravan routes leading to and from the coast in various directions, present a glaring example of the statement. They are grovellers, devoid of self-respect, and evince a shameless state of beggary; although they possess a most fertile tract of country, protected by its eminence from surprises by hostile tribes, their indolence and the prevailing demoralization of the women too often reduce this tribe to a sad plight of penury.

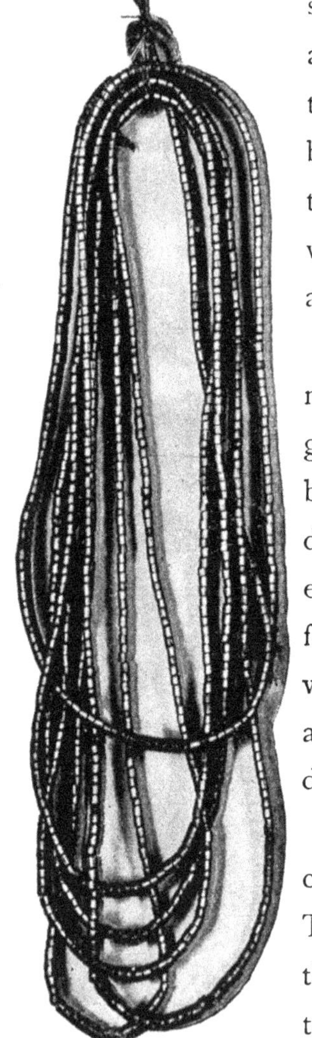
BRASS AND IRON BEADS.

The flagrancy of the women is most disgusting, from all accounts given by reliable travellers who have been forced to camp here for a few days. Food was too high priced to entice my porters to tarry long, therefore during the few hours we halted I was spared the humiliation of being an involuntary witness to their degradation.

Neither the men nor women are comely of feature or fine in figure. Their color is brown rather than black; they file and discolor their teeth and tattoo their bodies in a rudimentary way, without motive or any conventional fashion. The women artificially make their breasts pendulous, and shave their heads, all but a circular crown patch, which they strand and string beads upon; the prosperous or favorite women attach a number of strands of beads around their heads, in addition to the crown of beaded hair, and permit several strings to hang down over their ears and shoulders; they wear high masses of dark blue and red small beads, called large *sem-sem*, to distinguish such from seed-beads, around their necks, until their chins are awkwardly thrown up and pressed backwards; also a bead girdle, or simply more strands of beads roped about the waist; then a dark blue or brown — clay stained — cotton loin-cloth or kilt skirt, very short, coming only halfway between hip and knee, or a tiny scrap of cloth or goatskin hanging in front, or a small triangular flap of goatskin dangling behind from their waists; large pewter and bead armlets and upwards of twenty-four wire hoops two and one half inches in diameter, on which are strung all sorts of small beads, in one ear, and in the other a few hoops of large green and blue glass rings of the sort that are

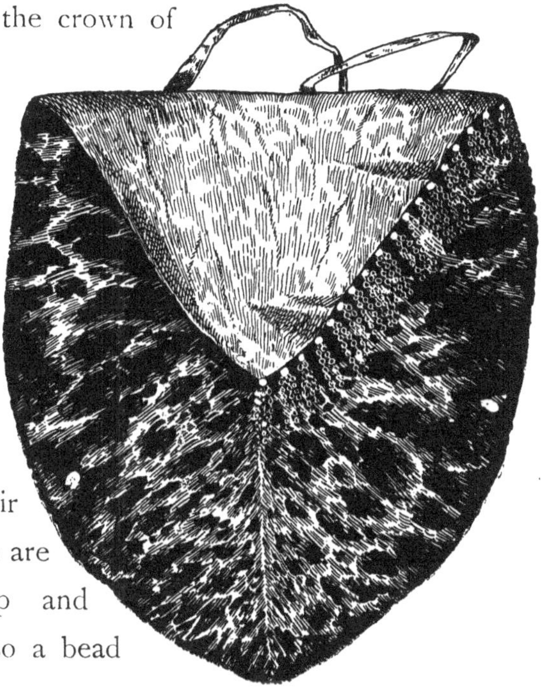

GOATSKIN FLAP WORN BY MANY TRIBES, ORNAMENTED WITH BEADS AND CHAINS.

prized by the Masai. In various punctures around the rim and in the lobes of their ears they thrust bits of sweet grass, circular pieces of ivory or bone, porcupine quills, brass, iron, and copper danglers ornamented with a few large showy beads. All these beads represent accumulated wealth. Occasionally women had followed the fashion of the Zanzibaris slave women, and wore little studs of various materials put through holes bored into their nostrils and lips and cheeks. When they are fortunate enough to possess a bright variegated bandana or handkerchief, they delight to display it on their person. Horn, metal, and goatskin rings bedeck their hands. Although their hands and feet are broad and thick, they are not long, and cannot fairly be called large. They, as other natives, detest ablutions, and use quantities of animal and cocoanut oil overlaid with yellow clay and accumulated dirt.

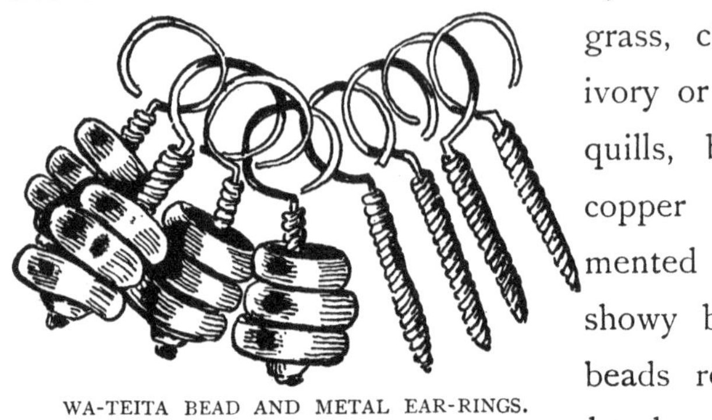

WA-TEITA BEAD AND METAL EAR-RINGS.
TWENTY-FOUR WORN AT A TIME.

The men wear odd bits of all sorts of calico, deck out their persons in ivory and bone and metal armlets and leglets, wear similar ear ornaments, arm themselves with bows and arrows, carry a hide quiver filled with poisoned arrows; the poison they use, and many other tribes in East Africa, is a vegetable product from the province of Gyriama, which they procure from the Arab traders, or direct through their own envoys from the people of the country.

Polygamy exists, and a degenerate outcome of the men's thriftlessness leads them to marry their own mothers and sisters and even their own children, because they are too improvident or actually in some cases too poor to purchase an unrelated wife; hence the offspring of these consanguineous marriages, which enervate alike their mental and physical forces, must retrograde and develop vicious tendencies in their degenerate progeny, if they do not in time happily become sterile. Their religion, such as it is, may be safely called fetich.

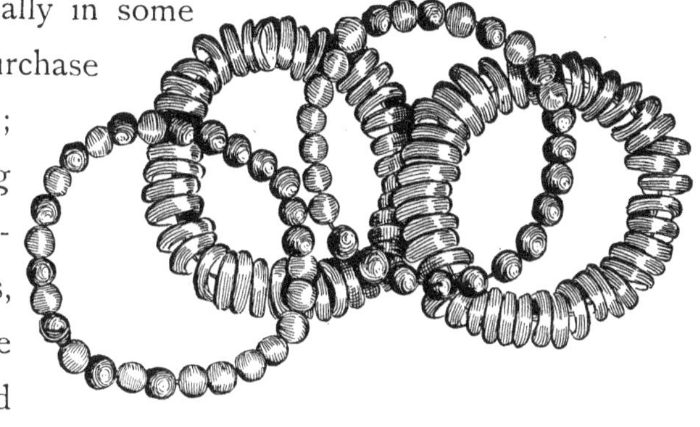

WA-TEITA EAR-RINGS.

As they depend largely, as one of their most profitable products, upon the yield of the calabash, which is the fruit of the baobab-tree, when a famine threatens they plant numbers of this tree to propitiate the elements, and regard as a bad omen the destruction of a baobab-tree if through accident or intention.

All the hair, as a rule, is shaved close to the skin. Magic doctors are held in high repute. Women are the *accoucheurs* and specialists for women. Puberty is attained at an early age, as in all tropical countries. The women may marry at the age of ten, and the youths at fifteen. The families are not large. Virtue here has no place. Men and women

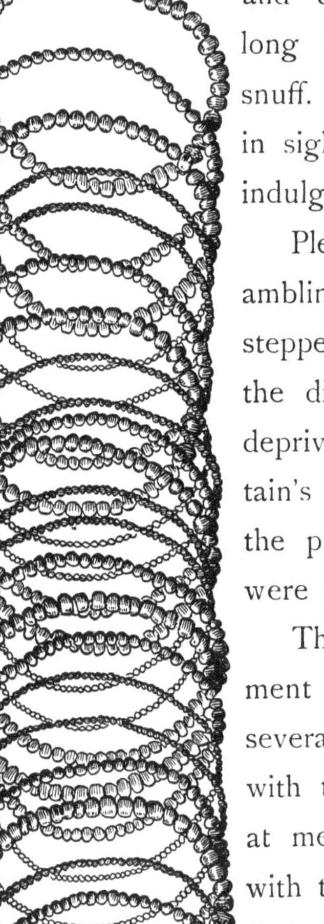
WA-TEITA BEAD HOOP EAR-RINGS.

and children drink *pombe*, and smoke long wooden or iron pipes, and use snuff. The inevitable snuff-box dangles in sight, for every tribe in East Africa indulge in the habit.

Plenty of game could be discerned ambling away on the outstretch of steppes beyond. A sudden mist shrouded the distant sight of Kilimanjaro, which deprived us of seeing the grand mountain's peaks. Rain portended, and despite the protest the natives made, we soon were in train to march.

The natives were struck with amazement to see the *white woman*, and several stood as if riveted to the ground, with their loads on their heads, staring at me for hours. Men squatted about with their bows and arrows clutched in their hands, mutely watching every movement I made. The Palanquin was a veritable surprise to adults and children. All wanted to see it carried; and when the bearers lifted it up to proceed on our *safari*, they ran in droves after them, shouting and screaming with delight, exactly as do street gamins pursue a circus caravan going through a town.

Shaba, the old chief of Sagalia, had presented me with a few of his ear ornaments, for which I had given in return an ample amount of beads; however, he expressed great dissatisfaction, and demanded some *Americana*, white cotton sheeting, which Hamidi peremptorily refused. He planted

WA-TEITA NECKLACE.

himself close beside me wherever I chanced to move, and commenced a nagging grumble, about being so poor and that I was so rich, and what the other travellers had given him. A more abject-looking creature can scarcely be depicted. His wives sallied about him to lend their voices to his bewailings, until for peace and quiet I came very near acquiescing to their demands. The women, to incite my pity, carried their wretched-looking babies slung over their backs in a hide or length of cloth, but Hamidi protested that he would satisfy and silence the "beggars."

Rather a sprightly bronze beauty — a beauty according to the accepted rule of that country — came racing up to me, repeating over and over again, "Bébé, Bébé," extending her arms, holding in her hands a sweet grass bead necklace, and a round bone ornament pierced in the centre, which she had worn on her own neck. I accepted her proffered gift, curious to know what she would demand in return. To my astonishment, she spit at me. In my disgust and indignation, I was about to return her presents, when Josefe checked me by saying in his merry way, "Quite right, Bébé, it is their way of paying you a compliment; they all do it in this part." So they do, as we shall see later on. Rather pleased at the little maiden's evidence of generous friendliness, I drifted into quite a revery, from

CARAVAN PATH.

which I was disturbed, some miles from the place of the scene, by her voice and her presence. She had repented of her free gift, and had pursued us to exact adequate payment for, or the return of, the trifles. She was pacified with the glitter of a few pice and a name ring.

Whilst I partook of my luncheon, sitting in my Palanquin, I confess experiencing great embarrassment in the presence of the large audience of natives who thronged about to gaze and comment upon the performance, wherever we chanced to halt, from beginning to finish of our *safari*.

The observances of little ceremonies and indulgence in certain refinements, as well as some few luxuries, conduced not only to my prestige in the natives' eyes, but to my personal comfort and self-respect. Requisite accessories add but little to the expense of a *safari*, and bring a threefold result: namely, in appearance, in instructiveness as to the white people's customs, and not the least, to personal convenience and comfort. All talk explanatory of such, not illustrated by actual representation, could not do half the service of certain observances adhered to consistently by a leader. It is not foolish. It is essential in studying traits of native people, and to provoke and develop the play of their intellect when brought face to face with strange manners and customs.

On we pushed, trying to reach a suitable camping ground for the night, despite the sharp showers that fitfully swept down upon us. Suddenly, as the sun neared the horizon, a bow of promise, with three reflected glories of its radiant self, made the heavens magnificent, and the storm ceased. Alas! photographs taken of this and similar manifestations of the elements proved utterly worthless, —vague, meaningless, and black beyond the recognition of a single outline or effect.

BEADED FIGLEAF.

Encased in a waterproof coat, rubber boots, and a cover over my *topee* (pith hat), I defied every storm, and marched with ease through violent outbursts of wind-driven rains. My head *askari* shouldered me to convey me across a muddy, leech-infested stream, swollen by the recent downpourings, and in his effort to obtain a foothold on the slimy, somewhat abrupt, yielding bank, slipped, and dumped me into the turgid waters. When fished out I certainly was a bedraggled-looking object, both eyes closed with mud which trickled down from head to feet, my mouth, nostrils, and ears resembling overflowing phials of pea soup.

Witnessing the event, Hamidi's *kibosh* (rhinoceros-hide stick) went whistling through the air as he impulsively plunged through the stream to chastise the frightened *askari*. However, in justice I signed him off, and made merry of the incident, protesting it was not the man's fault through any carelessness. Quietly I resolved never again to trust myself to the hazard of a similar ducking, and thereafter swam or

forded the streams, only making exceptions when we had to plod through short spaces of muddy, swampy ground, and there was no sense in making myself uncomfortable or hideous for hours by loading down my clothing and feet with tenacious clay and slime.

Straggling natives at first were very shy and half suspicious, although never hostile or reluctant to supply us with food when we would reach their settlements, although at Matata the prices were even more exhorbitant than at Teita. This can be accounted for from the fact that our reputation had preceded us, and we were heralded as a *big and rich safari*, and that Bébé Bwana was a white queen.

TWO BEADED GIRDLES.

The plantations were very fertile, and the women, who are the legitimate agriculturists of East Africa, bedizened with glistening beads and shining metal, tilled the ground, without apparently deeming their task to be any hardship. Somehow the natives' acceptance of the inevitable is very fine. Knowing that we were to traverse their country, they were evidently on the alert to see me, and were disporting their splendors in honor of the event. They were not surprised, and passed upon my anomalous appearance without hesitancy. My long hair was an unremitting source of amazement to all the tribes I met. They queried why I did not shave it off, like theirs. My crooked Alpine stock, with its blue pennant emblazoned with the magic device, *noli me tangere*, was much admired and I fear coveted. They innocently deemed it to be a badge of high rank, never having seen one before, hence inferred that I must be of supreme importance and possessed of limitless power, to pass over their idea of the inexhaustibility of my material resources.

On all sides I was besought for razors and clasp-knives, which I bestowed freely. An explorer's knife, worn attached to my belt, delighted them with its *multum in parvo* contents.

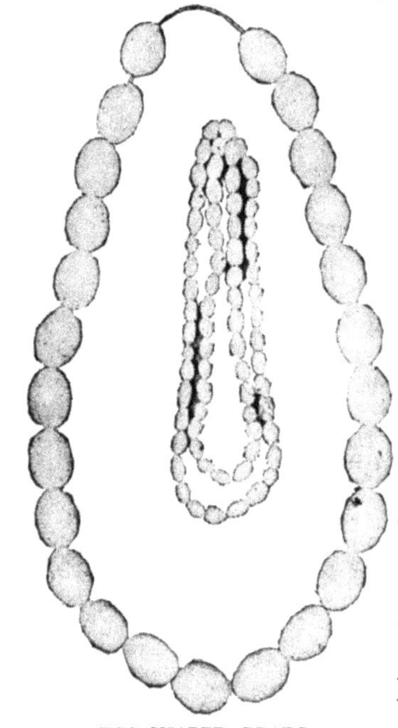

EGG-SHAPED BEADS.

They would peer around and into my tent if the flaps were fastened back to the guys, when fitted up with all of its paraphernalia, and stand, eyes wide open, fixed with amazement at the mysterious appointments thereof, for hours, without becoming weary.

At night I would set alight magnesium wire, red and green Greek powder, or send up rockets, and sometimes fire a volley for their amusement when they were bold enough to venture to defy the dark, of which they have an inherent fear, measurably shared by all African tribes.

On our route at Buru we found, curled up under the meagre cover of a few branches overspread with palm leaves and grasses, a poor, ill wretch dying from neglect and hunger, who had been discharged, it was said through his physical inability to proceed with a caravan destined to a certain station, and turned adrift, without adequate means to reach the coast as best he could or drop dead in the bush. Poor fellow, he managed to drag himself several days on his homeward journey, and then collapsed in his utter helplessness at this point. Although I was carrying a document from an authoritative officer to various subofficers, occupying stations in East Africa, ordering them not to deplete their stores, nor to provide me with supplies of barter goods, and under no circumstances to assume any expense in my behalf, or enlist in any of my undertakings other than to warn me of danger and if possible prevent me from incurring risk of life, common humanity asserted itself, and I provided one of their adandoned wretches with a temporary abiding place in the care of a native family well known to my headman Hamidi, and left him trade goods sufficient to get him to the coast when he should be able to travel. Three weeks afterwards, three natives from this village presented themselves in my camp to demand further payment for the maintenance of the fever-stricken waif. Their claim I promptly repudiated, as it could only be regarded in the light of sharp practice, for the man had died, by their own confession.

BEAD-INLAID DISH.

We were constantly coming across the fresh spoor of buffaloes and rhinoceros, and the bush was trampled significantly. The rear part of the caravan was put to rout by the dash of a herd of *wilde beeste* which had been disturbed by the noise whilst grazing, but after the panic subsided it was found that no one had been hurt; then they all boasted how they could have brought down the entire herd if Bébé Bwana had only given them permission to shoot.

WOODEN BASIN.

During the course of the day I was fortunate in bringing down a lovely gazelle at two hundred and forty yards, — a random shot I sent from my Winchester into a herd. This bit of luck was hailed with great acclamation by my men, and they boasted about it with as much fervency as if they, each one, had individually been the marksman.

Several porters started on a gallop to bring in the game. It was soon flayed, and the meagre portion of meat it afforded was dressed and sent to my cook tent. Selecting a few steaks, the balance was given to Hamidi, to distribute to the sick, after reserving the liver and kidneys for his own mess pot.

Although quantities of big game abounded, after a few

experiments it became obvious to me that it would throw my caravan into wild confusion to engage in sport which would not have had a brilliant result, as my men were not expert in the use of rifles. However, when we could not procure meat, and the men seemed to require a more generous diet than fruits, corn, bananas, and yams, I would try my hand. Partridges and Guinea fowls were plenty, and flew up from the bush when we were right upon them. One morning, in less than an hour, with my revolver, I shot for the pot nineteen, without the slightest tax of skill. The inflammation that had set up in my injured eye behooved me to avoid long-range sights. However, after my minor successes, I fully comprehend why it is that great sportsmen like Sir John Willoughby, Jackson, Chanler, and others, have expressed themselves with so much enthusiasm about this "hunter's Paradise."

RHINOCEROS.

A deplorable species of "buck fever," belonging exclusively to no particular country, experienced by me when in too close proximity to the ivories of elephants encountered on my *safari*, prevented me taking photographs of the admitted greatest source of commerce in Central, East, and West Africa,—a commerce which has a nefarious significance when one speaks of black ivory, or slaves; for it is the white ivory yield which is the very key-note of slavery for the ill-favored blacks who are captured and impressed into service by the Arab ivory traffickers to transport their hauls to marketable points, and then sold when their task is accomplished. Another plea for proper and humane transportation, to which obviously Christians, humanitarians, commercial promoters, colonizers, should lend unanimous voice.

JEWELLED PRESENTS FOR SULTANS.

Our caravan was constantly being joined by small Arab caravans, who were bound interior to the elephant regions, expecting to be absent from the coast for one, two, and three years. The paucity of their numbers, and seeming inefficiency of their barter goods, provoked me to make many inquiries which resulted in certain revelations as to *how it is done*.

A few Arab merchants, none of the number particularly wealthy, form a little band and pool their money to venture themselves or employ available men to go interior for ivory, and with combined forces procure the smallest possible number of porters requisite to carry their wares, and forthwith proceed. They do not hesitate to plunder the natives of their accumulated ivory, which they usually bury for safe keeping; or purchase at a rate barely removed from actual looting, or even employ native hunters to bring down the elephants and secure for them live ivory *tembo*. When they have collected sufficient, without hesitation, in the name of the Sultan, they capture strong natives to carry their ill-gotten gains to the coast marts,

The surveillance of the European officers over the posts and stations of their respective governments, in order to collect the duties of the incoming ivory caravans, has a judicial tendency to check the influx of slaves. The English, Germans, French, and Belgians, as well as the Sultan of Zanzibar and some others, have united and pledged themselves by the passage of a law to suppress slave raiding and to free newly made slaves.

CHAPTER X.

ON TO TAVETA.

USELESS to mark day by day our progress over a most variable, interesting route known to all caravans who hail for Taveta.

The scenery at times was superb, Lake Jipo shone like a copper mirror, and now and again we caught a transitory view of the snow-capped peak of Kilimanjaro, only to lose it in the great sweeping shoals of fluctuating mists. Excitement reigned every time there was a rift in the fluffy thick mantle, which would part like a curtain drawn back from the centre, in consequence of the saddle-like cut between the illustrious Kibo and Mawenzi; porters shrieked, "Kilimanjaro! Kilimanjaro!" From van to rear the call would leap from their lusty throats in quick succession.

The incomparable grandeur and limitless expanse offered the field of vision put my heart athrill, and I felt if only for this glorious sight I was more than amply rewarded for all the hardships incumbent upon the undertaking from beginning to those lurking along the line to the finish. Mountain ranges on both sides of us, behind us, and Kilimanjaro facing us, spaced and frontiered by long stretches of plains over which bounded magnificent wild beasts, varied by

LAKE JIPO.

ravines, sloping hills, silver lakes, and gushing streams turbulently rushing seaward. A defined tree line, the point where vegetation about ceases, the cloud line, and far, far above it all the peerless domain of sun and moon and stars! That picture can never be reproduced by word or color.

Again the Masai scare stirred my cowardly Zanzibaris. We reached a point by a dismal pool overshadowed with enormous trees, called Little Lanjaro, where the embers of the fires were still smouldering, and the remnants of a meat feed all betokened the recent presence of the bogy-men, so the porters acceded with a degree of alacrity to my command to go a few hours further on to Big Lanjaro, where we could comfortably rest during a day in camp to make a becoming entrance into the forest-locked arcadian Taveta.

Rain, rain, pelted down upon us with unlooked-for fury. With a howling gasp of wind that drove the rain into our faces, all was over, the sun peered out behind the clouds and soon put the storm to flight. Everything fumed and steamed, and the sultriness became almost unbearable. The men rushed and plunged into the stream, which coursed below our encampment, to cool themselves.

A TEST OF VALOR.

We were ascending a hill, trying to hold our footing on a slippery goat-path, when, without a loud spoken word, a dozen porters dashed down their loads, crowded by me, compelling me to halt, and at stated distances ahead each man grasped a sapling from the side of the hill above the path and stood on the very edge of the path overlooking a wild, dangerous ravine, muttered a prayer from the Koran, and closed his eyes. A strange rattling of stones, crushing of bushes, and clumps of flying earth came from above, followed by an enormous bowlder, which in the serpentine trend of the path, although I had not seen it, the porters on the outward curve of the hill had, and voluntarily were standing awaiting a doom that seemed inevitable to try and sheer the bowlder off of its destructive course, and save me.

One instant, and the first man must be crushed. He never winced, but stood his ground with feet firmly planted, and his sinews and veins standing out over his entire body like whipcords. My heart sank. I felt I could not endure the sight, and closed my eyes. The ground crunched, something gave way, a man screamed, and there was a new crashing. My eyes flew open in terror, but were greeted with the unexpected. Just as the bowlder reached within one foot of the first man, the earth crumbled, and it went swirling to the bottom, and the brave porter lost his footing and was clutching the shrubbery right and left as he rolled down to save himself, which he did, and all the other brave porters went to his assistance. I made a detour to photograph that bowlder as it lay innocently at the bottom, by the side of which a mountain stream went purling by as if nothing had happened. I christened the stone "A Test of Valor."

During the day I was more than astounded suddenly to experience several shocks of trembling of the earth, and upon inquiry was informed these manifestations of suppressed earthquake were far from being unusal in the vicinity of Taveta; and although there are no evidences of a recent eruption, the volcanic character of the country just beyond and the extinct craters of the Kilimanjaro range would seem to betoken that at some future day an eruption might recur. From those who are learned as to the geological character of this region, I could obtain no knowledge as to the existence of any fumaroles which might indicate smouldering or latent volcanic action.

LIVING TREE GATES OF TAVETA.

Natives are very superstitious about these tremblings, and are always thrown into a panic during their mild manifestations, and seek the shelter of their huts, close the entrances, and revive the fires, as they huddle together in their apprehension. The thunder rumbled in the distance, and the black clouds were cut zigzag across the dark heavens by blinding lightning flashes, until the cataclysm seems to relieve the surcharged heavens, at the same time gorging the throat of every ravine and water-way. These fierce outbreaks of the elements fortunately are of short duration, and immediately afterwards the country is smiling and fresh as possible, and the water has become absorbed by the porous earth and rocks; if storms have not been continuous, soon the earth is dry again, and the sands and rocks have been greatly cooled.

Hamidi, my headman, came rushing to me one day, pointing to a swirling black cloud in the heavens which seemed to be a centre of magnetic attraction, drawing impetuously to itself all other clouds until they rapidly coalesced as one mass, yet the greater part of the heavens was cerulean, fair, and sunny.

He exclaimed with considerable agitation, "Bébé Bwana, we must set the tent for you; that is a cloud-burst, you'll get drowned with the rain shortly." With considerable curiosity, I queried what he meant.

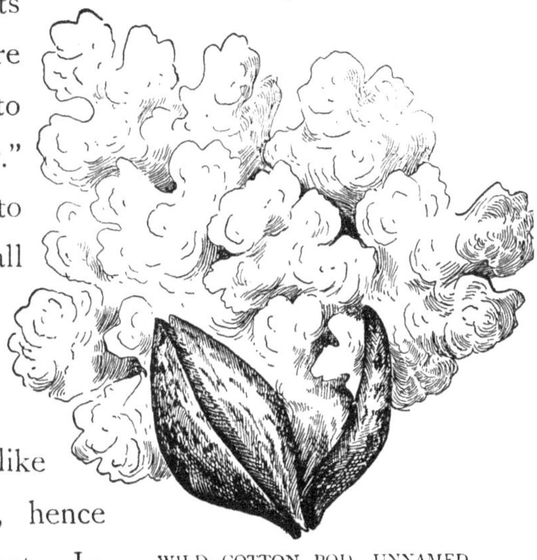

"That cloud will wing its way directly over where we are now marching and then fall to earth, a solid sheet of water."

As we were just about to leave a valley, and I saw on all sides the natives fleeing to the hills, and my porters all edging up towards the declivities, I concluded I should like to experience a cloud-burst, hence refused to have my tent set. In a moment the cloud did burst, and we were standing engulfed by the downpouring to our armpits in water in less than

WILD COTTON POD, UNNAMED.

three minutes, and in less than ten minutes we were able to proceed on our march with no evidence of the transitory deluge, save the moist, glossy appearance of the stones and foliage, and the balmy freshness of the atmosphere. This manifestation of the elements is not peculiar to Africa; but since my return one or two Peruvian travellers have imparted to me a similar experience. I felt well repaid for my obstinacy, and thoroughly enjoyed the adventure.

Hamidi informed me, with some hesitation, that it would be impossible to get my Palanquin through the forest gates of Taveta, as they were so low the men would have to push their ordinary compact loads through, then crawl in after them. Here was a dilemma. However, "the Palanquin must go where I go," that settled it, and it did enter Taveta more than once, despite the gates; twenty yards of unbleached calico paved the way.

Wa-Taveta men, women, and children came far on the road as we approached Taveta to bid me welcome, to bring me tributes of all kinds, to say to the *white queen*, as they persisted in calling me, that they had looked for me for two moons, and almost despaired that I would ever arrive. Then they asked about *bwana* this, and that, and the other who had visited them in years agone.

Presently we met, at the confines of the forest environing Taveta, a sentinel from the English post, who fired at least a dozen shots in salutation, and informed me that the officer in charge was absent, but had made preparations to entertain

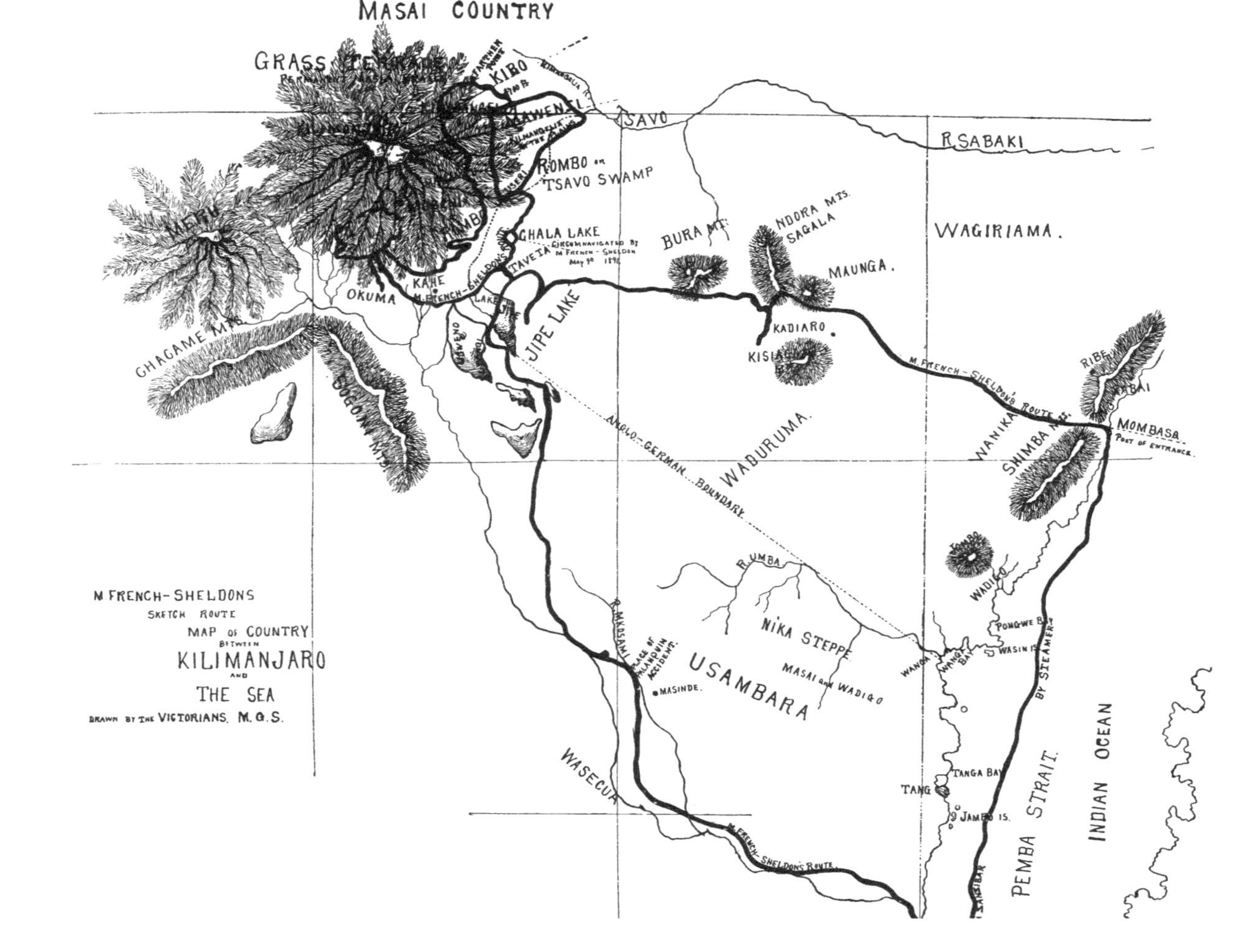
MASAI COUNTRY
GRASS
KIBO
TSAVO
R SABAKI
ROMBO OR TSAVO SWAMP
MERU
CHALA LAKE
CIRCUMNAVIGATED BY M FRENCH-SHELDON May 9th 1891
TAVETA
BURA MT.
NDORA MTS. SAGALA
MAUNGA.
WAGIRIAMA.
KAHE
OKUMA
M. FRENCH-SHELDON'S ROUTE
JIPE LAKE
KADIARO
KISIGAU
CHAGAME MTS.
UGONO MTS.
RIBE
RABAI
MOMBASA
PORT OF ENTRANCE
M. FRENCH-SHELDON'S ROUTE
WANIKA
SHIMBA MTS.
WADURUMA
ANGLO-GERMAN BOUNDARY
R. UMBA
WADIGO
NIKA STEPPE
PONGWE BAY
WASIN IS.
BY STEAMER
R. MKOSAMI
PLACE OF PALANQUIN ACCIDENT.
USAMBARA
MASAI AND WADIGO
MASINDE.
WANGA
WANGA BAY
INDIAN OCEAN
TANGA BAY
TANG
JAMBO IS.
PEMBA STRAIT
WASECUA
M. FRENCH-SHELDON'S ROUTE
ZANZIBAR
M FRENCH-SHELDONS
SKETCH ROUTE
MAP OF COUNTRY
BETWEEN
KILIMANJARO
AND
THE SEA
DRAWN BY THE VICTORIANS. M.G.S.

me in his *boma*. How strange this sounded, after having lived in the open under canvas!

We began to wend our way through the densest of forest, gloomy, dark, difficult to advance rapidly with the fallen giant trees, overhanging vines, and general tangle obstructing the way, and in places soggy and hideously muddy, after crawling through gates constructed out of living trees which evidently had been trained from their stripling period until their tall, thick, raddled branches and huge trunks in course of years constitute formidable barriers. There are, I was told, thirteen such gates, making Taveta impregnable to the attack of an enemy. The tiny cone-shaped entrance, not three feet high, and about the same in width at the bottom, is blocked by rolling huge logs against the gap. Not only is Taveta stockaded thus, but the tortuous maze-like paths diverging in all ways leading up to a stream to be resumed on the other bank, and the scattered *bomas*, instead of congregations of huts, would perplex, defy, and frustrate any strange invader.

TAVETA PINK AND WHITE BEAD GIRDLE.

An awe crept over me. The porters were hushed, as we struggled to thread our way, until we attained the splendid plantations of bananas, corn, sugar-cane, and tobacco. Arrayed in brave splendors, the belles and beaux, the husbands and wives, crowded about us. The porters greeted old acquaintances, and were welcomed in return with unmistakable fervor.

Almost all the huts and officers' quarters of the English post, which is the market place of the Wa-Taveta, were placed at my service. Great and many preparations had been made by the resident officer, who had sent a letter to await me, saying that he was on the road to Taveta, and would hasten if I sent him word. He arrived, with his assistant and posse of men, in a few hours.

My caravan was installed under cover, but I declined to accept any shelter apart from my canvas dwelling, although I found the new house of the assistant a convenient storehouse and agreeable to retire to and put up my personal attendants. I was deeply touched at the efforts made in my behalf to beautify and make convenient this little hut. It means more in East Africa than in great centres of civilization, where the refinements and accessories of comfort are easy to obtain.

Never was woman more indulged and fêted than was I during my sojourn. My eye had become greatly inflamed, and I was tenderly ministered to by men who did not hesitate to administer personally the *kibosh* to any wayward fellow under his command, and this care for me was delicate, sympathetic, almost reverential. Gentlemen, I publicly thank you now; you had not to do with an ingrate.

Caravans always make a habit of halting at Taveta sufficient time to string their barter beads, in consequence of the abundant growth of *raphia* palm, generally known as *m'whala;* its fibre is stranded into threads of various thicknesses. These incomings and outgoings keep the natives in a perpetual state of expectancy and fête, as it were. The market place and camping ground is within the *boma* of the English post, and in order to collect the duties upon the ivory there existed the somewhat arbitrary and uncomfortable law, when I halted at Taveta, enforcing all caravans bound

FOUR POMBE CUPS.

for the coast, no matter what their destination or purpose, to camp within the *boma* under the immediate inspection of the resident officer and his *askari*.

Wa-Taveta raise an excellent quality of tobacco, although a trifle coarse through lack of proper cultivation, which they do not habitually either chew or smoke, but use lavishly as snuff, and the habit is prevalent among the women as well as the men. This is universal among all tribes in East Africa.

Their snuff-boxes are most varied and highly decorated, often most beautiful. The ceremony of snuff taking quite outrivals the former court etiquette respecting the same in France and other countries of the last century. When the compliments of the day and polite salutations are at an end, snuff is proffered and taken all around. Having been informed of this custom, I had taken a large supply of snuff and tobacco with me. Whenever a snuff-box was presented to me by my request or voluntarily by any native of any tribe, every atom of the snuff was patiently extracted with jealous care before the donor surrendered it to me.

Their plantations are fertile, owing to the fact that their district never suffers from prolonged droughts. In good truth water can be obtained anywhere in this village by using an Abyssinian pipe, and the stream which cuts through in the woodland part of the settlement is reputed always to contain abundant water.

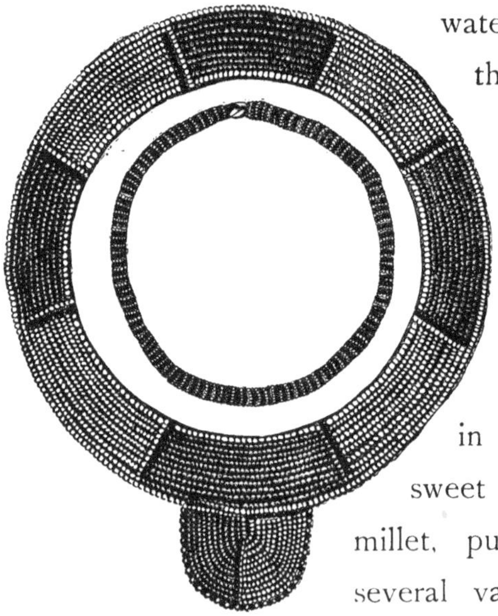

TAVETA BEAD COLLAR AND NECKLACE.

On all sides could be seen in thrifty condition quantities of sweet corn, — maize, — wimbe, or millet, pumpkins, tomatoes, sugar-cane, several varieties of bananas, a number of edible vines which are cooked as greens or eaten as salad, and sweet potatoes that were somewhat fibrous.

The English officers have placed a hand-mill within their

boma for their own use, but generously accord to the natives the privilege of using it to grind their corn and banana flour; this relieves them of the tedious process of pounding the grain and dried fruit in a wooden or stone mortar, with a heavy wooden pestle,—an advantage they evidently seem to highly appreciate, for the mill is never idle all day long. Heretofore the women were allotted the task of pulverizing the corn and bananas to an impalpable flour, and with maternal solicitude strapped their babes upon their backs, afraid to put the little ones on the ground on account of the ravages of the white ants, and they would be quieted and rocked to sleep by the swaying motion of the mother's body as she monotonously wielded the heavy pestle.

Honey bees thrive, and the Wa-Taveta manufacture quantities of beehives out of logs; they are cylindrical in shape, three to four feet long, and a foot and a half in diameter, hollowed out and then closed at one end, with a puncture at the other to admit the ingress and egress of the bees.

The honey is rather dark in color, but most delicious in flavor and plentiful. It is put in hide boxes or calabashes. We several times came across dead hollow tree-trunks, branches lopped, standing erect, covered over with a removable piece of hide, punctured to admit the bees, which were used for hives. These primitives are utilitarians by nature.

Made hives are hung in the trees on the track of the bee ranges, where honey flowers are most abundant. A similar utensil to the made beehives is used in which to brew their *pombe*, a concoction of sugar-cane, bananas, or cocoanut, wimbe, and corn. When the mash is fresh the beverage tastes very much like unfermented mead or beer, but in the course of three days fermentation has reached a point when the brew becomes a subtle intoxicant; and as it is profusely brewed by almost every native of the tribe, they are during harvest times in a perpetual state of jollification, and all the unamiable qualities and propensities of their natures seem to be strangely affected by this intoxicant. It is a mistake to say that the Africans have been polluted in this respect by the invasion of white men, because they have always, as far as one can ascertain, used *pombe* and *tembo* or other native drinks.

THE WOMAN OF TAVETA.

At Taveta I met a woman, whom I please to call "*The* Woman of Taveta," who was in sore trouble. Immediately upon seeing me, if I may use the expression, she adopted me into her confidence, and all her troubles were poured into my ears, and by her earnestness she so engaged my interest

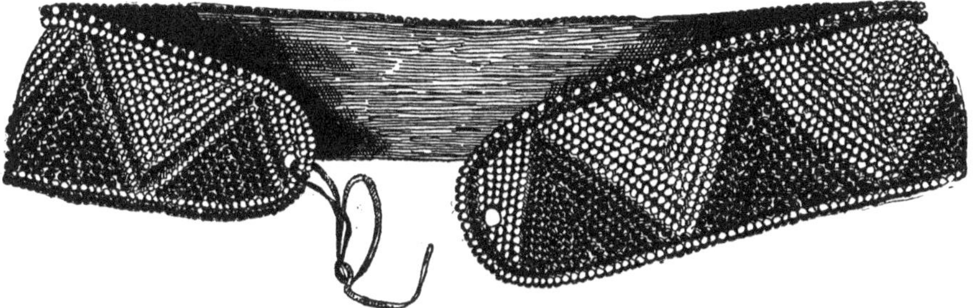

BEAD BELT PRESENTED BY THE WOMAN OF TAVETA.

and sympathy it was a delight to try and assist her to some better state of daily existence, which would preclude certain trials she was subjected to. She was a woman of intense feeling, a lover of power, indeed was a leader among women, and the wife of one of the elders. Her word seemed to be beyond dispute with them all. She was eager that I should be a friendly witness to all of the strange customs and habits of her tribe, and she had the power as well as willingness to give me the *open sesame* to them all. Twice at midnight, when the moon dances of the *el-moran*, from which women of the tribe are excluded, were in full swing, she stole to my tent, mysteriously signed me to follow, and silently led me through the forest to a sequestered spot to be an unseen spectator to the wild, riotous performance of the utterly nude fellows, who were unaware of the presence of an interloper. Thus I was enabled to become familiar with customs forbidden to the presence of white men. How they pranced, gyrated, leaped in the air, squatted on the ground and hooted, shook their long hair and waved branches or brushes made of zebra tails, their faces daubed, Masai fashion, with white chalk and red paint, splotches on their cheeks, chins, and their eyes encircled with broad bands of color, their bodies shining with grease under the rays of the moon as the perspiration started from every pore!

Through the Woman of Taveta's instrumentality, I saw a funeral ceremony in which the stiff corpse of a child was fixed in a sitting posture amidst blazing fagots, until all the flesh was burnt off from the bones. Meanwhile the men formed an inner circle around the funeral pyre, and gave vent in a lugubrious voice to a monotonous chant, slowly moving in an unbroken ring round and round, whilst the women, forming an outer circle, moved in a reverse direction, and as if in response to the threnody of the men, at stated intervals they would make a sweeping salaam, and while their heads were still bowed, utter a piercing wail. The little one's flesh was soon consumed; only the bones remained; the skull was taken and reposed

CALF'S STOMACH HEAD-DRESS, ORNAMENTED WITH BEADS AND CHAINS.

in a rude pottery urn, then carried to some distance and lowered into a hollow tree containing the skulls of the deceased members of the family. The bones were gathered up by several men bedecked in flowing red and white cloths and interspersed through the forest, evidently in places which were already consecrated for the deposition of such revered remnants of the dead, amid the exposed tree-trunks, but not under the ground. They have a strange idea that the cadaver pollutes the soil, and deters the fertility of crops. This habit of disposing of the bones of those who have died normal deaths, and the arboreal vaults with their accumulation of bones, account for the suppositions that there have been massacres committed, or that disease has ravaged the land when found by caravans. There exists another burial custom much more obnoxious. In a selected cleared spot not very remote from their *bomas*, well surrounded and hidden by thorn-bushes and trees with dense foliage, beyond the observation of casual passers-by, if it were not for the foul, fetid stench, in rude pottery urns turned up sideways are deposited certain parts of the viscera, the heart and the head, and there allowed to fester and decay, until in time nothing is left but the whitened skull. These burial places are not infrequently met with in all the villages I visited; they are entered

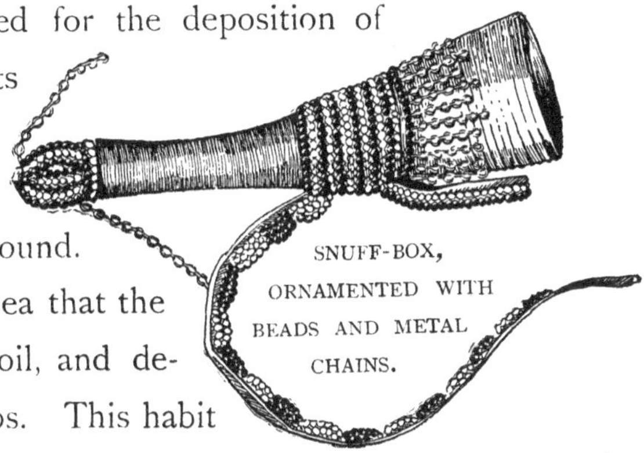

SNUFF-BOX, ORNAMENTED WITH BEADS AND METAL CHAINS.

by a very low squatty opening through the thorn-bushes, compelling those who seek to effect an entrance to get down and crawl through on their hands and knees.

The idea prevails that by the preservation of the skull the spirit of the departed is saved, and that the congregation in one place of the skulls of a family or tribe guarantees a future reunion.

Superstitions concerning death are decidedly obscure and extremely heterogeneous in East Africa, and yet there are little threads which have various origins, running through the tissue of what may be called their religion. They worship the moon and the sun, and revel in songs or chants addressed to the rain during planting seasons. The Wa-Duruma near the coast beat drums, but they are the only tribe in the part of East Africa I visited where they use drums.

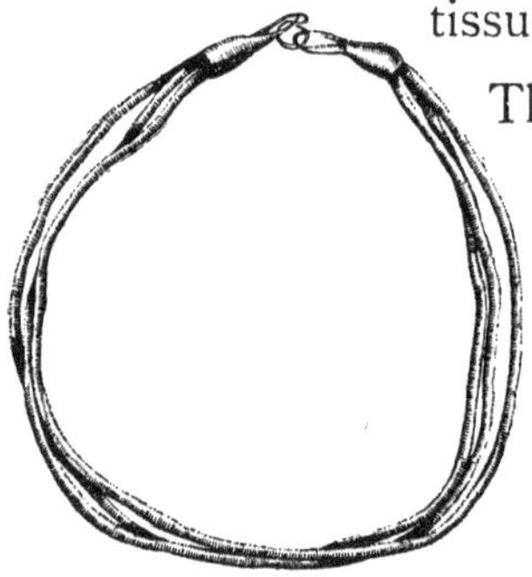

BRASS WIRE SPRING NECKLACE.

A decided aversion among all tribes exists in respect to permitting an outsider to know of the death of one of their number; if a familiar is missed, and an inquiry made concerning the absence of such a one, an answer promptly comes, "He has gone on a *safari*,"—doubtless to the great hereafter.

Among the Masai the corpses are often tossed into the open, where vultures or wild beasts soon devour them.

The birth of a first child is quite an event, but not so subsequent births. Children are not numerous in any one family or sections of families.

Elders, or the oldish men who formerly, before the occupancy of the English, exercised a dictatorship over their tribe, strut about in a majestic way, with as much sheeting as they can afford, ten, twelve, or fifteen yards of Americana or white or unbleached or clay-stained drill or cotton cloth, varied occasionally by Turkey red, or lasso bandana handkerchiefs,—which trail behind them, fastened over the shoulder, much like a Roman toga; and they have infinite grace both in manner and speech, which seems to marry well with their surroundings.

COTTON CAP MADE ON SAFARI.

Many wear slung over their shoulders, attached to a leather strap or chain, a little three or four legged stool, which they carry, as they do their bows and arrows, wherever they go, and, when paying a call or chatting in the open with their comrades, they plant it on the ground to comfortably sit upon, and take out from the knotted corner of a bit of cloth their bead work, just as might a young white girl engage in fancy work; these effeminate warriors leave the toilsome avocations of tilling the ground, and caring for the cattle, and packing loads, and the duties of the kitchen to the women.

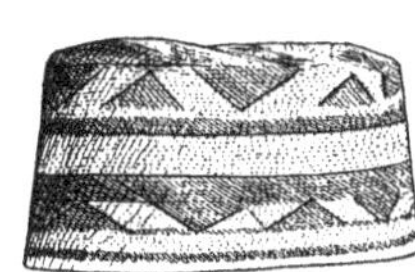

COTTON CAP MADE ON SAFARI.

Almost every individual, man, woman, and child, in the Taveta community or tribe, carries a pombe cup, made from a gourd, to which is affixed a long handle, sometimes beaded or ornamented with metal rings; the bowl of the cup usually bears numerous effective devices, which make an interesting study to trace their origin. Many of the designs have been adapted with more or less variation, prompted by the taste of the copyist, from the scroll work on the little cotton caps which porters delight in making and wearing when on *safari;* sometimes too they were of Turkish, again even Persian or Egyptian origin. I consider as a great acquisition the possession of a pombe cup which bears upon obverse and reverse sides the first attempt I found or heard of to represent the human form divine; and quaintly enough, the white man is distinguishable by his feet, which are indicated by awkward lines to counterfeit shoes, and a school-child's slate and pencil angular lines to represent European clothing; whereas, the native is represented with bare feet, and ears stretched out of shape by heavy ear-rings.

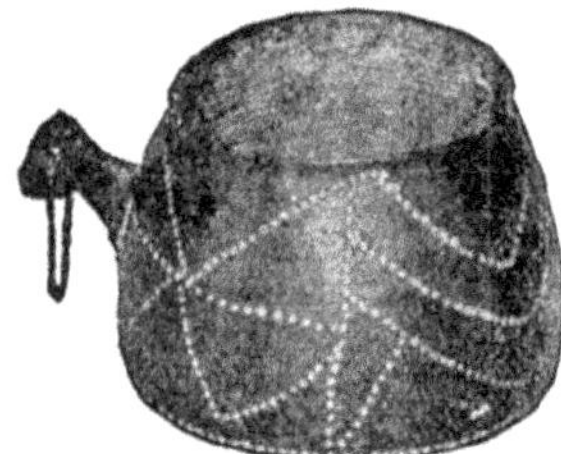

INLAID WOODEN BOWL.

Strange as it may seem, when shown photographs, natives have as a rule no real conception or appreciation of the photographic semblance of human beings or animals. Sultans Mireali, Mandara, and a few others are notable exceptions to this obtuseness. Photography is regarded as a species of witchcraft or black magic.

There are certain beans and some sweet grasses made into beads, and bits of horn, amber, iron, wood, animals' teeth and glass beads, musk and vanilla, which are universally worn as charms, alike to ward off evil as for *dawa*, or medicine, for all maladies. Their possessors are very reluctant to part with these charms, or *dawa*. However, they will lend them one to another, when suffering, but always reclaim them when the recipient has been alleviated, or before if personally needed. With some difficulty I procured a string of these beads from a magic doctor who had lost caste, in consequence of his misfortune in permitting a man of importance to die during his

DAWA NECKLACE.

ministrations, hence he desired to capitalize his stock of charms and bad *dawa*, and make haste to the coast, knowing that his own life was in imminent jeopardy. Peculiar black pine-like needles obtained from a huge forest tree, the name of which I could not ascertain, these are punctured, and when strung resemble the coarse teeth of a large rubber comb, and are much-prized *dawa* for *enceinte* women.

Strange native medical practices were revealed to me

through the auspices of the Woman of Taveta. The old women are all skilled midwives. Mothers suffer very little during the period of gestation or in the throes of childbirth. A girl reaches puberty at the infantile age of ten. Youths are circumicised by their own election when they no longer wish to be children, but aspire to the station of *el-moran*, as early often as the age of twelve. The custom of circumcision must have maintained for many decades, for nature frequently simulates it, and the parents boast of an offspring

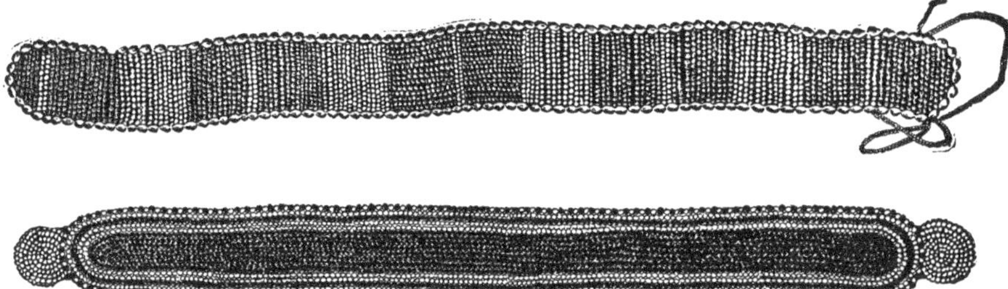

TAVATA BEAD BELTS.

so pre-eminently destined to be a warrior, and the favored boy is pointed out as one elect.

All the natives are most delicate about alluding to any complaints of their *tumba* (abdomen). All seem to possess a minor yet practical knowledge of the use of herbs and roots, and of imported medicaments. Sulphur, quinine, bluestone do they beseech the leaders of caravans for. They suffer from itch, ulcers, sore eyes, and fevers. The Woman of Taveta told me of bubbling hot-water *ziwis* (springs or pools) where those who were afflicted with various diseases, including smallpox and elephantiasis, made pilgrimages and were benefited, and of certain clays that the Wandorobo knew about and brought down country that possessed curative properties for coughs and stiff joints, a species of rheumatism, and sometimes progressive paralysis caused from excessive drinking and exposure to the elements. This paralysis, with marked and retributive selection, inflicts the sultans and important men of tribes, who are in position to command the largest harems, and indulge themselves like Sybarites.

Personal decoration attains a very great height at Taveta, especially among the young men, who are much given to dressing their hair in a very quaint fashion, drawing it in braided clumps, hanging down over the face and divided in strands made over the back of the head, hanging over the shoulders, which they plaster with grease and red clay, to which they frequently add bead and metal pendants. These young fellows, who represent the Taveta snobs, smear their

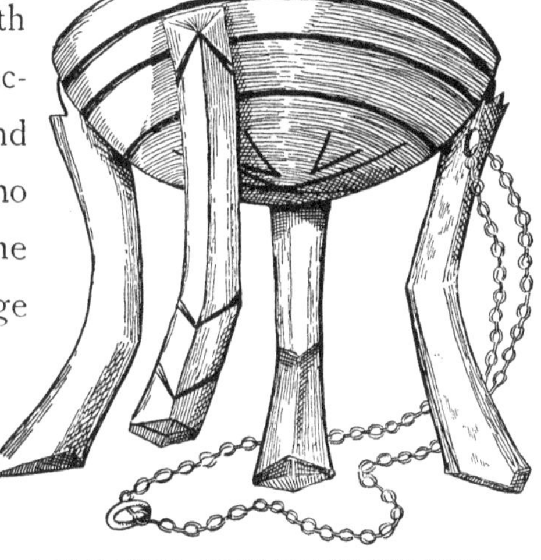

TAVETA STOOL, MADE OUT OF ONE PIECE.

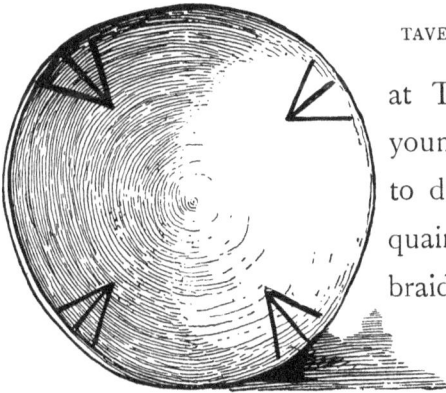

TOP OF STOOL, DESIGNS BURNT IN.

bodies with grease, and tint themselves with red clay. They are very self-conscious and great posers, the very princes of dawdlers and slaves of fashion. They divide themselves up into little bevies, almost clubs, and they wear as an insignia or badge of fellowship or brotherhood little armlets made of a strip of cowhide, upon which are sewn beads in special devices and chosen colors, which seem to indicate their particular faction or club. They are great dancers and merrymakers. The young fellows gather in groups and dance as though in competition, one with the other; a daring aspirant will dash out from the circle apart from his companions, rush into the middle of a circumscribed space, and scream out, "Wow! wow!" another follows him and screams in the same way; and a third, and so on. These men will dance with their knees almost rigid, jumping into the air faster and faster, until they bound with amazing velocity, and their excitement becomes proportionately greater, and their energy waxes more and more spasmodic, leaving the ground frequently fully three feet as they spring into the air. At some of their festivals at which I was a spectator, this dancing was carried to such a pass that I have seen during a crisis a young fellow's muscles quiver from head to foot, and his jaws tremble until his teeth chattered like castanets in playing a tremolo, without any apparent ability on his part to control himself, until he foamed at the mouth, his eyes swimming about, his head wâgging idiotically, from his drivelling lips issued moans and shudders, and as one drunk finally he fell in a paroxysm upon the ground, to be carried away to a place of retirement by his companions until he resumed his calmness.

This state of seeking artificial physical excitement bears a singular resemblance to the dances of other people outside of Africa. I am not purposing to make deductions, but I think there is considerable opportunity to study comparisons as to the motive which prompts various people to engage in this physical excitement. It would seem to emanate from an undefinable species of voluptuousness.

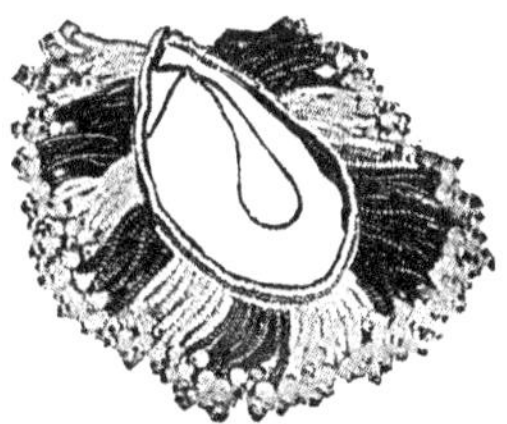
CHILD'S BEAD FRINGE GIRDLE.

The women also engaged in dances, and especially as guests, during wedding festivities, bedecked with all their fine toggery, they separate themselves from the men and follow in a procession, one after another, with their hands upon each other's shoulders or hips, beating their feet in time, and singing a strange, monotonous plaint, now and then interspersed with shouts of laughter when they resume their measured processional steps, jingling all the bells they have about them with a peculiar jerk and fling of their hips and shoulders as they go round and round, threading their way through the forest, back again to the *boma* of the host of ceremony, drinking and carousing quite as much as the young fellows. A certain amount of dignity is put upon these gayeties by the presence of the elders; however, there seems no viciousness in any of their games and pleasures.

They have a certain amount of animation and youthful exhilaration, which expresses and expends itself in an abandon to muscular exhibits and jocose explosiveness.

They are very jealous of each other in their attentions to the *mzungu* (white man), and seemed especially so respecting myself; one family would bring me milk and eggs, but seeing that somebody had superseded them, would immediately commence a tirade as to the bad quality of the other's gifts, and recommending their own with great vivacity. However, they were so pleased to have the "white queen" with them, there was nothing among their possessions which I really craved in the end they did not give me. Of course, it is well understood that these gifts were always reciprocated by me, if not in kind, certainly in excess of value, but that does not in any way detract from the fact that they were willing gifts, and presented with a free, open hand, without expectation of return, as a tribute to the "white queen."

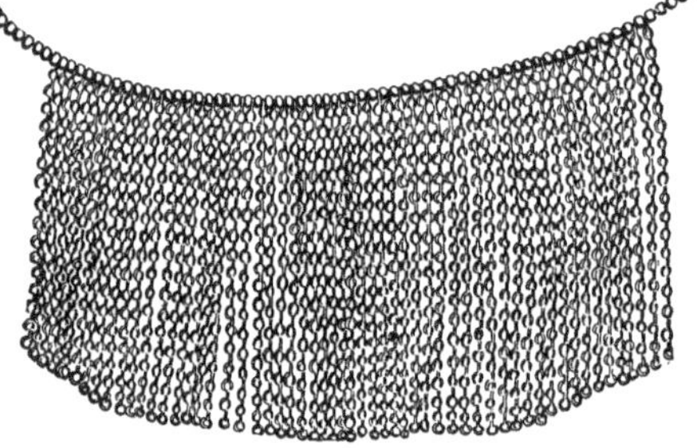

FINE CHAIN GIRDLE.

Finding the children very merry, I endeavored to amuse them in every conceivable way. Soap bubbles were failures, tops successful, and huge colored balls great favorites. Masks of animals' heads and grotesque human faces simply threw children and adults into paroxysms of glee, until the fun became rather too boisterous, and my porters overstepped the mark. As it was a gala day, and my four music boxes were playing, it occurred to me a fine opportunity to let fly some large Japanese paper kites, imitating birds and fish, from which floated long streamers of bright-colored tags. Taking the end of the strings of several at once, the brisk breeze inflated and carried them on their aerial flight far and swiftly into the air. True, the children were attracted, but lo! instead of inspiring the delight I had expected, quick as a flash the alert little chaps whipped their bows from off their shoulders, at the same time jerked their arrows from their quivers, and with deadly aim shot my poor kites, with imminent danger to me, as their arrows spattered about very freely. The volley was not discontinued until every winged bird and fish was brought low, the breath knocked out of it, falling vanquished to the ground, a shabby, shapeless thing, for the youngsters were animated more by the inborn traits of hunter than juvenile play.

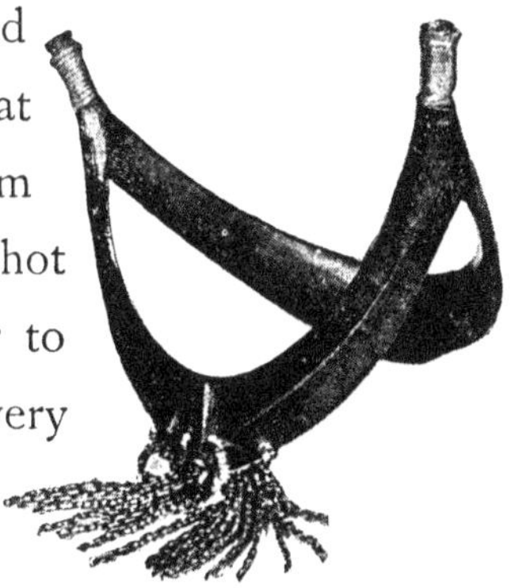

BONE ARMLET.

Not so with the adults. They queried with deep concern what kept the aerials mid-air, and with much excitement exclaimed and pointed to them as they floated serenely skyward when I ran out in the open, free from trees, with my arms outstretched over my head, manœuvring to keep the strings from becoming entangled. The vandal youngsters were summarily waved away from my encampment by the elders, who evidently thought it the most natural thing that I would give vent to great anger at the wilful destruction of my air birds and fish.

The children amuse themselves, as do other children, vying with each other shooting at a mark and at birds on wing with their bows and arrows, which they succeed in doing with great dexterity. They have some idea of forming companies and drilling, and accept a leader whom they are disposed to follow. Their education is a rudimentary one of imitation, and not of instruction. They are impressionable and observing. Their reasoning faculties naturally would be quickened and vivified by attrition and calling them into play, although at present they are, at times, somewhat slow to comprehend innovations to their old habits and customs. They are afraid of monkeys, and the lemur makes frequent nocturnal visitations to the settlements, to the distress of the people.

There are, in parts of these woods, the most beautiful butterflies, and some bright-plumaged birds and marvellous beetles.

Many of the men wear upon their arms jaw-shaped armlets, which are placed upon the arm in youth before the muscles are developed, and become imbedded in the expanded flesh to such an extent that removal is almost like amputation, so painful and difficult is the operation. Upon the three arms from which I took the armlets I have in my possession, the scars were so pronounced and disfiguring that the owners of the surrendered ornaments insisted that they should have a substitute of sufficient metal armlets to entirely cover the scars. There may be traced a great significance and analogy between these bracelets with the thyrsus of old. I was told by a very intelligent elder that the figures graven on the reverse side of these armlets represented the male and female organs of generation, and the armlet itself was of moon origin; and this was all I could deduce from them. But considering that the moon—Astaroth—was the goddess of the Phœnicians, and many of the mercenary soldiers who served the Phœnicians were reputed to be of East African origin, there seems something at least to investigate, wherein a close student may possibly draw some conclusive analogy. Since offering this idea, I have received from an American traveller a silver ring, presented to him by the late King Ja-Ja, of Opobo, West Africa, representing, as he was told, a shark's jaw, which is identical in shape with the East African armlet, however, displaying no distinctive ornamentation device, apart from a little rosette or flower form on the articulation of the jaw, with no motive other than decoration; yet it is African.

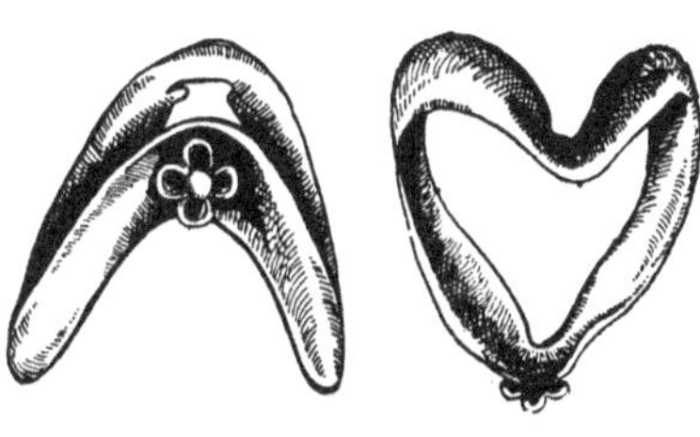

JA-JA RING.

With other tribes, they also have a great horror of insects and all creeping things; and there are constantly being met many small vipers, puff adders, and a few pythons. One of the porters of my own caravan was viciously bitten in the foot by a viper, while cutting grass on the plain.

They detest rain falling upon their bodies, and use three or four broad banana leaves spread out over their heads as arcadian umbrellas.

I found they were very eager to possess needles and reels of bright-colored cotton thread, which I had liberally provided myself with. They had never seen a thimble, and when I showed them those I had brought with me, they exclaimed almost immediately, "Finger hives," quick to recognize an analogy between the thimble and their hives. Then upon discovering the little indentations, they turned and said, "They have had smallpox." Scissors and razors and clasp-knives they were delighted to receive, and hand-mirrors. In this there was quite a difference between tribes, for I found some who considered the possession of a mirror as an ill omen, and would refuse to receive them, or if in a moment of temptation they had accepted one, lost no time in returning it with some apt excuse.

JOSEFE, THE INTERPRETER.

I was taken to their *bomas* in sickness and in their joy, and although I found it most difficult to breathe within these chimneyless inclosures, with a fire always burning in the centre of the room and their cattle stalled in one part, yet I never refused to enter, in order to show them that I did not spurn becoming acquainted with their habits and customs, and was most interested in everything they did.

CHAPTER XI.

ARCADIAN TAVETA.

GLINTS of the daily existence of the arcadian Wa-Taveta reveal many charming attributes of character, so untrammelled, so natural, that the town dwellers of other countries can but sigh over their own removal from a free pastoral life, apart from the perpetual worry and labor of money getting, or even bread winning. Although the Taveta damsels are very fine in figure, their faces are not so attractive as some of the highland tribes. I came very near being betrayed into supposing that certain scars upon their bodies were the result of tattooing, but after close inspection found that they resulted from cupping, which they resort to for their headaches and stomach difficulties; in fact, no matter what malady afflicts them, they are great blood letters, and the simple methods they employ I adopted with great service during my caravan clinic. After excoriating the surface with a little knife or a piece of flint or a piece of wire, they place over it a gazelle horn, with the pointed end cut off,

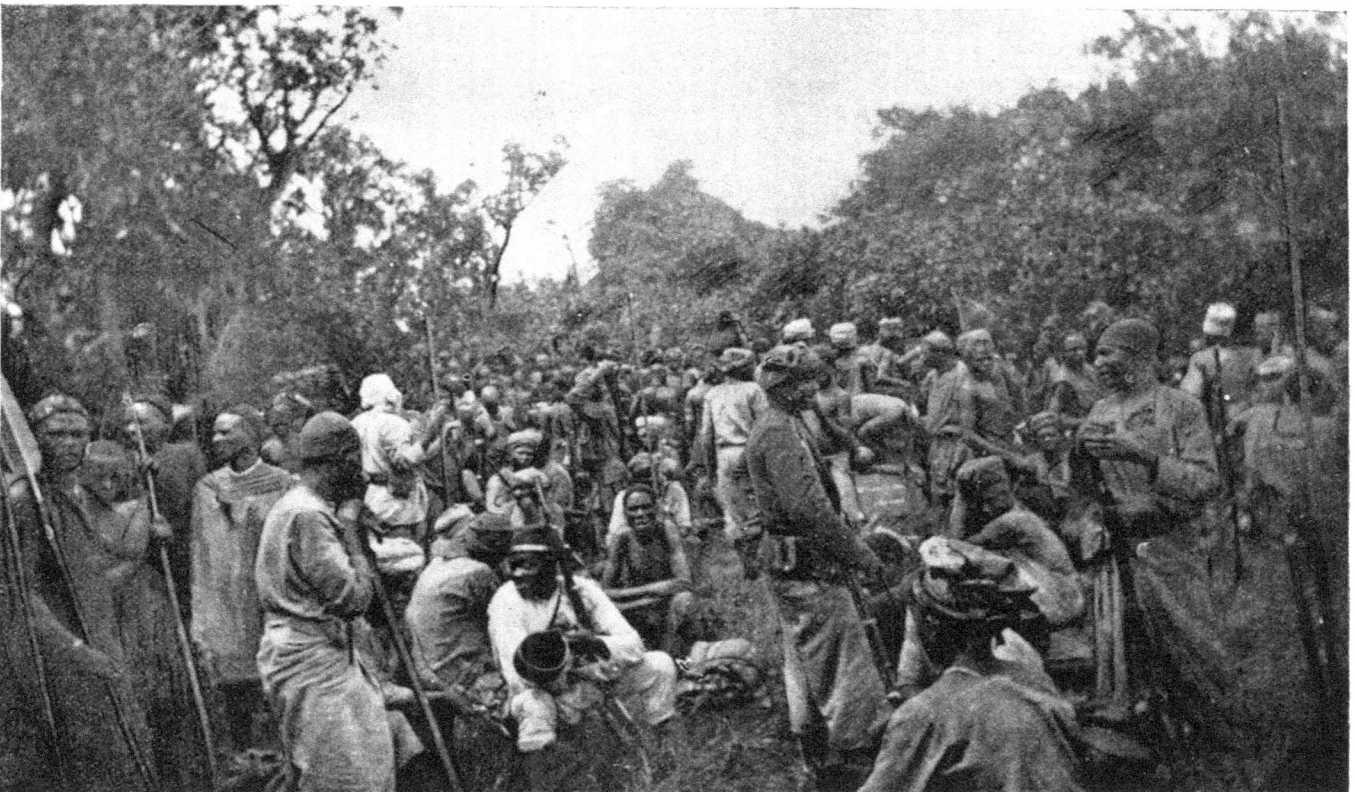

A PAUSE FOR BREATH.

when they apply suction by holding the horn, first wet, firmly against the part to be cupped, and then drawing with their lips the blood; and if the malady is serious, they make several applications, on different places, drawing as much as an ounce and a half of blood from the sufferer. Some Taveta wives file their teeth; however, this is not a tribal custom with the Wa-Taveta, but it indicates that the women who do so have been married from other provinces, and the casual observer is often misled in supposing it to be such. They also often color their teeth, finger nails, and palms of their hands and occasionally their faces with a red stain procured from the dracæne or she-dragon shrub; but as a rule the pure-blood Tavetas keep their teeth beautifully white and polished with tooth-sticks. These tooth-sticks are cuttings from small branches of a saponaceous shrub, and are also universally used by Arabs and Swahali.

WA-TEITA SWEET GRASS NECKLACE.

Caravans bring up from the coast nutmegs, which are disposed of to the natives by the porters as charms against disease, and taken internally to allay fever; they form one of the important stock medicines every *nepara*, or headman, carries.

Natives eat as a medicine, as a condiment, and as a stomachic great quantities of red peppers, which grow indigenously and abundantly. They are fond of raw plum tomatoes, which I discovered to be delicious, and identical in flavor to the cultivated tomato, perhaps a trifle more tart. Ears of corn or maize are spiked about their fireplaces, which consist of three stones canted inward so as to touch at the top, or placed upright, under which the fire is built, where they roast, bake, or boil the maize, which is most luscious. They also eat maize raw, and so did we before too ripe, when it is palatable and nutritious, full of sweet milky

VIEW OF KILIMANJARO.

juice which slakes the thirst. When they cannot obtain pure salt, which they always crave, and is an appreciated article of barter, they use chumvi-stone, which has a brackish, alkaline flavor, and answers very well as a substitute. Salt is found in great abundance in some of these highland districts, according to good authority. Butter they churn by rolling across their *boma* grounds or by shaking large calabashes, or oblong wooden dug-out cylinders, like their honey boxes, filled with milk. Butter made of cow's milk is very white and waxy in appearance, strongly flavored with banana, for the cattle are fed during the rainy season on banana leaves and the fruit that is unfit to keep or exceeds the native's wants. The taste for this butter I fancy must be acquired by a foreigner. They also make goat's milk butter, called *gee*, oily, strongly flavored, and odoriferous as the goat itself. This product is used largely in the cookery of native gormands, and adopted by caravans, but to my taste it was decidedly obnoxious.

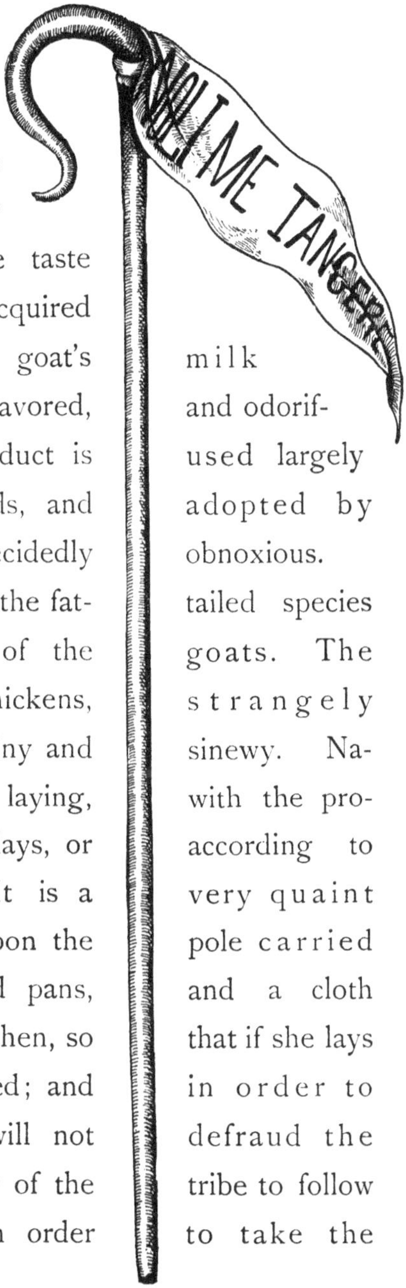

Mutton obtained from sheep of the fat-tailed species is very strong, as is also that of the goats. The beef is more or less tough. The chickens, strangely enough called *ku-kus*, are very tiny and sinewy. Natives frequently sell a hen that is laying, with the proviso that the eggs laid for four days, or according to arrangement, should be theirs. It is a very quaint custom to string these chickens upon the pole carried by the cook's mate, with pots and pans, and a cloth pouch is kept fastened under the hen, so that if she lays on the march, the egg is preserved; and in order to make sure that the purchaser will not defraud the seller, the latter sends some boy of the tribe to follow the caravan three or four days, in order to take the product on the spot.

Africans all have a particular taste and decided preference for rotten eggs. It has been often cited that as a reward for some act of kindness on the part of white men to natives, that the women, under the guise of gratitude, have brought as thank-offerings, eggs — rotten eggs! Could they do more? Even their gratitude has been impugned by almost every explorer and traveller, simply because the natives' expression of this sentiment is at variance with the white man's conception of what it should be. They gave what they valued most, yet this has been attributed to a mean trait of deception in their natures, which are judged so utterly devoid of gratitude. The civilized man is, after all, a thorough Procrustean, intolerant of the natural diversities of human nature, unjust and illiberal once he departs from the limitations of his own studied environments. He deliberately makes his reason impervious to new truths by a heterogeneous composite of principles and his own accepted theories.

TAVETA PEOPLE.

Domesticated and wild animals' hides they tan in a very admirable and sometimes unique manner. They put aloe juice upon the surface after having shaved off the hair, and the hides are hung up or spread out to dry in the sun, first carefully rasping from the inside all the fat and fibre. To obtain variety sometimes they cut or shave the skins, leaving lozenge-shaped squares as decoration, which are relieved by the bare patches. This style is much affected by the "smart" *el-moran*. They also make a species of chamois leather from goatskins, which they soften by friction and working in a large amount of grease. Domestic and wild animals yield them a large quantity of fat, or as they call it *mafuta*, which is valued highly; and, with a little instruction, they could soon be taught to make soap, candles, and especially ointments, for they much need medicament for ulcers and wounds.

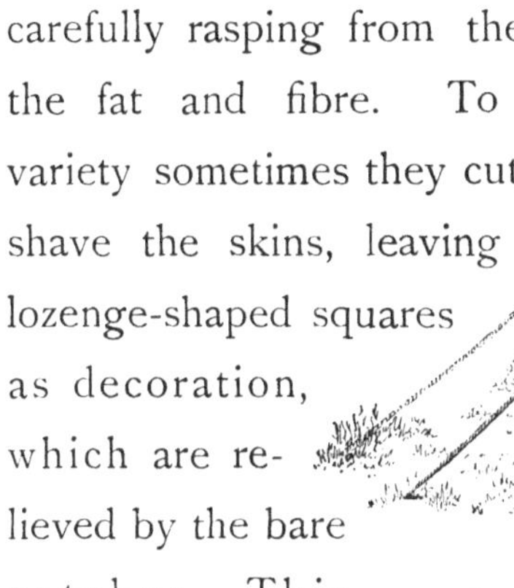

BÉBÉ BWANA'S CANVAS VILLA.

The cowhides and other hides are used for making loincloths, and togas for men and women, and shields and little three-cornered flaps which they sling across the dorsal part of the back, with no apparent purpose if not to brighten and whet the edge of their knives upon, excepting that of decoration; although some writers assume they are to sit upon, — a thing impossible in the anatomical structure of those whom I saw wearing the article. These they embellish with little rows of delicate beads, and sometimes metal chains. The lads carry wooden spears, artistically modelled after, in fact a perfect counterfeit of, the fine Masai metal weapons, and these youths are always posing as prospective warriors. They are experts in the use of bows and arrows, shoot birds and fish and at a mark in games of competition.

Men, women, and children are all equally good swimmers, but use very little water to keep their persons clean; in truth, in some East African regions, they suppose the white man's ablutions are part of a religious preparation before prayer. They substitute, instead of water, grease, yet with all of its nutritive and cleansing properties, by the aggregation of the red clay they universally affect, the decomposition of the oil, never prime even when fresh, renders them rather odorous, when stale it becomes foul and rancid.

Women shave their heads like the men, with the exception that they often retain a small cushion or clump on the crown, from which they allow to grow one or two long strands, on which they string beads; and even at times they strand in little pigtails the entire unshaven clump of wool with beads. The men frequently disport head-dresses made of cows' or calves' stomachs, stretched into shape upon their heads whilst warm and pliant, soon after the animal has been slaughtered; these hang down over their shoulders from their foreheads, completely covering their heads, and are variously garnished with beads and delicate metal fringes and dangling diamond-shaped or round glints of tin. The men are dandies of the most effeminate order.

Most of the bead work is done by the men, and it is not a rare sight to see an *el-moran* moving about in his own or a friend's *boma* with a leather scabbard upon which he works a glass bead ornamentation, or a woman's loin-cloth, leather bracelet belt, armlets, anklets, for some one upon whom he may have smiled, if not, in fact, for his lordship's self. The regulations of conventionality in the different regions seem to be so set that various shapes of beads lend a clannish caste to many ornaments and personality to the *parue* of each tribe. An expert looks at an approaching native, and at once he proclaims the newcomer

A QUIET SIESTA IN MY PALANQUIN.

to be either "Rombo"; "Taveta"; "Kikoro"; "Kiboso"; "Masai"; or "Kimangelia: aye, aye!" He seldom fails in the speedy classification he denotes.

Apropos to this, a camp story was current to the effect that Mandara, the Sultan of Moschi, detected among his women some Kiboso beads, the country of his dire enemy, Sina, and forthwith accused them of infidelity, and of having leagued against him, betraying his future plan of action to his enemy. Forthwith he stripped them of their bawbles, ducked them in the stream, daubed their heads with cow's dung, and threw them as bait for prowling animals in the forest, proscribing succor to them on penalty of similar treatment to the violator of his command.

Certainly the Wa-Taveta are most extravagant if not even luxurious in their love of decoration. Noticeably they, as most of the Chaga tribes do also, wear great heavy pewter armlets and leglets and necklaces, several at a time if they are fortunate possessors of a number. All the women wear a beaded belt of a set pattern, and those classed as the wealthy disport quantities of various colored beaded fringes as a cincture and fillets from which hang long strands of Chaga metal beads, or chains of copper, iron, and brass.

Polygamy exists. It seems almost as a necessity more than licentiousness, considering the environments. A man accumulates more land or more cattle than his first wife can attend; he purchases another wife, and so on. The wives are far from being jealous of each other; in truth, are delighted to welcome a new wife, and make great preparations for her. Each wife has her own hut, if indeed not her own *boma*. She has control of her own plantations, and has the supreme right to her children. Her moral standard is exactly the same as her husband's. A woman is only declassed when she holds *liaisons* with porters in a caravan or with the enemy of her husband. Marriage is by purchase; the wife is bought from her parents by cows, land, spears, etc.; then the marriage ceremony is consummated by capture. Her marital aspirant, with four or five of his comrades, pursues her, and after capture she is secluded four or five days; meanwhile the husband's friends have been permitted certain privileges before the husband claims her. This is simply atrocious. The wedding feast is held with great pomp and ceremony to every one but the bride, who is secluded and presumably undergoing a preparatory schooling in the hands of her husband's mother.

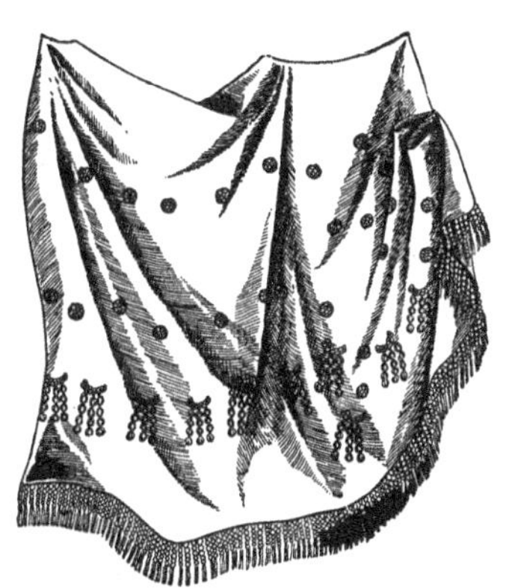

BEAD AND CHAIN EMBBOIDERED LOIN-CLOTH.

The established wives are full of merriment, and interchange many pleasantries with their lord and master, feeling that their daily toil will be lightened.

Frequently the Woman of Taveta would bring a man or woman to me and say, "This is my brother by my father, but not the same mother," and "This is my sister by the *el-moran* my mother lived with before she married," or "This is my brother by the same father and the same mother."

A Wa-Taveta elder, or *mzia*, requested me to visit the infant of one of his new wives and take my *dawa sauduki* (medicine box) with me. I went with him without the medicine, knowing that if the child grew worse, or perchance died, I naturally would be accused of black art, tabooed, and possibly arouse the natives to some retaliation which would expose me at least to embarrassment. Within the arena of the *boma* were congregated other of his wives than the mother of the sick child. The infant was held in the arms of his maternal grandmother. A throng of intimates were sitting and standing about, who had flocked there as much to see Bébé Bwana, as out of sympathy for the distressed parents, or to lend assistance.

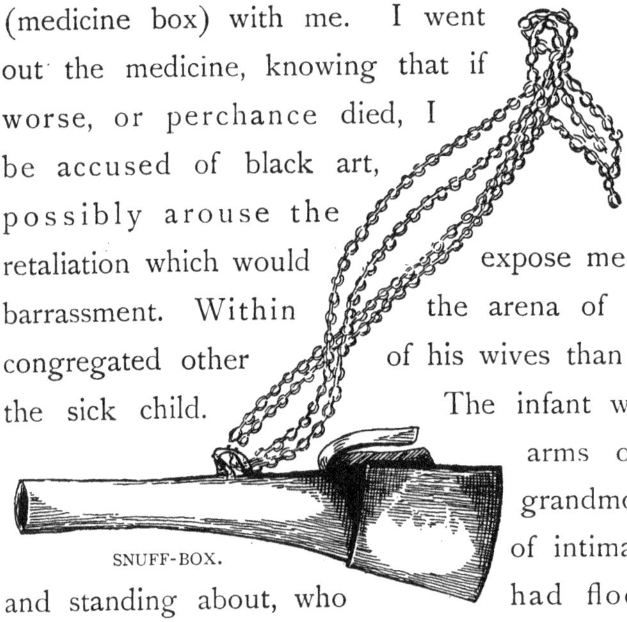

SNUFF-BOX.

The little one was a victim to a malignant form of dysentery, and I knew from the pallor of his visage that his doom was irrevocably sealed. Mercy would have dictated that the sufferer should be comforted in every way, most certainly not violently forced to take nauseous nostrums. The parents were not of the same opinion, for they determined without delay to administer another dose to the screaming, struggling child, who was on the verge of convulsions in his wild efforts to resist his tormentors. Tears suffused the mother's piteous eyes; her stoicism evidently was waning. The brave warrior father, seeing her falter, came to the fore, addressed a few peremptory and not very refined words to the grandmother, turned to me and said,

NATIVE MAIL CARRIERS WITH DESPATCHES FROM HOME.

"Bébé Bwana, this may make you sick; it is not nice, but it must be done."

Curiosity prompted me to protest that I did not object, for I was in a quandary to know what he proposed to do. The father took from his wife's hands a small gourd dish, stepped to the fire, filled his hands with the white ashes and mixed with a little water, thoroughly cleansed the vessel, then smeared honey on its edge, before putting into it the medicinal decoction, which emitted very strong herbaceous fumes; he held this to the child's lips to no purpose; despite the honey bait, the little one kicked and struggled. However, the relentless father concluded that the child must be overcome; the time for coaxing had passed. At a glance from him, the grandmother grappled the child and crushed him, plunging and yelling, flat upon her lap; two of the lookers-on clutched the little martyr's feet and hands, and the grandmother pinched his nose between the thumb and forefinger. I confess experiencing alarm lest I should, by my presence, be aiding and abetting a murder. The dusky father held the gourd to the self-sacrificing grandmother's lips. She took, with real abnegation, a large mouthful; it bulged her cheeks out. Ha! there was to be some vicarious cure. No, no. The infant scion of this African house of distinction must take his own physic. Soon the grandmother, without relaxing her grip of the child's nose, in order to force open his mouth, bent over him, and after fixing her lips against his, as he gasped for breath, squirted into his mouth, out of her own, the noxious dose.

Of all medicinal processes, and I have seen some strange ones, I never witnessed any to equal this in novelty and expediency, for the spluttering youngster had to swallow the dose or be suffocated on the instant.

The deed done, the panting child subsided; then fell

into a sleep of happy unconsciousness. No one seemed touched, even with pity. One must naturally deduce that there is no puerile nonsense among African families of good standing.

Possibly the sequel to this may be of interest. The child died.

Childhood's limit is very brief with the African children; in good truth, it seemed to me there were no real children

COAXING A FIRE DURING A COLD DAY.

after six or eight years of age. That is, they engaged in the pursuits of, and mingled freely with, the adults, in so far as their physical strength and adolescence would admit. They seemed also to be perfectly acquainted with the existent relationships held by their seniors, even to the extent of passing comments upon certain customs, and avowing their future intentions to follow or abandon a similar course when they should have become *el-moran* (young man) or *en-ditto* (a marriageable young woman). This fact comes from the mediocre limitations of the native adult mind, hence the children's accession to the same is comparatively rapid, although I must disclaim that it evinces precocity.

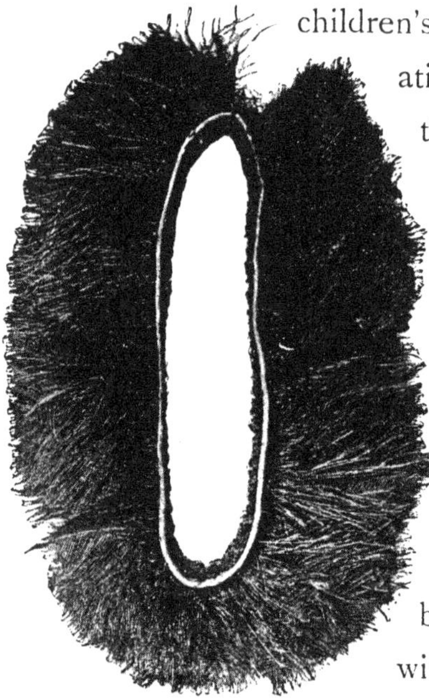

I heard a boy of about six say to a little girl no more than five years of age as he strode about, facing her, while he flourished his wooden spear, full of pride and impetuosity: "When I shall be *el-moran* and thou *en-ditto*, I shall win and wear the bearded collar, and thou wilt be my wife, aye! Thou shall have more beads than all of Endella's wives put together. I have spoken! Now walk with me and show to my fellows how a sultana should look." And the two midgets, with all the pomposity imaginable, made a circle round about the young people gathered in the market place, to become the object of merriment and joke, but good-naturedly they gesticulated and returned the pleasantries of the different groups, and seemingly had their own little fun and glory by thus emphasizing their rosy prospects.

BEARDED MASAI WARRIOR'S COLLAR, WON WHEN TWELVE FOES HAVE BEEN KILLED.

This bearded collar is worn by the Masai warrior who has twelve times "plunged to the heart of twelve focs his spear." Hence the ambitious, bellicose youngster proffered to his young Dulcinea no mean outlook, if his boast met with realization.

Throughout the section of East Africa I journeyed, I was in a constant state of wonderment over the happy, merry dispositions of the children, full of song and sport, like arboreal sprites. The region can well be called, as is Japan, the *Paradise of Children.* Archery clubs are formed among the youngsters and under the command of a leader, selected, or who asserts himself, because of his skill. They practise shooting at a mark, and vie with one another with a pardonable zest. They participate in games of running, become competitors in swimming, diving, and dancing. In imitation of adult blacksmiths, they make wooden spears, the precise counterfeits of the metal ones. They are venders of all sorts of produce at the markets, especially of chickens and eggs.

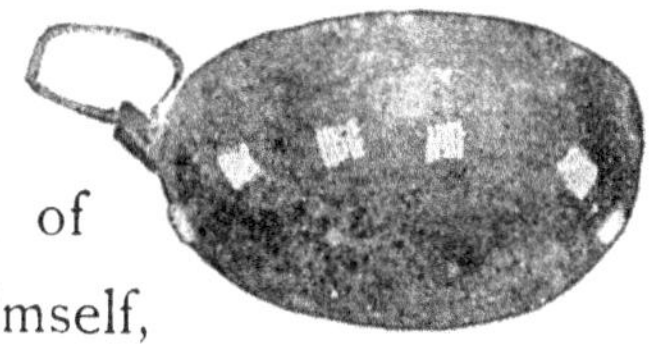

INLAID GOURD.

Soon as they attain an age and have strength to endure journeys, they are sent as couriers, and, when experienced, as guides. Their early existence is spent in a perpetual sort of rudimentary kindergarten, and their education is acquired by observation, imitation, and object lessons. Like all aborigines, and animals, left to their own resources, they are constantly on the alert, more or less wary, even to a degree of suspicion. In their primitive condition they affect the mannerisms, adopt the customs, and aspire to the estate of their seniors, as have and do the children of all nations.

The fact of the natives' simplicity, despite their detractors, fills me with an abiding hope that if at the outset these particular, amiable, and amenable tribes of East Africa have sagacious, peaceful, fair treatment, and their natures are enlarged and they are led at a gradual pace to accept the ways of civilization, there is much to hope for in their intellectual unfoldment. Every move, every gesture, every word, is scrutinized by these natives, and this habit of concentration imparts a contemplative seriousness which characterizes the expression of their eyes. Strange, too, a traveller among them soon takes on the same expression, in the endeavor to fully interpret the natives' eloquent sign language, with which they vivify and supplement their circumscribed vocal utterances. With a vocabulary of two hundred and fifty Swahali words it has been affirmed that an observing person could travel, with a dialect interpreter, all over Africa. As Emerson has truly written: —

"The eyes of men converse as much as their tongues, with the advantage that the ocular dialect needs no dictionary, but is understood all the world over."

'ARRIOR'S SPEAR.

Several ostriches belonging to the officer of the English

NATIVES AND OSTRICH ABOUT MY KITCHEN.

post flourished at Taveta, to the natives' great annoyance. Apparently the natives never became used to them, although they saw them dozens of times during the day, as they passed through the *boma* bent on work or pleasure. If the gawky birds flapped their wings or made a rush, they would scatter, yelling, and striving to make a speedy exit, in clamorous terror. These birds with the famous stomachs would swallow with impunity cartridges, old shoes, and all sorts of rubbish tendered them. An ostrich breeding farm could be advantageously maintained thereabouts, and stocked from the wild birds that haunt the country in great flocks. We encountered a number whilst on the march.

CATHERINE WHEEL DOUBLE BRASS EAR-RING.

They dry fish and jerk beef, which they cure by hanging in their huts, exposed freely to the smoke of their fires. Everything they possess, even their bodies and hair, smell strongly of smoke.

An elder of unexcelled intelligence and standing among his tribe told me that the fires were never allowed to go out; that is, in the village; a single family fire might become extinct, but this could be resupplied or reignited by getting a blazing fagot from some friend's fire. But in the history of the tribe, as far as he knew, they had always vigilantly preserved the fire, as doubtless did their prehistoric ancestors. On a march or when hunting or visiting from tribe to tribe, they carry with them fire-sticks, which they deftly use by twirling rapidly in the hollow of a bit of hard wood in which is placed dried fibre until the friction. They also are acquainted with the use of flint, and by scraping the fibre from the *m'whala* or other fibrous trees they make a pulp which is quite as inflammable as tow.

A FUTURE WARRIOR.

The children are very skilful in the use of bows and arrows, and when I presented them with fish-hooks and lines, to please me they would use them at the end of a reed pole; but no sooner was my back turned than they would resume their old practice of obtaining fish by shooting them with wooden arrows in the water, or by using weirs.

Taveta's grand forest as well as its mountain, and its ready access to the plain, or *bara*, give the Wa-Taveta ample security from invaders and scope for their plantations and grass land for fodder for their stall-fed cattle, making theirs almost an independent province; and although it is said they are of Masai origin, they are so gentle, pastoral, and peace-loving I could but doubt the supposition, always going back to the fact that their environment showed a long line of antecedents of like ilk. During the period of my sojourn in East Africa there was considerable friction between the young dandies, or *el-moran*, and the elders, in Taveta, on the matter of *hongo*, or tribute exacted from caravans passing through their country. This has been abolished by the English government throughout in their protectorate, also by the Germans in theirs, but it is evaded in an ingenious manner by the natives, who impress the newcomer with the idea that they will receive certain advantages and surety from molestations in giving them presents; and in former days the elders received this toll, and made distribution as it suited them. Now the young men personally desire to receive this tribute, whenever they are able to exact it, and they are continually holding palavers between themselves to determine what effectual course to pursue. However, this exaction must be short-lived; the government will doubtless succeed in totally abolishing it as an imposition and an indignity. However, I did not pay *hongo* to any tribe during my *safari*. When approached respecting this, I said, "I am your guest; I am as a white queen coming to you. Would you ask *hongo* of the sultan of such and such a tribe should he visit you?" and it successfully relieved me from further parley or exaction.

They are very tenacious as to the quality of the cloths they receive; and although they are very much attracted by bright colors, you will see them take a piece of cloth and hold it up to the light, to test its texture, and if it is too thin they do not want it; and the old habit of forcing upon the native any trash as good enough for the negro, at least in East Africa, does not at present answer.

They are kind to their children; however, I found no children in act or intention in any tribe I visited in East Africa, after the age of six; they were little men and little women, who, of their own accord, daily trudged to the noonday market with a load upon their heads, happy and delighted to be in the swim with their parents; and the only child I heard cry during my expedition, who was not an ill baby, was a little one who was restrained from going to market, and he howled, and kicked, and yelled in such a fashion, alarmed, I paused to inquire the cause of his uproarious distress.

The utter freedom with which the men and women mix together, and the homely intercourse between parents and children, reveal a trait of their social life that is most genial and certainly not looked for. Possibly this leads to a certain amount of familiarity with matters and things in civilization removed from the knowledge of the youth and the maid;

but then one must admit that natives are naturals, and that ignorance with them concerning natural things is as much of a crime as innocence is a virtue in civilization. Although they are not purists by any manner of means, let me say I saw in Taveta no manifestation of licentiousness, excepting the matter of their dances. In talking with them as to the English occupancy in their country and the benefits to accrue therefrom, they would answer rather dubiously, "Aie, aie; yoh, yoh," and I fain discovered a tinge of regret, and in their hearts I believe they would be content to go on in their happy, pastoral way, without bothering their brains about education, government, and all the confusing principles of civilization. They live to enjoy, and enjoy to live, and are as idyllic in their native ways as any people I ever encountered.

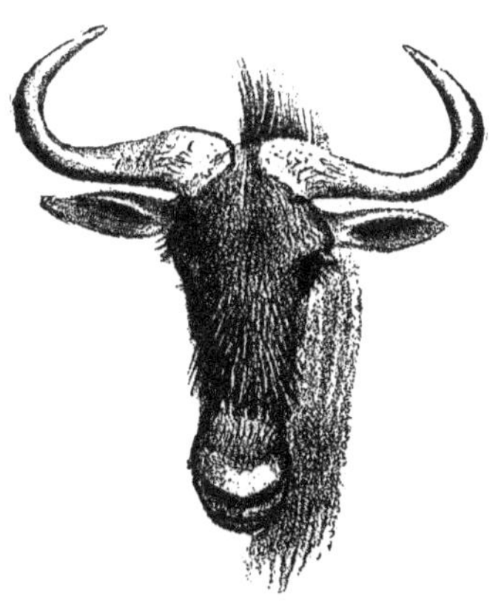

CHAPTER XII.

CIRCUMNAVIGATION OF LAKE CHALA.

WHILST the majority of my caravan were busy stringing barter beads for *posho* at Taveta, I sought the opportunity of starting on a little tour. Accompanied by the resident English officer, Mr. Anstruther, but at my own expense exclusively, with my own selected corps of fifty porters, solely as my own private expedition, the last of April, 1891, I made my first visit to the crater Lake Chala, and descended to the water's edge. Under the same circumstances, *en route* to Kimangelia, a fortnight later, with my entire caravan, we returned, and on May 9, 1891, circumnavigated this lake. Through the courtesy of the Germans, Mr. A. was the fortunate possessor of two sections of a copper pontoon, which were the original property of Count Teleke, and abandoned by him as cumbersome *impedimenta*. These were conveyed between ten and twelve miles on the shoulders of my porters, the distance from Taveta to Lake Chala, in order to make the venture.

I feel prompted to offer an explicit statement of certain facts, to exonerate Mr. Anstruther from criticism of having in

LAKE CHALA. SOUTHWESTERN VIEW.

any way violated the covenants of his legal and moral obligations under his iron-clad official commission with the Ibea Company.

Finally, it will be well to state that absolutely in no instance was my rule and order of command relinquished to any temporary guest or friendly escort during my entire expedition, nor in any way have I to acknowledge the successful carrying forward or completion of my expedition to the auspices or patronage of any European resident in East Africa, however grateful I may be for certain courtesies. At this period I owe to Dr. Baxter, formerly of Moschi, hearty thanks for surgical care given to my eye, and for the medical supervision he bestowed upon the unfortunate fever-stricken invalid of the caravan. Every time a white man chanced to be with us, my porters were discontented and at times positively sullen; they seemed somewhat apprehensive lest the white men might be installed in my place as leader. Like children they would flock about me to express their delight over the departure of a guest. This spirit of displeasure was likewise evinced by many natives, who seemed to have a latent suspicion that the white man would make some demands upon them, or might be desirous of subjugating them, or fighting with them. So it was proved disadvantageous for me to entertain or to be joined, when on the march, by white men, no matter who they might be.

Leaving Taveta during a great downpour about three P. M., the ten or twelve miles' march was a great hardship to all of the men, who were more or less demoralized and out of condition in consequence of the long encampment. Night overtook those who were in the rear, and after delays and tumbles into animal pits, those belated straggled in camp at all hours until after daylight. Wood for fuel was scarce, as there was nothing growing immediately about the stony place of our encampment, close beside the rim of the lake, but thorn-bushes, and the rain had soaked everything. It was a night of discomfort and anxiety, for we were in the immediate haunts of wild animals and the so-called fierce Rombos.

The gradual ascent from Taveta to the rim of the crater lake on the western side is only a little above the level of the plain, and on the southwestern end there are abrupt peaks two hundred to four hundred feet high; the level of the water, as shown by our aneroid, attained a level of one hundred and ninety-five feet below the encampment, and about four hundred and forty-seven feet above Taveta. And the temperature of the water near the surface was only one and one half degrees lower than the atmosphere registration. The lake is near the western side of the stream Mfuro, or, in the Masai language, Naromosha, but according to some travellers misnamed the Lumi. We find Lake Chala north of Taveta on the northeastern side of Kilimanjaro, about 3° 22′ south latitude, 37° 17′ east longitude, over three thousand feet above the sea level.

The crater's crest rises above the surface of the lake eight hundred feet at its highest point, and at its lowest two hundred and fifty feet. The lake, roughly estimated, is two and one half miles across at its widest point, and from six and a half to eight miles in circumference. It is environed by massive blocks of perpendicular rough rocks, which extend like a subterranean wall far beneath the level of the water.

Interminable vines and thickly grown forest trees present a forbidding appearance on all sides.

The late missionary New was the first white person to give an account of this lake and of his difficult descent to the water's edge in 1871. However, the explorer Thompson writes of this lake with reference to its inaccessibility: "I went all around it; and although I am not deficient in enterprise or nerve, I saw no place that I dared descend, not even if I could have swung from creeper to creeper like a monkey."

Standing on the crest of the rim of this crater, looking down upon the crystal water which was cupped therein, at first I was well impressed with the impossibility of descending to the water's edge, unless some means could be devised as a substitute for flying. Nevertheless, on the assurance of Mr. A. of Taveta, who had some months previously descended to the lake edge, nothing daunted, I determined to make the venture. There was a weird attractiveness overhanging this place that overawed even the natives. All accounts I could glean about it were so vague that I wanted to taste of the forbidden fruit myself. With an advance guard of only two men, alone, for Mr. A. remained at the top to direct the pontoon bearers, I found myself attempting to penetrate through a girdle of primeval forest trees, tossed, as it were, by some volcanic action against the rock base, and seemingly as impenetrable as any stockade. With bill-hooks and knives they cleared a slight opening through which I managed to squeeze, on emerging to find myself standing on a bowlder, which was balanced upon another bowlder, and every moment's tarriance seemed to imperil my equilibrium; and as I dared to venture on other uncertain surfaces which presented a footing, it required cat-like agility to crawl or slide down,

LAKE CHALA. NORTHEASTERN VIEW.

sometimes landing in a bed of leaves, which must have been the accumulations of centuries, and into which I frequently sank up to my armpits, and had to be hauled out by main force by my men; and then by clinging and clutching to the branches of overhanging trees, after great effort and considerable peril, succeeded in laboriously attaining some other foothold, step by step advancing, again and again to be opposed by gigantic trunks of trees, which, lightning-smitten, had fallen as a barricade, or through some potent eruptive force had been uprooted and turned themselves top down in solemn humiliation. Anon, a bowlder, loosened from its scant earthy holdings, would come crashing madly down from the top and shiver into fragments the white skeletons of these trees. The weirdness of the scene was intensified by the strange whirring of birds frightened unceremoniously from their hitherto undesecrated homes, and the whisking of myriads of monkeys as they leaped from branch to branch without emitting a chatter in their fright. A whistling eagle beat the air with its wings directly over my head, scattering its feathers like storm-flawn flowers in its wild flight, and white-hooded owls peered out from sequestered nooks and twoo-hooed in solemn amazement. The extreme sheerness of the rocks made the descent hazardous, tortuous, and very tedious. Constantly obliged to turn back on my path, searching and groping, creeping on my hands and knees through tangles of interwoven tissues of rubber-vines, and so was compelled to cautiously feel with my feet, and be content with the greatest slowness. The danger attending every movement and the spectral weirdness of the place inspired me and even affected my men with awe. My advance guard would sometimes whisper words of warning, afraid to utter a sound, and extended his hand or arm to prevent my plunging headlong to the bottom. All this filled me with an excitement and imparted fresh courage, and re-enforced my determination to overcome the difficulties of the uncanny spot, cost what it might, so long as I should be able to climb, or crawl, or slide, or step, or simply let myself go with utter blindness, and risk the incumbent results; for the goal bewitched me in anticipation.

Through gaps in the massed trees, through which the sun could scarcely filter, the arboreal darkness was pierced by a radiant gleam of light, and the flashing lake greeted my expectant eyes. There arose a general shout from the men, "Chala!" "Chala!" and behold! I found myself rewarded by being upon a rugged, rough tangle of prostrate trees and wild tumble of white and gray rocks, whilst the limpid, restless waters were laughing and dashing themselves into a jubilant foam at my feet. The scene was one of which I became enamoured. It was truly overcast with a sublime sense of a holy sanctuary. Losing myself in the spectacle, I forgot that Mr. A. and porters, with the two sections of pontoons we had taken the precaution to bring, were waiting eagerly for me to give the signal agreed upon when once I should be safe at the bottom on the lake shore. After a moment's revery, recovering myself, I sounded the whistle. Then the deafening crash and yell and rush commenced, as the porters struggled valorously with their precious burden down the narrow, serpentine, rugged figment of a path, which we in the van had essayed to make.

The marvellous ingenuity with which these porters manœuvred their metal loads, and the stoical way, when they would slip and their burden fall upon their shoulders, and cruelly dig out chunks of flesh, the blood trickling from their wounds, they would struggle to their feet and go on without complaint, called forth from their comrades screams of applause, whilst the leaders sung a wild, weird strain full of rhythm, just as we find men who are moving heavy loads always instinctively do in order to keep time with each other's movements.

Finally the two copper sections of the pontoon were in the water. They were immediately examined to see if there had been any puncture made through the thin metal sides in their difficult transit. They were scarcely large enough, when lashed together and covered with a *m'whala* door, which had been converted into a platform, to hold myself and men, and presented to the onlooker a most unsafe maritime structure. The moment came to embark, and on demanding, "Where are the men who are to accompany us?" not one would respond for the first excursion; subsequently Josefe and a headman were perfectly willing if not eager to distinguish themselves by going. Presently they murmured among themselves, "No, no; we will not go on Devil's water. Just see the crocodiles, and hear the monkeys, and look at the breath of the devil. *Inshalla* (God willing), we will remain with our feet under us on shore," as they pointed to the water which was in some considerable commotion, revealing here and there its amphibious denizens.

After going through the usual process of calling them goats, and cowards, and jungle-men, my interpreter, Josefe, who was somewhat of a daredevil, and ready for an adventure, stepped forward, saluted me, and said quite gallantly, "Bébé Bwana, at your service." So Mr. A., Josefe, and myself, with our guns and photographic instruments, embarked upon the bobbing pontoon with two long improvised paddles. We pushed carefully out from the shore, amid the shouts of the bewildered porters, who eagerly watched the performance, fully persuaded in their own minds that it must end disastrously, having taken the precaution to attach a hawser several hundred feet in length to the uncouth craft in case of accident. The crocodiles were very curious, not knowing what to make of the invasion of their haunt, and came in close proximity to our uderpinnings, as with one paddle I manœuvred to guide the craft and Josefe awkwardly propelled with the other, whilst my guest kept a sharp lookout for the obtrusive aquatic creatures. After moving the length of the hawser, we found the craft was manageable, and cut loose, to the horror of the men grouped on the rocks.

At every turn there arose from the midst of the crater forest great flocks of birds, which had all the appearance of being ducks, but which have since been named by the late Mr. Bates, *Phalacrocorax Africanus* and *Phalacrocorax carbo*, a species of cormorant but edible. They cawed and screamed and whirred about, making a great commotion, and, upon our approach, would dive into the water, when the crocodiles would immediately give them chase, which was obvious on account of the extreme limpidness of the lake. I was enabled to bring back several specimens, shot from my craft on the lake, as well as a specimen of monkey which has as yet not been named.

Gazing up at the steep cliffs on all sides, the vines hanging in theatrical festoons, and the weird, weird beauty of the various foliage contrasting with the grand trunks of whited trees, the strange murmur of the waters, the remarkable outbreak of waves crested with foam, the small circle of sky as I looked up, and the mad tumble of rocks, all contributed to make it seem as though I was in some phantom land.

PHALACROCORAX AFRICANUS.

Everything was most eldritch and immense. At the firing of a gun the reverberations came back like a thunder-clap—sharp, crashing. I should not have been surprised to have seen the whole lake covered with some uncanny creatures, or to have seen the apparition of some mammoth forest king issue forth and assert himself as monarch of all we surveyed, and crush us out of existence as invaders. The hours spent upon this lake at different times held me in a thraldom of wonder. There was little said, very much thought, and imagination thrilled my brain with the ineffable pleasure which I had craved and sought for years, of being the first to visit a place undefiled by the presence of man before.

AFLOAT ON LAKE CHALA, MAY 9, 1891.

The thing which surprised me most was the fact that when I plunged my paddle two or three feet under the water at various points, the suction was so great it would be drawn away from me, and only with difficulty could I recover it and resume control; and at other points it would be drawn beneath the float, and again I would have to tug lustily to pull it back. At the same time the entire lake was in agitation; it was bubbling almost like a hot spring, and yet there was no rift in the rim of the crest through which currents of wind could sweep down and cause this commotion. After trying to make a sounding with a plummet and line of two hundred and fifty feet, without success, I determined that it was the reservoir for the meltings of the snow from Kilimanjaro, and that these under-currents and counter-currents were due to subterranean in-takes and outlets, and that this body of water fed the streams of the plains, and was a water-shed subsidiary to Kibo and Mawenzi. Another remarkable thing, although the dashing of the water at different times must have reached a greater height than its level when I was afloat thereon, as shown by the moisture upon the boundary rocks, they were unstained by decayed vegetation and uncolored by mineral deposit. It was perfectly clear and clean, as evidenced by the specimens of rock I took the pains to bring home for analysis. The water to the taste was not disagreeable, but was soft and sweet, a trifle warm, 72°, whereas the atmospheric mean temperature was 74°. As we cast about the margin of

PHALACROCORAX CARBO.

this lake, with its seductive little insects making unrevealed bays, until one was fairly upon the turn of the margin, it was so exquisite and beautiful! and as far as the water scene and the surrounding forest of vegetation, I could scarcely believe it possible such beauty could be encompassed within the precincts of the crater lake, nor have I ever heard or read of a parallel crater.

Although this is doubtless one of the last evidences of a volcanic eruption in this region, it has survived the memory of the people. The fabulous tradition concerning it is that

KILIMANJARO.

when the sun sank into the mouth of Mawenzi, the Masai village which was located upon the site of the lake when Chala was a mountain was tossed into the air, and great rush of water rose, filling up the space and making the present lake, and had swallowed the people; and that the strange murmur, which is almost unaccountable, is caused by the spirits of those unhappy wretches, and the soughing of the trees is the lowing of the cattle and bleating of the sheep, and the clapping of the reeds is the cackling of the fowl. Another version of this tradition is that the people of the Masai village that was once located here had committed so many depredations against other tribes, became arrogant and ungrateful, and refused to pay tribute for years to Kibo and Mawenzi; so the angry God of the Mountains inundated their village, and swept them far away out of existence.

> "What length of far-famed ages, billowed high
> With human agitation, roll along
> In unsubstantial images of air!"

Capt. Sir John C. Willoughby says: "Making a slight detour, by climbing the lower slopes of Kilimanjaro, which enabled us to visit the curious Lake Cala [Chala], no sooner had we ascended the low hills encircling its eastern shore than we were rewarded by a glorious view. At least a thousand feet below us nestled the lovely lake, somewhat triangular in shape, and from one to two and a half miles in its widest diameter, completely embedded among hills and cliffs,—a basin in which the great Masai Mountain God could always wash his hands. From our position its shores appeared inaccessible, but the natives declared a descent was practicable." Notwithstanding this statement, I was not enabled to find that any of my porters had heard of any one descending to the surface of the lake, or to meet any native who had gone to the water's edge or who could be induced to descend thereto; and instead of being the subject of curiosity, which I had apprehended and was desirous to avoid, when the natives knew I intended to descend, and witnessed my preparations, they flew back, terror stricken, into their mountain villages, and not one intrusive eye would gaze upon the white woman on the Devil's water.

Bewitched by Lake Chala, I made several descents at different times, and floated my little American flag from the pontoon craft during its circumnavigation. To facilitate matters at some future day, when I hoped to return, the historic little craft named for me was buried in a bed of leaves, and I retained a key describing its secret hiding-place. Several slabs loom up at various intersections of the lake margin, defiled by red paint, which emblazon my name and the date of this exploit.

Having completed for the time being my explorations of Lake Chala, I turned my attention to the people who inhabit that section of Africa.

My ears had been filled with warning as to the hostilities of the Rombos, consisting, in four or five provincial divisions, of a tribe known respectively under the names of Rombo, Rombo Chini, Rombo of the Bara, Rombo Colis, inhabiting the plain and hills between Lake Chala and Kilimanjaro; so with justifiable precaution my men were well armed, albeit I was fully determined, unless the most desperate events should compel defence, under no pretext to use firearms, and had impressed this upon my porters before making the venture, giving strict orders to my headman to punish any porter severely who violated my command, and under no circumstances to fire at natives, or even the wild animals haunting this region, without word of command from either myself or himself. My first impression of the physical aspect of their domain environing Lake Chala was most inauspicious, presenting great gloomy hill slopes, with basaltic formation and rotted lava stones interspersed with thorn-bushes, although overshadowed by the majestic twin peaks of Kilimanjaro,—snow-capped Kibo, crenelated Mawenzi,—which certainly lent a scenic splendor to the horizon. The plantations, which are unquestionably fertile, were so far removed from my line of march that they were scarcely discernible.

A succession of animal pits ranged immediately below the point where we were to encamp, which were set by the Rombo

ROMBO SPEAR.

people, who are trap hunters rather than hunters of chase. The curious construction of these animal pits is worthy a word. The Rombos and other native trap hunters dig a pit of about four feet wide, six to ten feet long, six to eight or ten feet deep. This is covered over with brush, and presents no appearance of a trap to the casual eye. They are spaced at the distance of say a foot between, ten or twelve in a row, so as to intersect a path to a water course or water pool. These traps are baited or not, and the Rombos beat the bush and jungle thereabouts, and drive the animals who are seeking water or prowling for food into them, and afterwards kill their prey with spears or arrows. However, they frequently leave the traps undisturbed, and withdraw to their hillside *bomas*, and await the chance of the animals straying untowardly into them. These are used for elephants, lions, and all other big game. Mischief not infrequently befalls an unwary traveller or a caravan passing through the country during the night, who may fall into these pits and become seriously injured; and there are credible accounts that men have tumbled into the very jaws of lions which had already become victims. Another method of making a trap, especially for elephants, is by excavating a large pit on the usual caravan route, covered with an ingenious intertwining of vines, upon the top of which is placed a covering of sod and sand, to all appearances no different from the rest of the path. These are excessively dangerous, because interspersed beneath the outer covering are sharp spikes, made of tusks or spear-heads, or even giant thorns, to step upon which is most injurious and painful. These are incidental disadvantages to pleasant promenades, and can be warded against by the judicious employment of native guides, when one desires to pass through regions known to be habited by native hunters.

To reiterate, the Rombos living in this region have ever been deemed a very ferocious people, tricky in their dealings with other natives, and the marauders of passing caravans. Some of their villages have been closed even against the Arabs, and they bring their products to barter down upon the *bara*, or plain, rather than admit strangers into their kraals. With the warnings which I had received, I felt imbued with a sense of precaution and unwillingness to enter their villages until I could decide from their manifest attitude as to the likelihood of their looting my caravan and probably murdering me. However, after being beset with earnestness by the prime minister of one of the sultans, I concluded to go and see for myself; and at an hour when the men were all resting and I could safely leave the camp without observation, I selected four of my most trusty headmen and an interpreter, and visited one of the Rombo villages, to find the delighted people most civil, and eager to do Bébé Bwana homage. They were neither uncouth nor unkind nor ungenerous, and certainly far from being hostile. They loaded me with gifts of beautiful furs and such other of their worldly possessions that I chanced to admire. Although, with few exceptions, men, women, and children were in an absolute, state of nudity, the men carrying shields

ROMBO SHIELD. OUTSIDE.

made of hippopotamus hide three feet long and a foot wide, bossed and with pressed designs, they brandished spears, the blade end not a foot long and narrow, carried bows and arrows, their deportment was as manly as one would naturally expect from civilized people. When they were presented by me with cloth (and this I wish to explain fully, because I have been very much misquoted on the subject), they looked about and saw in what manner my porters were bedecked. However, instead of putting their cloth on from a sense of prudery or shame, they were as likely to hang a piece of four or five yards trailing from their shoulder, or try to twist it about their heads as a turban, or tie it on to their arm or leg, as much so as they were disposed to use it as loin-cloths or surround their bodies. The idea which evidently prevailed with them, as in fact it does the world over, was simply to follow a fashion, and to imitate what they thought was fine in some one else. They have no consciousness of their nakedness. They bore themselves with so much dignity, and I grew to regard their color as abundant clothing for them in their primitive simplicity. Truly they were clothed with *toga virilis*, a robe of manhood unfashioned by any mode of civilization, but inborn.

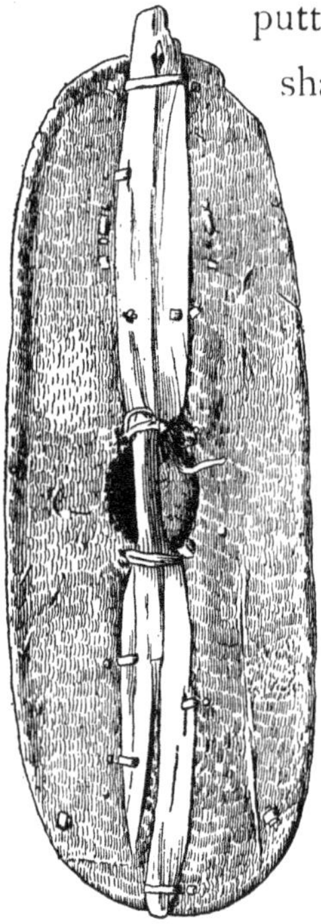

ROMBO SHIELD. INSIDE.

In passing, as an illustration of the effect of superstition upon these people, which reduces them to a timorous, suspicious state, the following may be interesting.

By the suggestion of a man who had gone from coast to coast of Africa, subsequently spending a year in East Africa, holding a position which should have given him full insight, one would suppose, into the habits and tastes of the natives, and who should have known what would have amused them, I took a dozen bright feather toy birds, which, by means of a rubber bulb and tube, are made to hop about with great animation. The dull day came when, quite at my wit's ends to amuse some visitors from one of the tribes of Rombo, suddenly I recollected the birds. The case containing them was opened, and with great flourish I wound up my music box and set the birds to gambol before the wide-open-eyed guests, as they squatted expectant on their heels around my tent.

TOY BIRD.

Presto! in two seconds that robust vision of dusky warriors, yelling at the top of their voices, presented nothing but heels. They ran like the rushing wind, terrified by the innocent toys, and as if pursued by his Satanic majesty.

The next morning, through the prime minister of the tribe, they indignantly requested us to leave their sultanate. Unwittingly I had actually betrayed my entire caravan to imminent peril, as the performance was looked upon as black art.

Nothing more of these natives was seen; and after exhausting every resource in my efforts to induce them to return and accept of our amity, they persistently refused, and I was unable to procure food for my men. This threw us into a very sorry dilemma; for we were quite depending upon reprovisioning the caravan at this village, for food was scarce and cattle dying off rapidly several marches beyond this point of our journey.

HOSTILE ROMBOS.

Having to submit to the folly of my experiment, so innocently made, it opened up a new field of consideration as to a characteristic in their nature of which I had previously been entirely ignorant.

This recalls another incident which shows the importance of striving to understand the peculiar characteristics of different tribes, in order to know what impression they are likely to receive when experimented upon.

ROMBOS. VICTIMS OF GERMAN GUNS.

Observing a bevy of young warriors and girls hovering about one of my tents, I took a hand-mirror and through the ventilator of my personal tent, unseen by them, I caught the sun's rays and threw the reflection upon the group, never for a moment thinking of the cross-lacing in front of the opening. This made the reflection fall in checkers or squares. An instant sufficed. They scrambled pellmell away, thinking it was a devil's tattoo that I was directing against them, to enslave or put them under a magic spell.

In connection with this I must add, these little traits of character, based upon superstition, are like stepping-stones to the index of their character; and one who is careless in the study of what may on the surface appear to be frivolous and unimportant, will miss the finest points in the individuality of any people.

Whereas these natives, with the cited exception, treated me with so much courtesy and gentleness, I still recall the circumstance which has been blazoned throughout the world, that when six weeks after I had safely traversed that country as a lone woman, the celebrated Dr. Carl Peters, in order to pass safely with himself and armed soldiers through this district, felt obliged to turn his guns on these Rombos, armed in their simple fashion, and kill a hundred and twenty before breakfast one morning. It makes one's blood boil with indignation! This, then, is how Germany proposes to civilize and colonize Africa.

I am constrained to say either there must have been some

peculiar power vested in me of a quality almost superhuman to have enabled me to subdue these so-called hostile Rombos, or else Dr. Peters's methods are simply brutal, atrocious, and unnecessary.

This distinguished man reveals his belief in despotic measures throughout Africa. The following citation from his "New Light on Dark Africa," respecting his manner of proceeding in Uganda, is a satire on the title: "As I well knew that in case of possible Arab enterprise I should have to rely principally on moral impressions, I had taken care that our reputation should precede us, and had been careful, above all, to bring with me from Usoga a band of war drums, which should send the signal of war resounding before us over the far-spreading heights. Three drums tuned in fifths on which the roll was beaten, and the big drum coming in between, the whole produced a solemn and threatening effect."

If an alien provokes by coercive measures the native in his own land and develops all of the worst propensities latent in his nature, it is not fair to lay the blame upon the poor untutored native and call him "savage."

CHAPTER XIII.

VULCANS OF CHAGA.

VULCANS, *fundis*, or craftsmen in metal work, have attained a great degree of skill and perfection throughout Chaga land. The renowned blacksmiths all have been or are celebrated chiefs or sultans, whose deftness in the forging of spears, knives, pipes, agricultural implements, tools, bells and most delicate little charms, necklaces, armlets and leglets, as well as various metal ornaments, has given them a distinctive prestige in other spheres of tribal significance.

Mireali of Marungu, and Mandara of Moschi, have held their own, generally speaking, with the belligerent Masai in consideration of the fact that, although great warriors, they are dependent upon the skill of these two sultans for their spears.

Mandara does not now personally forge any weapons, in consequence of his physical disablement; those made in his sultanate, however, are practically his ware, and bear the stamp of his original skill, temper, and patterns. He has rendered the metal work of Chaga land the envy of other districts, as well as the wonder of white men.

The simplicity and poverty of the native tools make their skill all the more remarkable. One of their finest spears, with its blade three and a half feet long and four inches wide at the broadest point, and an inch-square metal pike about four feet long joined with a wooden rod from one to three feet long, requires forty rings of iron the thickness of telegraph wire. The texture of the metal becomes fine and durable as it is heated, in order to weld, in charcoal fires, and necessarily wrought very slowly, hence it is the gradual process, coalescing the iron wire into a mass, and its carbonizing makes the temper very fine, and converts the metal into an admirable semblance of steel. In lieu of an anvil, the metal is forged upon a piece of close-grained ironstone by a heavy stone or iron hammer. The hot iron is grasped and manipulated with a rude pair of long-handled pincers; the fire is kept alive by a pair of native bellows alternately inflated with and expressing the air as operated by a man sitting between them on the ground opposite the fire. The nozzles of the bellows are made of pottery, and are plunged into a small clay oven; the charcoal is doled out in small quantities, and treated

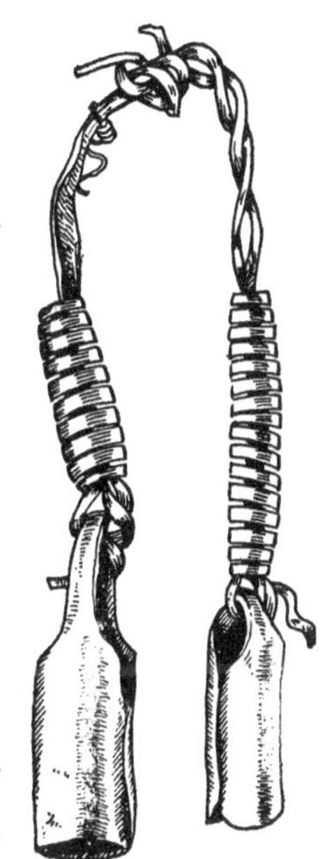

BRASS AND IRON BELL EAR-RINGS.

sparingly as something precious; in fact, a long roll of grass, neatly disposed, contains the fuel, opened at one end, from which an attendant picks out with his hands, lump by lump, or in handfuls the black diamonds to revive the fire; his miserly care impresses the onlooker with the idea that he is dealing with an article of great price, as in fact it is, in consequence of the primitive manner it is charred on the mountain. A tree is fired about six feet from the ground, and wet grass plastered in a hummock over the burning portion to smother the flames. When the smouldering trunk is charred, the tree topples over, and when a fresh supply of charcoal was required, the body and branches were treated in the same method.

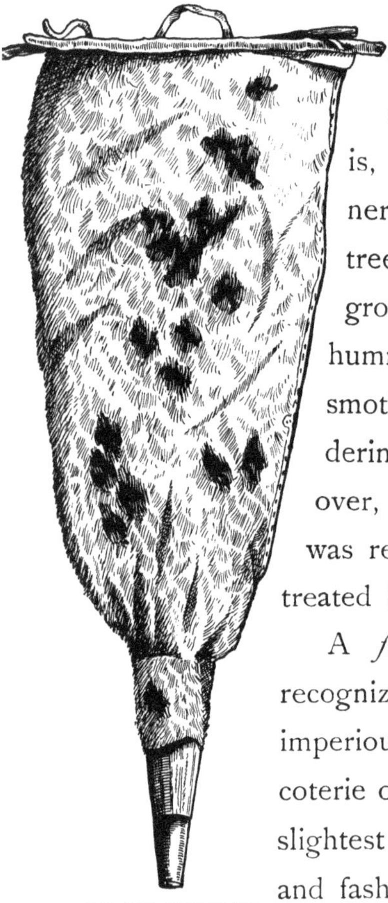

NATIVE CALFSKIN BELLOWS.

A *fundi* is an autocrat, accounted and recognized to be a great man; he bears an imperious mien, and is always attended by a coterie of followers and henchmen who do his slightest bidding, as he bends over his work and fashions the articles of his craft; thirsty, some one gives him a drink of *pombe;* tired or hungry, he pauses, even betakes himself away for refreshment. No one presumes to suggest aught to him; no one dares to gainsay him. He is master of his craft; he realizes his own power; he exercises his prerogative of superiority upon every trivial occasion. Then, too, he has certain privileges and perquisites not accorded even to the chiefs who are not also *fundis*.

During an evening's chat a *fundi* said to one of my interpreters, "Come now, good man, where would the warriors be, if it were not for the spears and knives that the *fundi* make?"

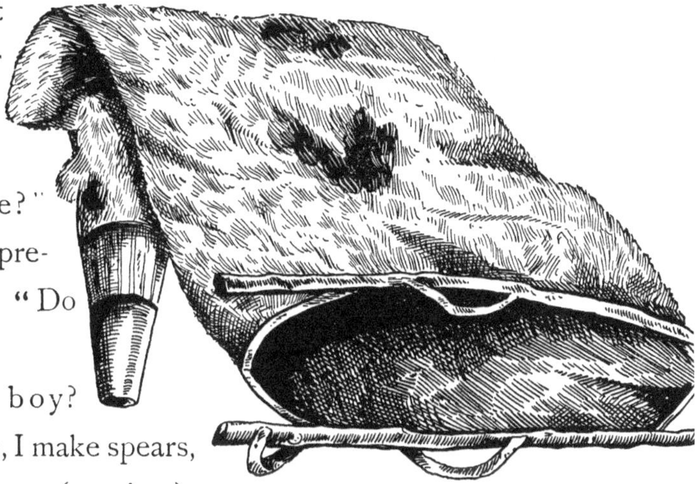

The interpreter queried, "Do you fight?"

"Fight, boy? Me fight? No, I make spears, so that *el-moran* (warriors) fight in the right way; fight to kill."

NATIVE CALFSKIN BELLOWS.

At this he seized by the middle the wooden part of a spear which he had stuck in the ground erect in front of himself when he had squatted down before the crackling camp-fire to chat.

"See! see, boy!" He cleverly balanced the double weapon, spear-head one end, pike the other, plunging forward with an upward sweep the fire-flashed metal, describing a broad arc, yet he did not let go of the wooden centre, but rushed ahead until it had reached its limit, then whirled the weapon out, and vaulting backward forcibly drove the pike into the ground behind him, when, with a glow of satisfaction over his own prank, he exclaimed, "See, boy! see!" quickly uprooting the quivering weapon, again violently swirling it from right to left in the same wild manner, leaping sideways with agility as if parrying a blow; "this, boy, this is the way I, the great *fundi* of Fimbosa, teach the warriors; they may kill a foe in an eye-look with my beautiful spears." Poising the heavy weapon on the forefinger of his right hand until it gently swung like a pendulum, he sauntered away, evidently loath to remain in the presence of Zanzibari who was ignorant of his noble calling and of the brave fabrications thereof.

In good truth, to be a spear or sword *fundi* requires admirable skill and practice alike of eye and hand, in order to shape, balance, set, edge, and polish the blades, much more so certainly than is required to make their agricultural implements and small knives, although they are more or less all made according to tribal conventional shapes, gauged by the requirements of utility.

Still more delicate and nimble, but not so masterful, must be the fingers of those who are the jewellers amongst the *fundis*, for the fine wire they make by repeatedly and laboriously drawing when heated with long, slender pincers through the *chamburo* or perforated metal or stone screens of various sizes in order to reduce to a delicate size to make the slender link chains which are so pliant and marvellously

MASAI SPEAR.

TALL GRASS.

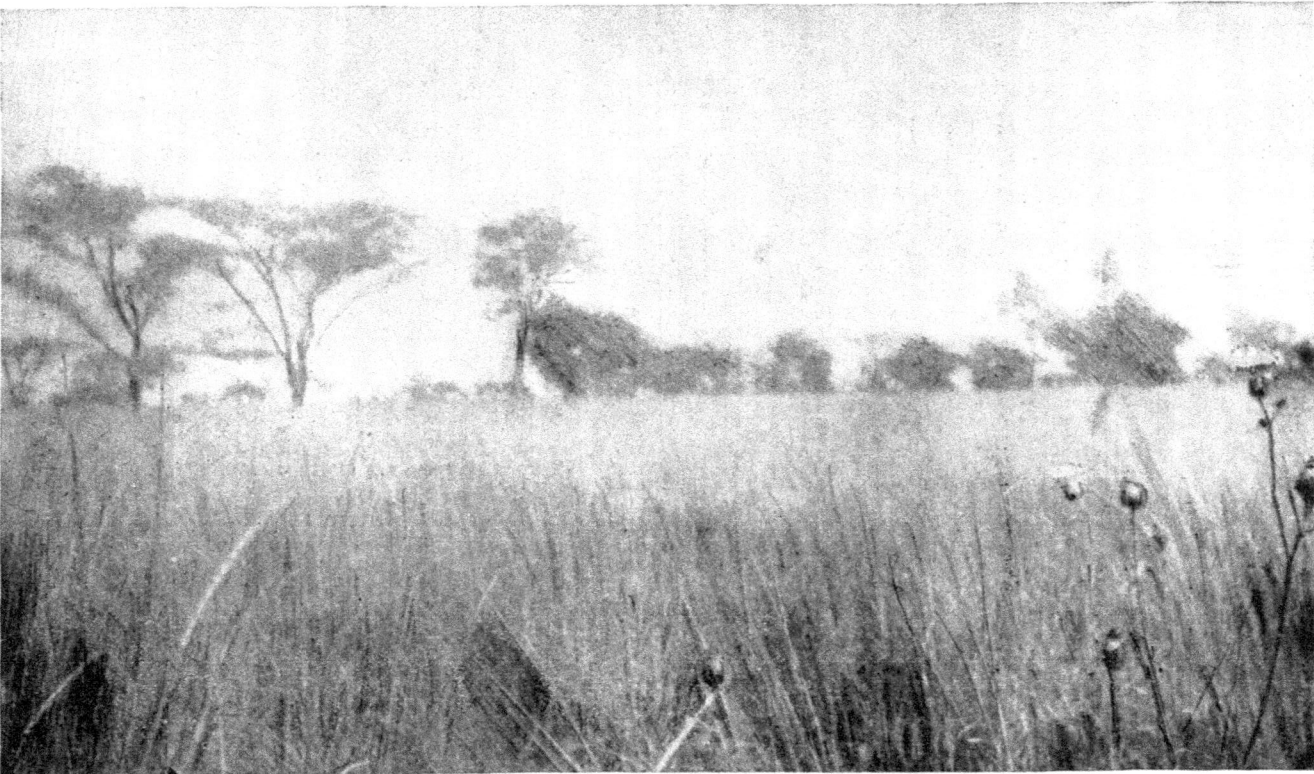

dainty, and the many sizes of metal beads they manufacture by cutting from a wire cubes of certain length, then, by beating them thin and flat, turn them into little cylinders, pressing the edges so close the union is scarcely noticeable, at the same time keeping them round. Some square dice-shaped metal beads are also made by them.

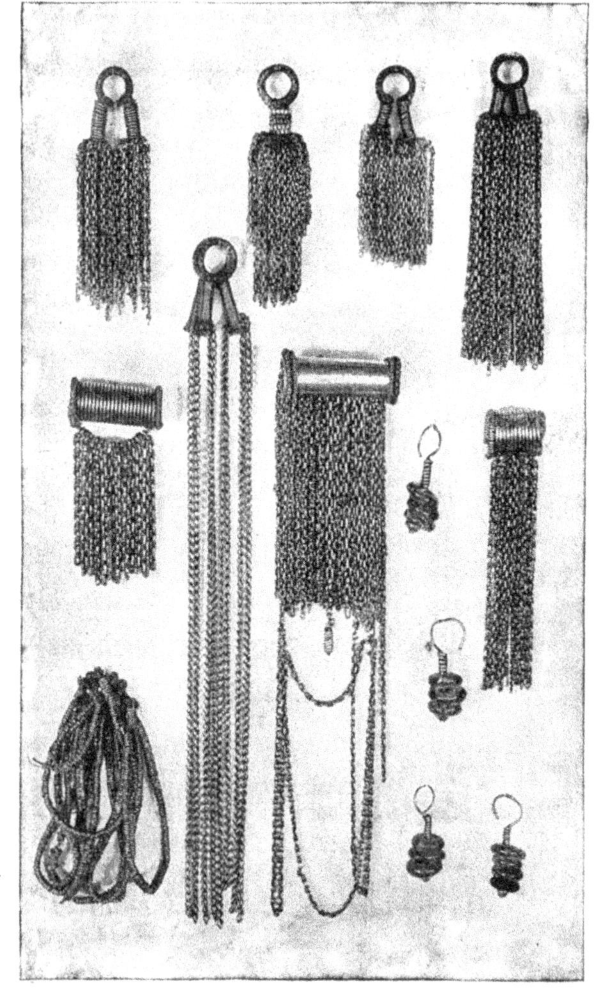

METAL CHAIN EAR-RINGS, BRASS, COPPER, AND IRON BEADS.

It occurs to me that if caravans would carry for barter suitable tubings of different metal and different sizes, it would vastly reduce the labor of the native metal workers; although it is questionable if more accurate and symmetrical forms of machine-made tubing would lend beauty to their present fabrications. They have an odd habit of placing around a staff rings of iron wire, and stringing together links of chains to be used when required.

The only crucibles I could discover in the regions I visited were stones hollowed out and a fire built all around them, inside and out, until they became white hot, when the inside was brushed out and iron, brass, copper, and solder put in, then kept hot by the surrounding fire until it melted, when they would pour the liquefied metal into a wooden mould the shape of the bracelet or necklet required, which they had previously soaked until thoroughly saturated, first in grease, then in water; but this method is not held desirable. The native connoisseurs prefer the hand-forged articles of jewelry, in the same manner as do civilized folk prefer anything hand wrought to that which is cast or machine made. I am not speaking of the people far up on the mountain, who use great furnaces and smelt native iron, but of the people of Chaga land, whom I was privileged to see at work. Hence I hope I will not be understood as assuming there are no furnaces in East Africa.

REAL SIZE SMALLEST CHAGA BRASS BEADS.

Their graving tools are very primitive, generally consisting of a piece of iron they have welded, having a narrow chisel edge with which they cut into the articles, much as do the artisans in civilized countries, by tapping the instrument with a metal or stone hammer when held on the article to be embellished, and follow the pattern, thus graving out the design intended. All of their processes are slow, requiring great patience,—a quality patent to native peoples the world over. They insert or incrust bits of silver, gold, and other metals, bits of ivory, bone, beads, into wooden vessels and gourds most cleverly. This is done in a style durable, finished, and artistic, far from being trumpery, and certainly not slipshod. They finish off with spiral rings of fine copper or brass wire or dainty rows of beads the ends of all objects, or where there are two parts joined, or one material used for embellishment or it merges into another for lack of quantity, or prompted by the selection of taste, displays the trait of perfection which is the acme of all crafts. Ear-rings five inches in diameter, of double circles of brass wire, like Catharine rings, are most perfectly shaped and highly polished; and this without any tools except pincers or hammers, pieces of flint and pumice stone, and perchance when they are fortunate enough to possess a file procured from some Arab caravan. The art of buffing or polishing, smoothing off and brightening, is effectually done in the

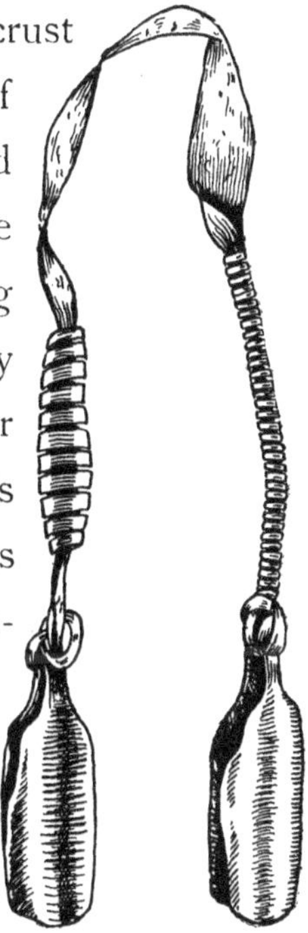

METAL EAR-RINGS.

first place with pumice stone, in which this volcanic region abounds, wood ashes, using as buffers goat, sheep, and cow skins, as well as the palms of the hands well moistened. If you will take the trouble to watch a group of this dusky people before a fire which has burned long and the ashes accumulated, you may see some of their number spitting into the palms of their hands, which they dip into the ashes and afterwards vigorously rub their bracelets or anklets, and the brightness and glitter which their ornaments preserve, although coated with grease and clay, I have never been able to procure without using burnishing irons and pumice powder mixed with kerosene or lye.

NATIVE SEMÉ AND SCABBARD.

Ornamentation appears as a species of religion with them, and they never seem to be content with their possessions to the point that they cease to strive to accumulate more.

Vanity and love of finery, in Africa at least, are free from being exclusively feminine, for the men are quite as prone to indulge in personal bedeckment as the women, if not more so, and amongst some tribes the warriors and *paterfamilias* do all the strutting about and fancy work, whilst the women toil, till the plantations, carry wood, carry the fodder for the cattle, care for the stall-fed creatures. They stick with marked tenacity to a mode in decorations, and seemingly avoid exercising originality in design, in order to follow a fashion. Very true, this fashion may change or become diversified when the people of various tribes mingle in friendly association, and possibly exchange, present, or barter their trinkets to some enterprising youth or girl. Anon, frequently when they cannot get what they crave in gewgaws, they will not refuse what is proffered, unless it is in lieu of a purchase; then they will not as a rule be swayed, save by their own will. To their native metal work they frequently subjoin charms, *dawa*, or medicine beads, animals' teeth, which are worn for various complaints, and frequently loaned by members of a family one to the other. Their bells have various uses and various significance, beside that of ornamentation. A warrior's bell, six inches long, turned over in shape, with a metal bullet or metal piece within, is attached to a leather beaded band, which is worn below the knee by the Masai during times of war. A little iron bell, three inches long and two in diameter, with a long bar-shaped tongue, constructed somewhat after the pattern of a lily, is worn by a woman during her first pregnancy. It serves as a warning to those who approach her: the herders driving home the cattle, and youths dancing, and all those who might suddenly frighten her, take heed of the warning tinkle, are silenced, and let her pass unmolested. Then the majority if not all of the people in most of the tribes wear little jingling bells, affixed to thongs strapped around

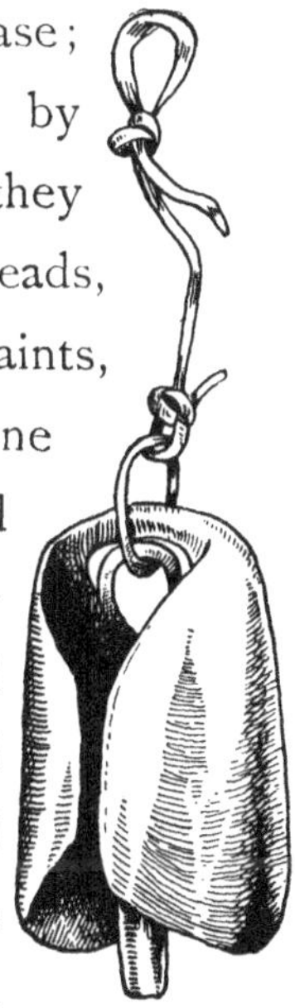

IRON BELL WORN BY A WOMAN.

their ankles or arms; and in the tribes on the mountain, if a woman or man is found at night outside the *boma* without these bells, they are supposed to be on some evil errand, and must suffer accordingly. Then they wear little bells, like turnover pies, in their ears, around their arms, around their dancing wands. They put bells around the necks of one or two of their cattle in a herd, when they are grazing in the open, and hang them about the fringes of their bead ornaments; and they all have a peculiar sound of their own. They use a circlet of bells to teach the children how to walk.

BELLS WORN BY INFANTS.

Catching sight of and hearing the jingle of a string of cowrie-shaped small iron bells attached to a leather strap around the ankles of a mere toddler, and observing the little one constantly looking down to her feet striving to see them, apparently to the great danger of her equilibrium every time they tinkled, I asked her mother why she allowed the child to wear them, at the risk of having her fall.

"To make her walk," was her prompt reply.

Then she pointed to the little feet, and I watched the child's performance only a minute to be convinced of the cleverness of the maternal trick. The little one would move a foot in an undecided, unsteady way to put it to the ground, when the bells would tinkle, and with frantic efforts she would wriggle her body in every direction to see where the noise came from, and half losing her equipoise, up would fly the other foot, then she would hear another sound of bells; and so on indefinitely going through with the same performance, one foot and the other alternately, until she had crossed the broad ground of the *boma*.

By a happy chance I had a large supply of table and call bells and small sleigh bells, which were received with delight as gifts, and the natives were even anxious to barter for.

Their knives are sometimes oddly shaped, sometimes rude enough, again works of artistic cutlery. Frequently they wear them on their arms in a leather band, with little tubes of arrow poison strung on to them by delicate metal chains or strips of leather; they also thrust them into their belts for convenience in case of defence, as well as to be able on the instant to cut the thorns, bananas, corn, grass, and to dig out their wooden utensils.

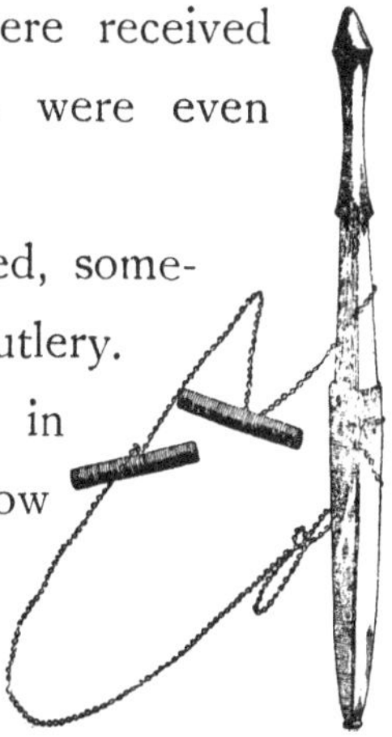

MEDICINE MAN'S KNIFE AND POISON TUBES.

Banana knives are rough, heavy blades, set in short, straight wooden handles, sharpened on the inner groove, so that they hook them around the stalk of a bunch of bananas and deftly with one sweep detach it from the main branch.

Rings and bracelets, leglets and neck ornaments, in the case of the Masai women, consist of great coils like exaggerated multifold continuous bangles or car springs, finished off with other metals; the body of the ornament, which is usually iron, garnished with copper and brass by way of contrast, always with the idea of accentuating display. Almost every man understands in an amateurish way something of metal work. He makes for himself, his sweetheart, or wives rings and bracelets and anklets, but he is not a master, not a *fundi*.

They showed me the source from which they pattern the splendid Masai spears, and I was delighted to find it was the

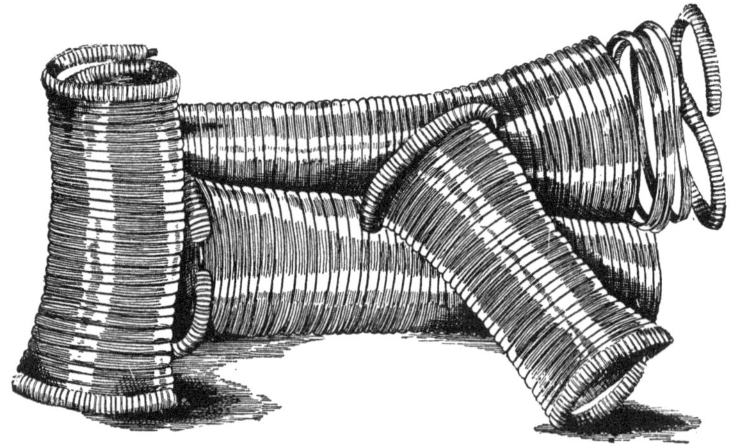

ORNAMENTS WORN BY A MASAI WOMAN. IRON COILS FINISHED WITH BRASS AND COPPER.

leaf of the same species of cactus as the Spanish sword bayonet, indigenous to various tropical regions, and when a leaf of this cactus was held beside their implement, the accuracy of their eyes and gift of reproduction were evidenced, for the shape was a complete copy, even as to the little peculiar roundness of the point, and the ridge running through the centre of the spear, which puts the stamp of grace upon a masterpiece; and their smaller spears, that are used by the Rombo and other tribes, are imitations of rubber and magnolia leaves.

They make crude bullets and spoons, arrowheads, rude razors. This latter is not to be wondered at, as it seems to be one of the traditional coat-of-arms of all negroes. However, their razors have no wings; they do not fly, as in America.

The way in which they turn to account every bit of shining metal is sometimes amusing. Every tin can, when emptied, is carefully preserved to present to them by the porters, who make efforts to win a smile, obtain a favor, or procure a tidbit for their pot they could not otherwise afford. One day after discarding the metal tube upon which had been rolled surgical plaster, spindle shaped, with circular ends colored bright red, I was pleased to see a pretentious young warrior sally about the camp with the article thrust into his ears. The tops of the cans they would convert into dangling dice, scalloped, diamond shaped, round, square, to add a lustre to their own finery. Watch and clock wheels are likewise extracted from timekeepers to mark the rapid pace of fashion in ornamentation.

WARRIOR'S BELL.

Soda-water bottles were pounced on with avidity, and the men would squabble until blows ensued for their possession. They liked to have the bottles to carry water or milk for their own use, as well as to barter with the natives. In sauntered on a village palaver ground a native, in truth a so-called crown prince, with twelve soda-water bottles attached to a leather girdle; the dozen represented his accumulation of possibly years, but this moment in my presence he thought the proper occasion to disport his *soi-disant* treasure. For this delicate tribute I held a full-dress reception, attired in my court gown and all the splendors of my jewel box and portable wardrobe. As usual, the function was a very distinguished social success, and exalted me far above mortals of common clay in the estimation of sultan, crown prince, courtiers, and plebeians. All the world over tailors and dressmakers hold a rule and reign wherever civilization dares stride. Decency and style with the enlightened, the spirit of monkey-like imitation with the untutored primitives, make votaries to the tyrant Fashion.

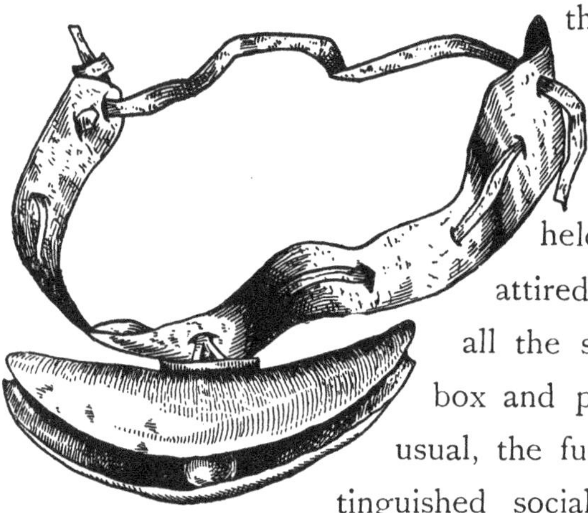

DANCING BELL.

Soon after a splendid Masai spear had been received by me, the chief of camp story-telling made it the occasion to

NATIVES NEAR KILIMANJARO.

flourish before his comrades, after scornfully listening to a green porter's yarn about some cruelty practised by the Somali, burst out vehemently:—

"What! you call that worth the telling, man? Come now, listen to a true story. It will put warmth into your blood, and make you sleep with your eyes open. When I first

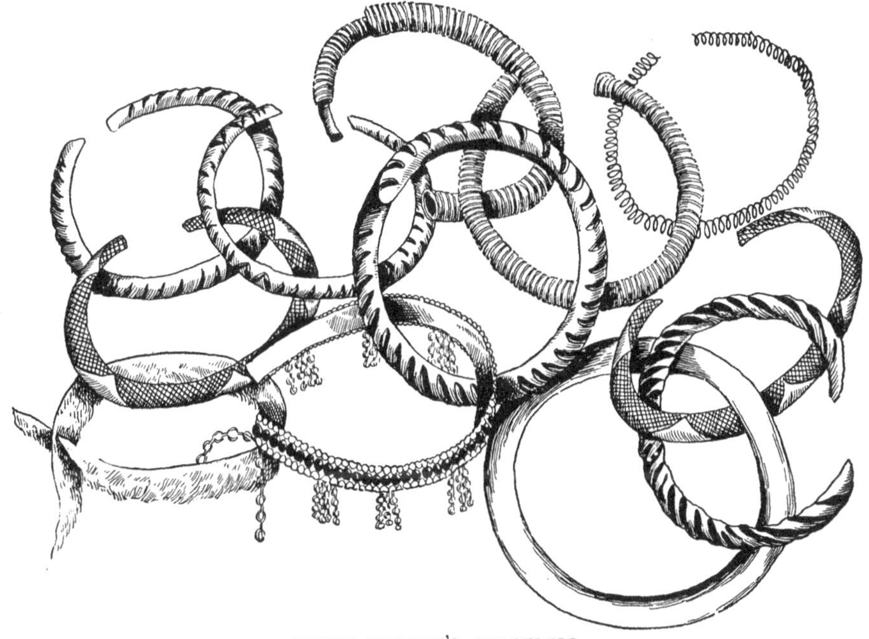

NATIVE VULCAN'S BRACELETS.

came to Masai country, aye, before you had stopped tugging at your mother's breasts, coming from the winter's sun-bed, we saw two men carrying—"

He turned and darted a fierce glance of defiance on the group of porters certainly uncalled for, as they sat mutely engrossed in the progress of his story, never vouchsafing to lisp one word. "Do you know what?" he said to one;

"or you? or you? or you?" and he pointed with his knob Kerry stick rapidly from one of his followers to another, never expecting an answer. "Ha! ha! I might have known you couldn't guess. Well, mark you! keep your ears open as the day. Upon a spear—a spear like this!"—and he took up a large Masai spear—"two Masai carried between them, upon which swung the bodies of three Rombos, spitted like fish to bake! right through the middle, on the same haft! Hey! who dares gainsay that? You see, lads, I have travelled. A man must travel to see and to tell."

And he swaggered on down through the camp, quite satisfied with the horror he had inspired; and it occurred to me that a white woman must travel at the head of a caravan to hear such yarns.

CHAPTER XIV.

PRIMITIVE KIMANGELIA.

KIMANGELIA, at the height of four thousand seven hundred feet above the sea level, in the mountain forests on the northeastern slope of Kilimanjaro, between the second and third degree south of the equator, forms the frontier of Masai land, was the objective point of a two or more days' march. It became necessary to repose considerable confidence in a native guide bearing the geographical appellation of Mombasa of Taveta,—a perfect dandy in his make up, handsome and self-conscious, faithful and inoffensive. He had been born at Useri, but lived at Taveta. The hue of his complexion betokened the intermingling of white blood in his veins. Mombasa of Taveta insisted, and was right, too, that the forest village was above Useri on the mountain, whereas an English official, desirous of floating the English flag and enter a first claim in behalf of the English, recognizing the established fact that all territory above the plains must be German, and having sited in the distance from Lake Chala the plantations of Kimangelia, had concluded that it must be below the lake region, which was a theme of dispute then, but since has been admitted to be German. He had laid out another route, by following which, in spite of Mombasa's protests, the caravan was compelled to make a long tedious detour.

Lake Chala was then debatable grounds in consequence of the gradual slope of the plain from Taveta to the lake which is so gentle that the rim of the crater approached from Taveta seems almost on a level with the plain. Dr. Myer has expressed an opinion that even Taveta should legitimately belong to the Germans. There is much striving to encroach on all sides in the establishment of territorial lines throughout Africa, which demonstrates the importance attached to African possessions, especially in this particular section of East Africa. The Chaga language is almost universally spoken after leaving Taveta on the slopes of Kilimanjaro, and I was informed throughout Masai country. The agreed governmental plan of allotting the highlands and mountain of Kilimanjaro to the Germans, and the plains and all territory to the east to the English, it would seem cannot be consistently adhered to, for the reasons that the highland habitants must have access to the grassy plains for fodder and to hunt, whereas the habitants of the plains should have recourse to the highlands for their plantations, hence with strictly maintained dividing lines there must

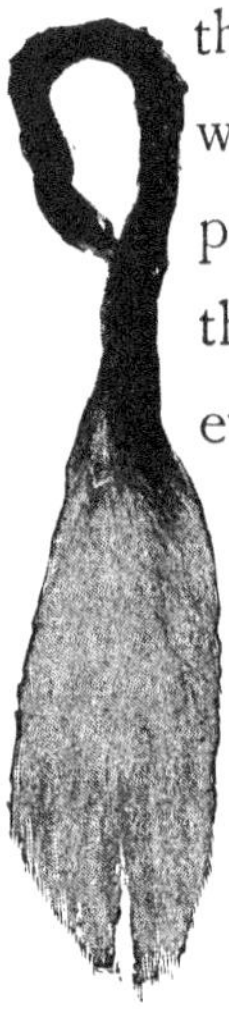

MASAI LEGLET.

constantly arise friction and worse; for it can hardly be expected that either the English or the Germans will complacently submit to the rigid enforcement of territorial lines, or the collection of imposts in these primitive regions, with mainly a native constituency to levy upon.

From this point I took guides from the tribes, with the idea that I would hold these guides, in case of attack or hostility, as hostages, and the instant the first tribe made an assault on me or my caravan, I would punish these guides in some unmistakable manner that would stand as a warning to all further aggressors. They were also useful to point out difficulties, avoid traps, and show the most accessible paths. Before I got through with my journey, I had attached to my little army forty of these half-prisoner guides, who were perfectly happy, in their unconsciousness of the motive which actuated me, to jog along day after day enjoying the fellowship of the porters.

OSTRICH FEATHER MASAI MASK.

The people of Useri were somewhat disturbed in their minds upon the appearance of the white woman's caravan. They were under German protection, flying the German flag, and hesitated in giving to me the welcome other tribes had extended. I sent two messengers to the Sultan Malimia's *boma*, saying we would await him half an hour, or, as they quaintly say, "until the sun is there," pointing to a special place in the heavens; and while I was waiting it gave me a little opportunity to study the people.

The women were decorated very much after the fashion of the Wa-Taveta, with the exception that they wore from a clumped piece of hair on the centre of their forehead little circular bone ornaments, terminating in metal fringes, which hung down over the nose; and some of them wore metal chains around their heads, which hung like fringed veils to their eyebrows; and their ears were pierced at every point possible, into which were thrust beads and pods, and long ivory or bone pendent rings. The men were shy and had a hang-dog look about their faces, which might have arisen from their recent subjugation by treaty of the Germans, and the presence of German soldiers in their midst; they seemed uneasy and on the lookout for a surprise.

Sultan Malimia did not make his appearance at the stated time, so we proceeded on our journey to be overtaken, when five minutes beyond the confines of his province, by a message through his prime minister to say that if Bébé Bwana would only return he would receive her, and he had some fine presents. I promptly said, "Bébé Bwana never returns. If the Sultan of Useri wishes to see her, let him follow her to the next encampment." This resulted in his sending after me a meagre quantity of presents, which I did not accept. In any country but Africa this would assume the appearance of surliness or contempt on a traveller's part, but in Africa the prestige of the white man or woman must be maintained through certain current conventions, which are well known with all the natives.

We passed the fountains of Useri, which are more in the name than in fact, and more like pools than fountains.

From this point, passing through many villages and small tribes, we directed our course to Kimangelia.

Wart hogs and other rather wild beasts abounded, and the fresh spoor of rhinoceros, the occasional bellow of buffalo, and the crushed grass showing evidences of beds just forsaken by recent denizens, made our march somewhat anxious. Every one was on the alert, and not one dare say he could complacently encounter a buffalo

USERI HEAD ORNAMENT.

My personal mishaps became stupidly frequent. In quick succession I tumbled into three deep holes, newly excavated by the wart hogs, never profiting by a first tumble on account of the tangle of grass that covered them.

Then the caravan parted, and it was a long time before the stragglers were reunited, one of the porters broke his shin bone, another had a chunk of flesh gouged out of his shoulder through a tin box slipping off from his head and cruelly striking him in its tumble; fever prevailed, and for some time all sorts of trying incidents flocked unceasingly like birds of ill omen.

A Masai woman's corpse was nosed out in the bush, with all her armor of iron wire leglets and armlets upon her stark stiff body untouched, however much coveted, through superstition. Personally I nerved myself to the removal of her leglets, which had become so imbedded into the flesh and muscles of her legs, amputation was necessary. Josefe only was ready to assist me to perform the unpleasant business. Certainly I could have commanded any of my porters to attend to this matter, but they were possessed by nameless superstitions; and such an exaction on my part would have put a damper on their exalted estimation of me for so outraging their sentiments. I endeavored to maintain a policy of harmony when consistent.

MASAI EL-MORAN.

Daily the temperature was so alterable that it was with difficulty the porters could keep warm at night, although sweltering under the direct tropical rays of the sun in the noonday. Towards three or four o'clock P. M. the hot air would suddenly ascend to the mountain region, and be displaced by a rush of cold air, and a constant atmospheric current swept over the country. The

ENTERING THE FOREST.

regularity of these breezes suggested the idea that windmills might be profitably established, which could be used for irrigation and cistern purposes. Although the natives have ingeniously and methodically constructed ditches and erected irrigation troughs, made by digging out tree trunks, with which they surround their plantations on the top of some of the mountains, and on all sides could be heard the purling of the water, sometimes hidden beneath the vines or by the dracæna hedges that divided the plantations by lanes. The recent downfall of rain had converted the ground of these lanes into very tenacious, slippery mud, and often we would sink up to our knees in a black, pudding-like mixture, and the suction offered great resistance to rapid progress; or in descending a slight slant with feet together every one would slide down, or in ascending we were forced to cut foot-holes and clutch frantically to the shrubbery to ward against backsliding, and avoid being washed along in the resistless current of an unspent swift gush of gurgling water that would bound down over rocky beds, seeking the bottom of the cañons, or leap and tumble into cascades to join swirling rapids seaward bent.

The moisture which rises from the ground at night makes a singular phosphorescent mist, which carries sufficient dew to bathe and nourish all vegetation and, in fact, the land around, to bring about certain results which are almost phenomenal considered from an agricultural point of view. It is from these heavy dews that most of the *ngurungas*, or stone reservoirs, are kept supplied. It is one of the great disadvantages to the traveller in Africa, subjecting him to much discomfort and rendering him liable to fevers, if the greatest care is not observed to ward against the insidious dampness. The moisture causes to exhale from the shrubs, flowers, and grasses a sweetish odor, which at times becomes stifling, and it is no uncommon thing to find almost every man in a caravan afflicted with asthma, and as he marches along his snorting, wheezing breath is very perceptible.

MASAI EL-MORAN.

In countries of such a climate the usual practice suggested by all good military tacticians, of surrounding a tent with a ditch, in case of rain, is a great mistake, excepting when absolutely necessary. Making personal observations on this point, in the hope of ameliorating my personal condition, — being a victim to chronic asthma, — I found that the newly upturned earth at night would emit a phosphorescent glow which would hang and hover about the little trench as if reluctant to part from its maternal source; and all sorts of crawling things would issue forth and revel in the unhealthy place. Another strange manifestation of these mists was evidenced in passing my hands through the thick, wavy veil and rubbing the palms together in a dark spot removed from the trench, they would glow with phosphorus as if I had dipped them in fire; and when one of the porters stepped out of these trenches he would leave his fiery footprint on the solid ground for some minutes after walking thereon. Such a miasmatic condition certainly cannot be conducive to the well-being of human creatures. I have also seen mists in Africa which were luminous and had certain powers of refracting the rays of the moon, which became iridescent and full of prismatic sheets and gleams. The effect was very much like a terrestrial aurora borealis, and the foliage would stand out bright, glistening, and green, as if the sunlight had fallen upon them after a rain. The appearance is very weird, and I inferred of common occurrence, as none of the men in the caravan noted it with any degree of surprise, which would indicate that they were accustomed to it. It had a very strange effect upon my eyesight, and I discovered that the porters in moving about at night would always hold their hands over their eyes, as one naturally does to avoid the sun's glare. A certain amount of superstition affixes to this strange manifestation, which perhaps may account for the porters reluctance to speak of it, and I only noticed it in Chaga land, and not on the plains or in the jungle. Sometimes when a man would come rapidly through the mist, which would float and settle down in a vacillating way without any apparent reason, here and there his garments would be illumed with spots and flecks of the phosphorescent particles, making him look as if clad in spangled armor; upon observing the effect upon his own garment, he would shake his cloths and *kanzu*, causing the particles to dart off in globules, leaving behind them streaks of shimmering light through the air. This same mist betrayed me into numerous absurdities; for at first, not realizing how vagrant was its course, and seeing strange lights in the woods, I would insist on one of my guards accompanying me thither to make closer observation, and although I would find something similar to a will-o'-the-wisp, it was different, inasmuch as the light would be in sheets. Josefe, who was always ready for a game, once placed around his staff a wad of cotton, which he took the precaution to wet, sallied into the midst of one of these mists, twirled his staff about as if to accumulate the phosphorescent qualities, and stood out in the clear, dark atmosphere whirling his staff rapidly around until it displayed a succession of fiery circles that lasted for an instant, then faded into nothingness.

BUFFALO BULL.

Observations made by me in East Africa at night were most unusual if not unique, and made me acquainted with certain peculiar revelations which nature seems to keep mysteriously concealed during the day. Creeping things, prowling animals, were ever on the alert just outside of the encampment, deterred from coming in by the numerous fires and the sentinels on watch. One night, experiencing great fatigue, I fell in a profound slumber lying in my Palanquin within my tent, when suddenly I awoke with a shuddering apprehension of danger, and possessed by an instinctive feeling of the presence of some harmful thing; involuntarily seizing my knife and pistol I cried out, "Who is there?" No answer. Then I called out for the *askari* on guard, at the same time tried to penetrate the darkness surrounding me, when I became aware, through the atmospheric conditions, that a cold, clammy, moving object was above me, in truth almost touching me, on the top of my Palanquin, the rattans of which were cracking as if under the pressure of a mangle. I was struggling to slide out of the Palanquin without rising from my recumbent position to avoid touching the thing, when the alarmed *askari* entered, carrying a lantern, to my abject horror revealing to me the object I had intuitively dreaded. My blood fairly seemed to congeal in my veins at the spectacle: it was an enormous python, about fifteen feet long, which had coiled around the top of the Palanquin, and at that moment was ramping and thrusting its head out, searching for some attainable projection around which to coil its great, shiny, loathsome length of body. Seeing the python, the *askari* immediately yelled wildly out for help, and in a moment, a dozen stalwart porters pitched in a merciless way with their knives upon the reptile, slashing and cutting its writhing body into inch bits. I am not ashamed to confess it was the supreme fear of my life, and almost paralyzed me. I came very near collapsing and relinquishing myself to the nervous shock; but there was no time for such an indulgence

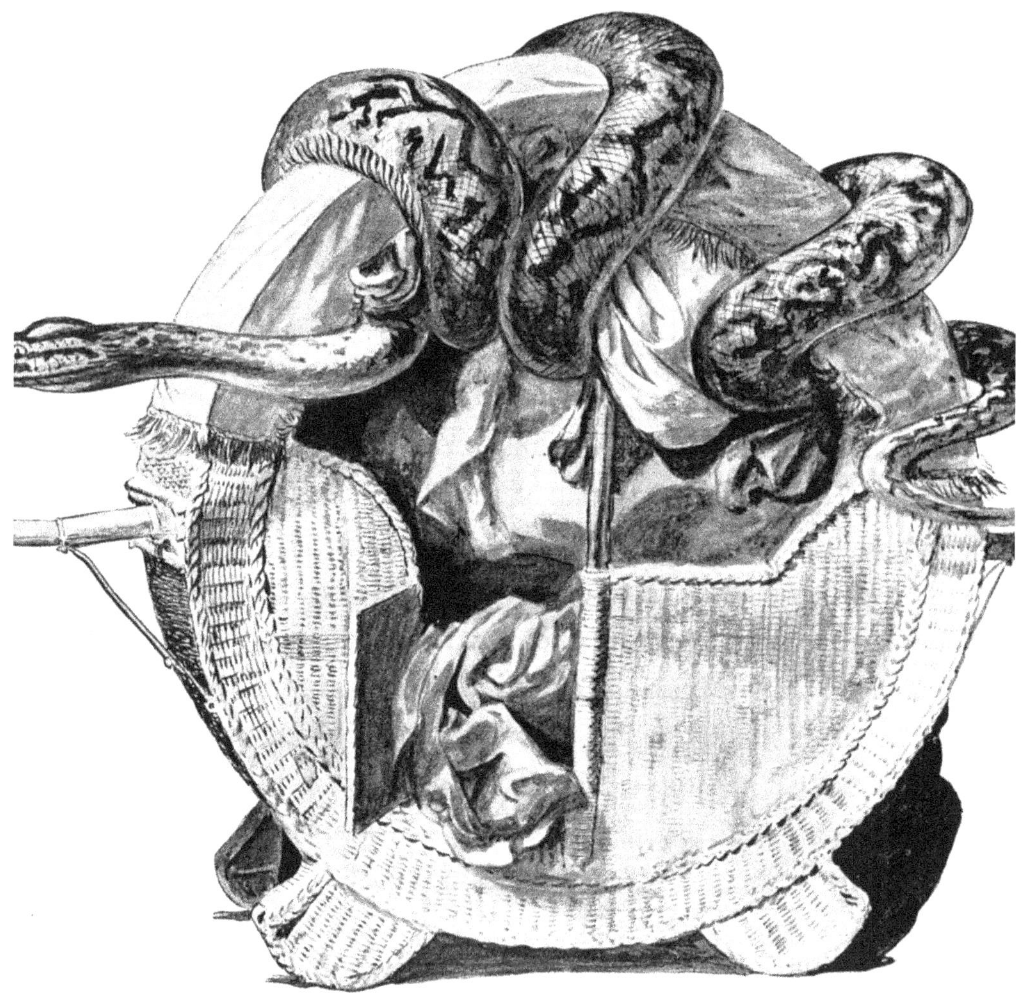

PALANQUIN AND PYTHON.

of weakness; there were other sequences to be considered. However, during my *safari* in East Africa, I only saw one other live python, wrestling inconsequently with all of its might with one of the invincible dead giants of the forest, without any visible success, as the majestic, unyielding tree gave no evidence of weakness under the pressing coils of the maddened monster, which was being overtaken by the realization that all was futile, and in the end it must be thwarted and admit defeat.

We encountered some small water and land serpents, a few puff adders, but with few exceptions were never molested, barring the fact that occasionally we missed a goat or sheep, and they might have been the prey of audacious hyenas and jackals, only for the reason that we heard no commotion in the temporary sheds where the animals were stalled, which indicated the work of reptile garroters.

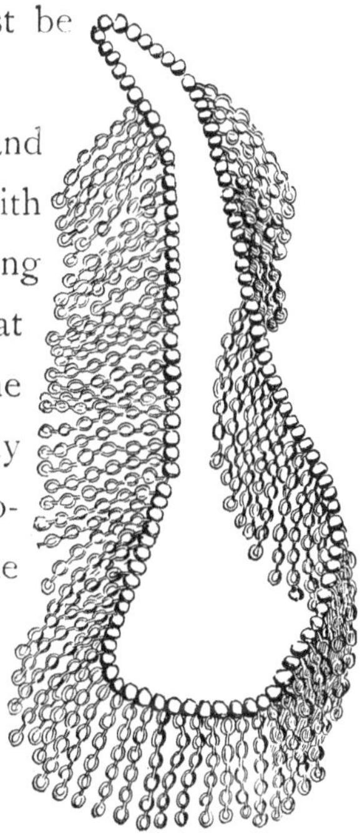

CHAGA CHAIN FILET.

Reaching Kimangelia on the plains, the natives swarmed down from the mountain fastness and urged us to visit their mountain village, previously never entered by *mzunga*. Difficulties arose; there was no cut or road through the forest environments; the porters could not force a way through. This was soon overcome, they assisted cutting a way through the gigantic trees, and as we plunged into the depths of a foliage-twilighted thicket, the hippopotamuses grunted and shambled away, disturbed for the first time by a paleface or the commotion of a caravan.

The sultan was a victim to his own debaucheries, and was paralyzed and unable to meet or personally welcome Bébé Bwana, but he had placed at my disposal his great circular palaver grounds cleared in the centre of a primeval forest, and overlooking Masai land on the north and the long stretch of

CAMPING GROUND, KIMANGELIA.

country we had passed over, and beyond, overhead, grand Kilimanjaro.

Their habits and customs, in matters of dress, superstition, marriage, rites, fêtes, and pursuits were a cross between the Chaga people and the Masai. At that particular time they were disturbed, not knowing whether the Germans or English were going to claim them, and inclined towards the English, having been prejudiced against the Germans by the accounts given by the Masai.

In consequence of the cold blasts which swept down from Kilimanjaro, the women wore, as do the Masai women, cow-hides around their waists and over their shoulders, and the great masses of iron and brass coils about their necks, arms, and legs that the Masai do. Their plantations are thrifty, and their *fundis* do splendid chain work; live stock was kept very scarce by the Masai. Honey and *pombe* were almost poured down upon us; and the heads of the tribe ordered dances, and as the moon shone, ventured to sally from their huts and pay nightly visits to the encampment. Greek fire delighted them, and a volley of musketry gave them a foretaste of real paradise. As usual, a full-dress reception was in vogue; their admiration surpassed anything of the kind I had ever been the recipient of. And as for the *music box*, they wagged their heads and addressed barbaric prayers, called it *ngăi*, and called me *ngăi*, their equivalant for God, as in fact everything mysterious is to them, *ngăi*.

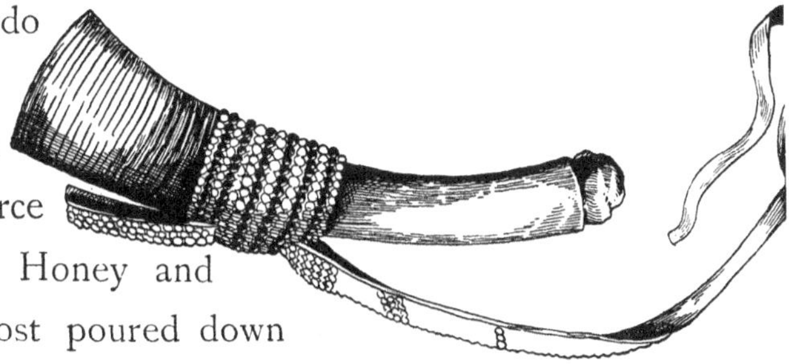

CHAGA SNUFF BOX.

Masai women flocked to see me, and secret messengers were sent to ask Bébé Bwana to visit a certain village not remote. The import of this was to say that I would accompany them alone about a distance not exceeding five miles, I would be shown something that no *mzunga* had ever seen. These envoys were not of Kimangelia, but from another tribe. Whilst a couple of guests I had for a short time with me were indulging in an afternoon nap, I accompanied the natives, escorted by Josefe and Hamidi. Arriving at the place of destination, with a display of great secrecy I was shown by the chief, after all but two of his own attendants had been dismissed, a stone spear-head, the exact size and shape of a Masai spear, which was kept secretly buried and unknown to any one but the chief and two or three of his confidants, including his prime minister, and which he told me passed in line of descent from chief to son for decades. I asked him how long it had been in the possession of his tribe. "Since the sun made day and the moon lighted the night."

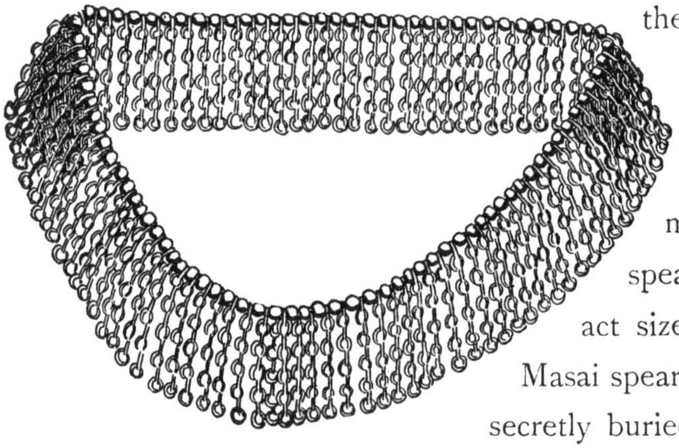

CHAIN AND BEAD GIRDLE.

"Was it before Kilimanjaro spit fire?"

"Oh, long before that," he replied, "when the streams run fire."

He begged me not to reveal the place of concealment, or the name of his province or his tribe, as he said the "Dutch"

NATIVES CROWDING AROUND CARAVAN.

would take it from him. It illustrated a very important point in the history of the origin of these people.

Another day, quite inadvertently, while my men were halted eating, smoking, singing, and talking at the top of their voices, according to my habit I was strolling about hard by to get away from the din and confusion, seeing what I could discover or taking photographs; after reaching a point about half a mile from my caravan, I stepped upon what seemed a firm surface and tumbled amidst a perfect screen of vines and shrubbery into a cave. I brought away pieces of the stone which made the body of the cave, and a small piece of a stone mortar which I unearthed, for it stood in one corner concealed by its cover of moss and lichens, so long had it been undisturbed. The cave was an irregular oven shape; part had been artificially made and part was a natural cave, and it undermined the surface of the earth above it, which came over sharp to the edge, wherefrom the vines fell as a pent and down to the ground, trailing in long lengths beyond and obscuring the entrance. It was about four feet square and five and a half in height, and evidently had been a smith's workshop, a primitive vulcan's forge. There were several stones standing up against the wall, upon the floor, which seemed to have served as forms to work upon, and what must have been used

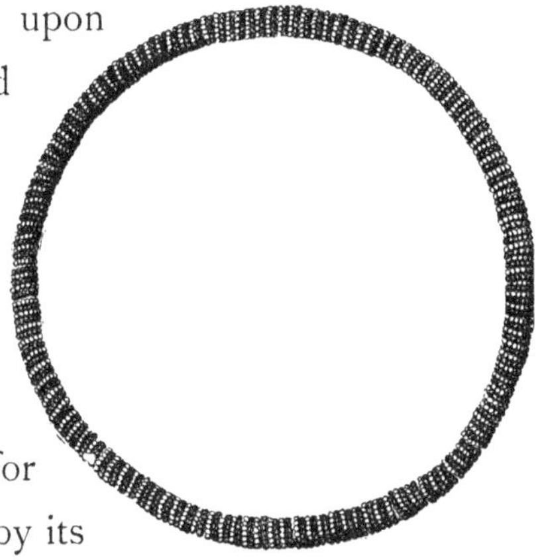

METAL BEAD NECKLACE.

as an anvil bore the abrasions caused by wielding heavy blows that spent their extra force upon the stone and was much discolored with smoke. Jealous of my discovery, and eager not to be surprised by my porters in this cave, I hastily withdrew, fully intending some day to make fuller investigation, as well as to search elsewhere for similar evidences of the Stone Age or of the Cave Dwellers. Just here allow me to digress and call attention to the excavations at the foot of the hill upon which Mandara's *boma* is founded, and which I subsequently entered only to be summoned back without time to make a full investigation by the warning of my headman who stated it was a death's trap to be shunned.

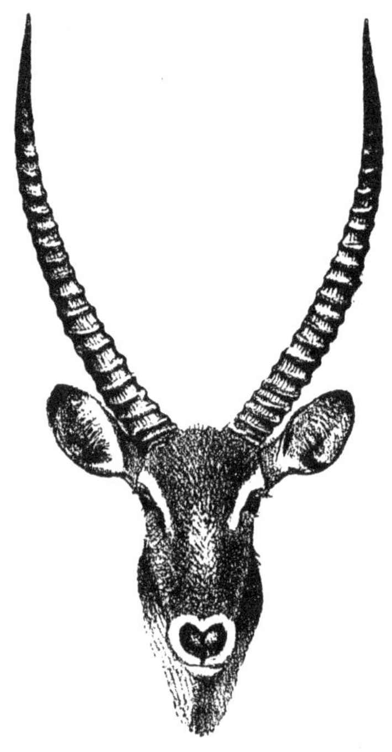

CHAPTER XV.

MASAI.

BLUSTERERS that the Masai are, they cannot be seriously looked upon as true warriors, or as possessing real bravery; but rather as African Jack Shepherds. Their vocation is cattle stealing, freebooting, and raiding their neighbors, after terrorizing them by their merciless onslaught. With theatrical make-up and hostile manner, they succeed in creating a panic wherever they list to carry a high hand, not only in the hearts of natives, but by compelling Germans and English to defence, and are soon put to rout by gunpowder.

They recognize no law but capture and victory. They have frequently attacked the arcadian Wa-Taveta with a fierce hatred, although the Wa-Taveta are deputed to have descended from the Masai.

They will not work; they have not the pride of the Wa-Chaga in forging their own spears, but depend upon the vulcans of Chaga for their fine weapons and almost all of their metal work. Donkey breeding seems to be their only legitimate labor. They make demands upon the services of the Wandurobo, a semi-subject nomadic tribe, which, although servile and subjugated by the Masai, is not actually in slavery. They hunt and engage in agricultural pursuits only to the extent of barely supplying necessities which the Masai cannot loot from other tribes, who, in return, give the Wandurobo their protection, and secure to them an immunity from their own persecution. These people are most insignificant in appearance, low of stature, almost dwarf. "Durobo" signifies stumpy. Among those we met there was no man who attained a height of over four feet and a few inches, and some were considerably shorter.

ARMOR FOR NECK.

The Masai have a quaint way of forbidding passage through their territory. They place in the middle of a path likely to be traversed by an individual or a caravan, a bullet, over which they cross two twigs stripped of foliage, with the exception of a tasselled brush at the top. The first person trespassing beyond this barrier is usually speared or shot without hesitation by some warder who is in ambush. Not knowing of this custom, inadvertently coming to such a forbiddance, I kicked it aside. In consternation one of my headmen sprang forward, urging me to pause if I valued my life, for the moment I put foot beyond that point I most likely would be assassinated.

Before he had concluded his words of warning, about thirty Masai warriors abruptly made their appearance in a great state of agitation, with uplifted spears, frantically gesticulating, as they ordered us to halt, and demanded from me the payment of a large amount of *hongo* for the depredation committed. Every porter in my caravan was terror-stricken and quite ready to drop his load and take to his heels. However, the fierce Masai were soon appeased with a few lumps of bluestone, which they prize as highly as they do donkeys or cattle. These were given as a present, and not admittedly as a penalty, for I felt to recognize, even in such a slight matter, their arbitrary right in prohibiting a passage through a tract of country not actually theirs, might in the end result disastrously not only to myself, but to other caravan leaders who might follow.

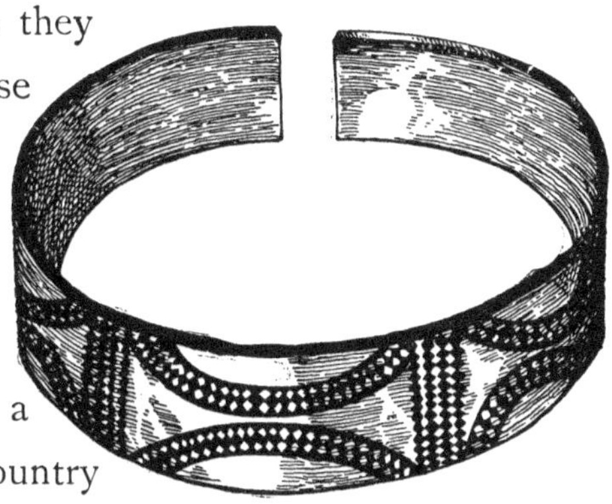

MASAI BRASS BRACELET.

Their costumes and habits have the most distinctive personality of all the tribes I met. The women paint their faces with white and red splotches, and often wear a close-fitting cowhide hood, embellished on the margins with iron and blue or green glass rings, which covers their foreheads and chins, exposing their ears with their heavy brass Catherine wheel ear rings, and falls down over the back of their heads upon their necks and shoulders, beneath their ponderous brass or iron coil collars. They present a most hideou appearance. The men, also, indulge, upon occasions mor or less frivolous, in paint, decorating their bodies by daubin on masses of color.

The women are not well made, and are far from bein up to the standard of physical comeliness of the women o other tribes, but rather taller, even more so than the men They wear quantities of ponderous iron coils like greave about their legs and also their arms, weighing as much a fifty pounds. These are placed on before the bones an muscles have attained full growth, and naturally the enormou weight and constant pressure of the ponderous metal orna ments retard the normal development alike of bones, muscles and flesh, hence the women are angular, lank, sinewy, an yet fleet as deer, and very strong.

Grass used as a truce with the Masai is more genera than with other tribes, possibly on account of the exigencie which are the outcome of their belligerent habits; an an essential part of the attire of the Masai women, who ac as purveyors between tribes, and move about generall unmolested among even hostile tribes, seems to be a bunc of grass, which they fasten to their cowhide belts, or ti to some of their iron coils, in order to have convenien when as occasion arises, wherewith to manifest amity. I is one of the most significant and delicate symbols univer sally recognized through Chaga land, to ignore which mus naturally curtail any traveller's opportunities to see and to b

PART OF AN ENCAMPMENT.

trustingly welcomed; the adoption of which proved most serviceable to me at almost every turn, for frequently I stepped apart from my caravan to parley with natives, holding in my hands and extending towards them a bunch of grass without any flowers intermingled, always to meet with a genuine welcome, albeit the natives might have at first evinced a measure of suspicion and over-caution, if indeed they were not absolutely inimical. When several Masai women approached me with their upheld hands full of grass, clutching in the middle the stems, which were turned from both sides toward the centre, and the heads of the grass waving outward, I thought it one of the daintiest exhibitions of symbolical friendliness I had ever witnessed. Grass is likewise used as a prayer for mercy when an offence has been committed. Anon, when the cross-paths are perplexing and a leader desires to forfend against the chance of his caravan going astray, grass is thrown across the divergent path.

MASAI WOMEN CALLERS.

The Masai also use salt stone, *chumvi*, and tobacco stone as peace offerings. I brought back with me quite a quantity of both sorts, which had been presented to me at various times, and have had them analyzed at the Royal College of Science, London, through the joint courtesy of Professor Judd and Professor T. E. Thorpe, February 22, 1892.

ANALYSIS OF SALT STONE.

Carbon dioxide	39.47
Soda (Nag.°)	39.95
Ferric oxide	1.59
Common salt	A trace.
Water	18.99
	100.00

Salt stone is simply a hydrated sesquicarbonate of soda or fona (2 Na_2 O 3 W_2 4½ O), containing a trace of common salt and oxide of iron.

(Signed) T. E. THORPE.

ANALYSIS OF TOBACCO STONE.

Soda (Nag.°)	29.92
Carbon dioxide	30.48
Magnesia	2.28
Lime	1.52
Alumina and ferric oxide	1.97
Chlorine	1.83
Water	15.31
Clay	16.69
	100.00

The substance is mainly fona, or hydrated sesquicarbonate of soda mixed with the carbonate of lime and magnesia, a trace of common salt and clay.

(Signed) T. E. THORPE.

Tobacco stone they mix with their tobacco and snuff; it is also advantageously bartered to caravans for the same purpose. Salt stone, called *chumvi*, is not a bad substitute for pure salt; however, pure salt is abundant throughout portions of Masai land, and many contests and battles have grown out of the fact that various other tribes have been discovered by the Masai in the act of looting their salt fields. Some of the lagoons or pools are decidedly brackish, and an incrustation of salt, caused by evaporation, forms on the surface of the stones about the water's edge. This renders the water of numerous pools unfit to drink. The wild animals naturally seek the waterways and the salt fields, and can be readily tracked by hunters to their lairs, as well as reveal to the observant individual where to find both water and salt.

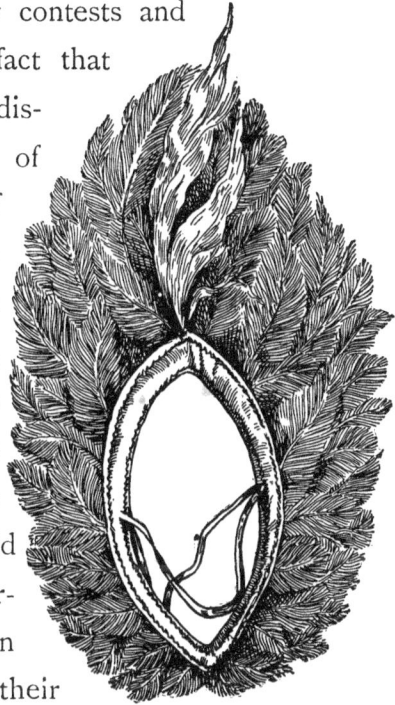

MASAI WAR MASK.

A Masai woman's regulation dress consists of four metal spiral coils for the legs, four similar coils for the arms, and a metal coil collar supplemented by brass and pewter collars or necklets representing an average weight of forty to fifty pounds, to which is added several pounds in metal and other beads. Usually they wear a cowhide as a skirt, and a second one as a cloak over their shoulders; even sometimes disport for this purpose fine Hyrax furs, monkey and goat skins, and sheep fleeces to protect themselves against the diurnal winds. Their shrewdness has been developed

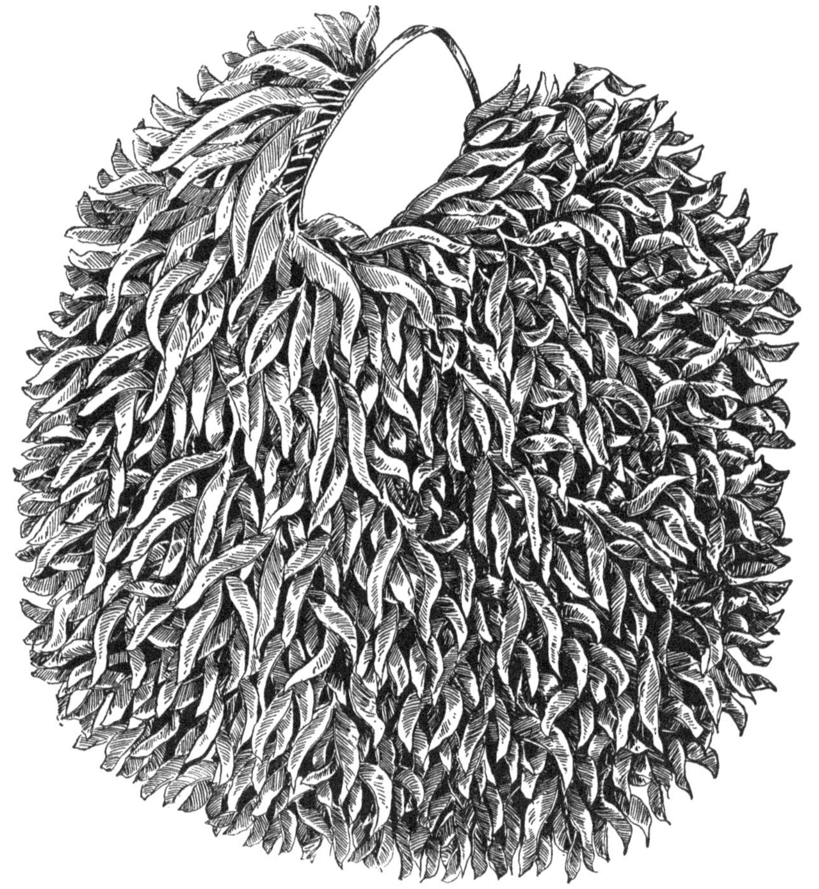

VULTURE FEATHER RUFF, PART OF MASAI WAR UNIFORM.

in a marked degree. Doubtless this is due to the fact that the men, with their freebooter propensities, are constantly embroiled with other tribes and Europeans. However, whilst war is proceeding, the women have free, unmolested access between the combatants, and constitute the bearers of despatches as well as are the purveyors, unless the attack is to capture women and children to sell to slave dealers to transport to the coast, when the traditional neutrality for woman is totally disregarded. And I heard many pitiful tales of such captures. The Masai men frequently sell their own women into captivity, or barter them away, which is the equivalent. The men are exceedingly crafty and are great braggarts, indulging in bluster and threats that can be put to rout by fearless use of the same measures by one conversant with their characteristics; totally deficient in any tender traits, never exhibiting any signs of affection, and keep their women under foot. They are laughterless, mirthless, having no songs but those of war. They are the heavy tragedians of Africa, full of theatrical display in manner and personal get up. When a plain intervenes between the Masai occupancy and other provinces, contention occurs over the pasturage nature so abundantly provides, which is above the necessity of cultivation, and coveted by those who are too indolent or possess no ambition to indulge in a pastoral, peaceful life. For some unknown reason the Masai lay claim upon all the land and all of its products, wherever they list to set foot. They are most brutal and more licentious than the Chaga mountaineers. Prompted by sheer wantonness, they capture women from tribes they have accepted truce with, to bestow as a mark of favoritism if not to sell as slaves upon some of their comrades or subjects when they have personally wearied of the poor creatures.

Their numbers and overruling spirit of despotism and cruelty put fear into the hearts of all lesser tribes within the radius of their excursive periodic raids. However, they have met their match in the Germans, and must either accept subjugation or stand a chance of being annihilated.

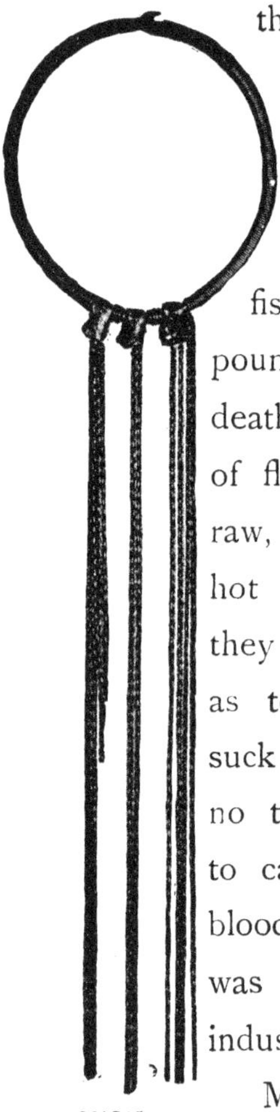

Contrary to most of the other tribes I met, who live as a rule upon vegetable and fish diet, the Masai are meat eaters, and will pounce upon an animal yet in the throes of death when being slaughtered, and hack chunks of flesh out of its quivering body, and devour raw, or cut the throats of cattle and drink the hot flowing blood. When meat is scarce and they are about to enter battle, they go so far as to make an incision in their own arms and suck the blood. With all this there is no trace, no tradition, that they have ever been addicted to cannibalism pure and simple. I partook of blood brotherhood with them when a white goat was the sacrificed bond. They engage in no industries, have no avocation but fighting.

MASAI NECKLACE.

Masai warriors were sent in deputations to warn me of the belligerent, disturbed condition of their territory, and I was afforded the extraordinary opportunity of seeing over one thousand Masai armed and ready to enter battle, having as an objective point Arusha-jue in the German territory which they had but recently been forced to evacuate by the Germans. The sight was certainly a magnificent spectacle, equipped, armed, and adorned with their picturesque paraphernalia, faces daubed with paint, splendid masks made of masses of ostrich and vulture feathers, plumed at the top with fine sweeping feathers, lions' manes, and white bits of Colobus monkey hair; huge vulture feather ruffs about their necks, and even encircling their faces, and enormous feather panniers around their thighs; here and there a warrior with an entire Colobus monkey-skin, slit in the centre, through which he had thrust his head, and the tail and long hair blowing straight out in the wind; from his shoulders wildly floated in the breezes a *nebara* made of stripes or figured red and white cotton cloth, and a long hyena tail decorated with a lion's mane, and Colobus monkey tails swinging from his shoulders as an emblem of war,—forsooth, the African shoulder chip! About the warriors waists was strapped goats' hides, into which they thrust their knives; below their knees, and over long oval iron bells a strip of Colobus monkey-skin, with the long white hair standing straight out like a pennant, and similar adornments on their ankles; and the leaders wore strapped across their

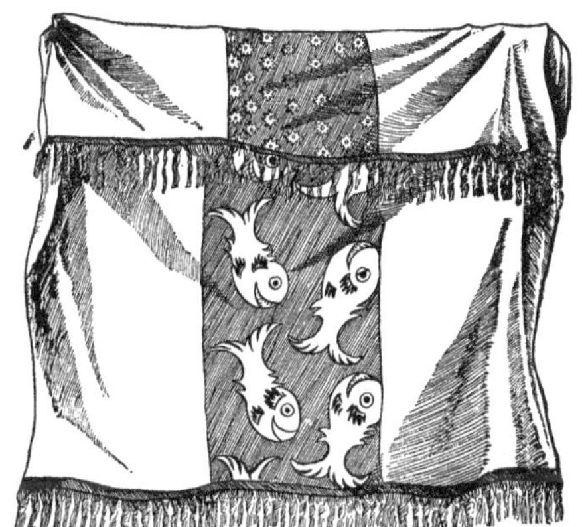

MASAI NEBARA, WHITE AND RED COTTON.

shoulders a leather quiver, containing a supply of ostrich feathers to refurbish their masks; they all carried a long fine Masai spear, which they *never* throw like Asagai, but run and thrust at their victims, always retaining the weapon in their grasp; and use to parry blows splendid cowhide elliptical shields from three to four feet high and a foot and a half broad, embellished with archaic designs somewhat varied, but the colors employed are invariably white, dark red, and black.

"Wow!"

The bells jangle as the yelling, fierce men dash and manœuvre. With all their ferocity there is, as I have said, a great deal of sham and bluster about the Masai. Although considered the bogy-men of Africa, I am of the opinion that any leader of nerve and self-possession need have no fear when they threaten an immediate attack. A warrior, hideously bedecked in his war paint and war toggery, having heard that I refused to pay *hongo* to the Masai who tried to exact it from me whilst at Kimangelia, and not in Masai land, came rushing up to me brandishing his spear violently, then uplifted it as though he aimed to cleave me in two, planted it into the ground before me,

GROUP OF TAVETA NATIVES.

yelled in a deafening tone as he bounded high in the air, "Wow! wow! wow!" Quick as a flash, I reached behind me and seized my gun, rushed forward with it, pointing the muzzle towards him, and in turn yelled, "Wow! wow! wow!" discharging it in the air. Suffice it to confess, I own that spear. It was never called for. It cannot be denominated as either a gift, or a find, or a capture.

MASAI WOMEN.

At this moment I became greatly excited in my desire to take photographs, and betrayed myself into a ridiculous situation. From a lurking place where I sought to evade observation, for more than all other tribes the Masai have a dread of a camera, suddenly a large body of warriors, all accoutred, passed in full view. Impulsively I turned, seized what I presumed was my camera, pulled off the supposed cap, and lo and behold! it was the stopper of my water bottle! I was perfectly deluged with the contents, and the only picture I could claim was an *aquarelle*. So much for blind zeal!

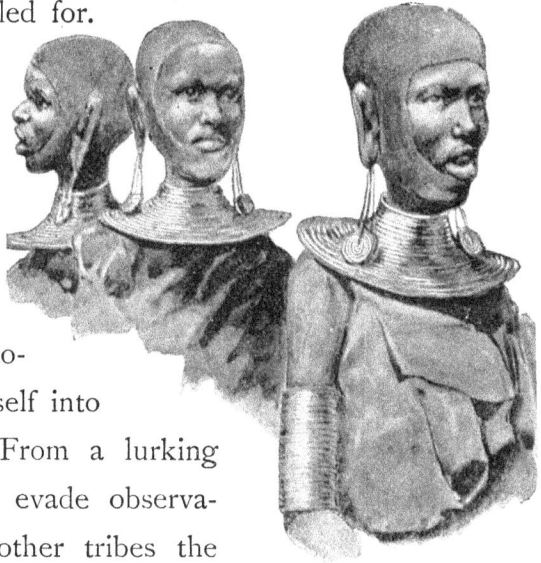

Spitting on gifts and upon faces and at people is carried to a great pass among the Masai. They are polygamists; their religion is fetish. They indulge copiously in the wassail bowl, however; intoxicated or otherwise they are aggressive, quarrelsome belligerents, quite in contrast to their arcadian neighbors. Their features are not specially negroid, and their color is variable; hands and feet small. But on the whole rather an impossible, barbaric people to effect much by way of civilization upon, for a long time to come, meanwhile they may be annihilated.

Masai women have not the privileges or rights that exist among the more pastoral tribes, except as spies and purveyors. They own no property whatever, whereas the Chaga and Taveta women hold and keep their own property and may acquire more. So disregarded are women, that in some Masai districts five large pigeon eggs, blue or white, green or amber colored glass beads will purchase a woman, whereas it takes ten of the same beads to purchase a cow! They milk cows and goats in the dark. They avoid catching the last glance of a dying person's eye, alleging that, if they do, after death the spirit of the departed will hold the unfortunate victim under a spell for evermore.

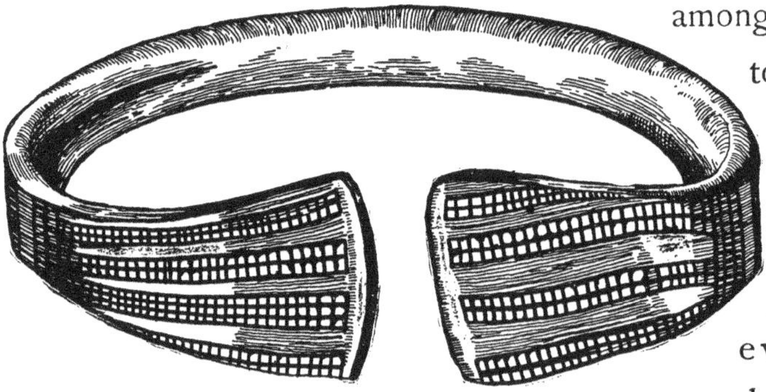

MASAI BRASS COLLAR.

My full-dress reception, among the Masai, came very near attaining the proportions of a calamity, as it incited some of the audacious young warriors with a desire to carry me off, and they had made a plan which was secretly imparted to me by a Masai woman, who had taken a great liking to me. Hence the little unpleasantness was averted in good time. The annexation was not effected.

The greetings and salutations are somewhat more poetic than that of other tribes. A *mzunga* is met, a woman cries out, " Good morning, son of a good mother, father of good sons"; and to me they said, " Good morning, mother of good sons."

All the Wa-Chaga have a poetic way of measuring time. When they speak of noon it is, " When the sun is as a brother," meaning there is no shadow; morning is, " when sun flies as an arrow to there," pointing over head, and when the sun is sinking and one walks towards it, it is designated as " an enemy skulking at one's heels." All tribes mark time by pointing when the sun shall have or has reached a certain part of the heaven. A messenger replied to my demand to know how soon we should reach a certain point, " To-morrow and the to-morrow of to-morrow and the night of another morrow you will get there."

CHAPTER XVI.

HEROIC HAMIDI AND OTHERS.

HEPARA HAMIDI BIN ALI, my headman of headmen, a freeman, born, I believe, at Pemba Island, near Zanzibar, a Mohammedan, endowed with amazing attributes of refinement and intelligence, upright, strict, possessed of just the right order of qualities to manage the affairs reposed in him, a man who never shirked duty or danger, whereas he never injudiciously courted the latter. The Sultan of Zanzibar particularly recommended this man to me as faithful and far above the average headmen. He had by his thrift accumulated considerable wealth, and was generally accounted to be among the Zanzibaris a *mzai*, or wise man, a *bwana*, or master. Although I made a rule not to commit even to Hamidi my real object in visiting Africa, other than the *safari* was destined for Masai land, I was obliged every night or every morning to inform him what I aimed to accomplish during the next twenty-four hours, in order to secure harmony in the caravan and have

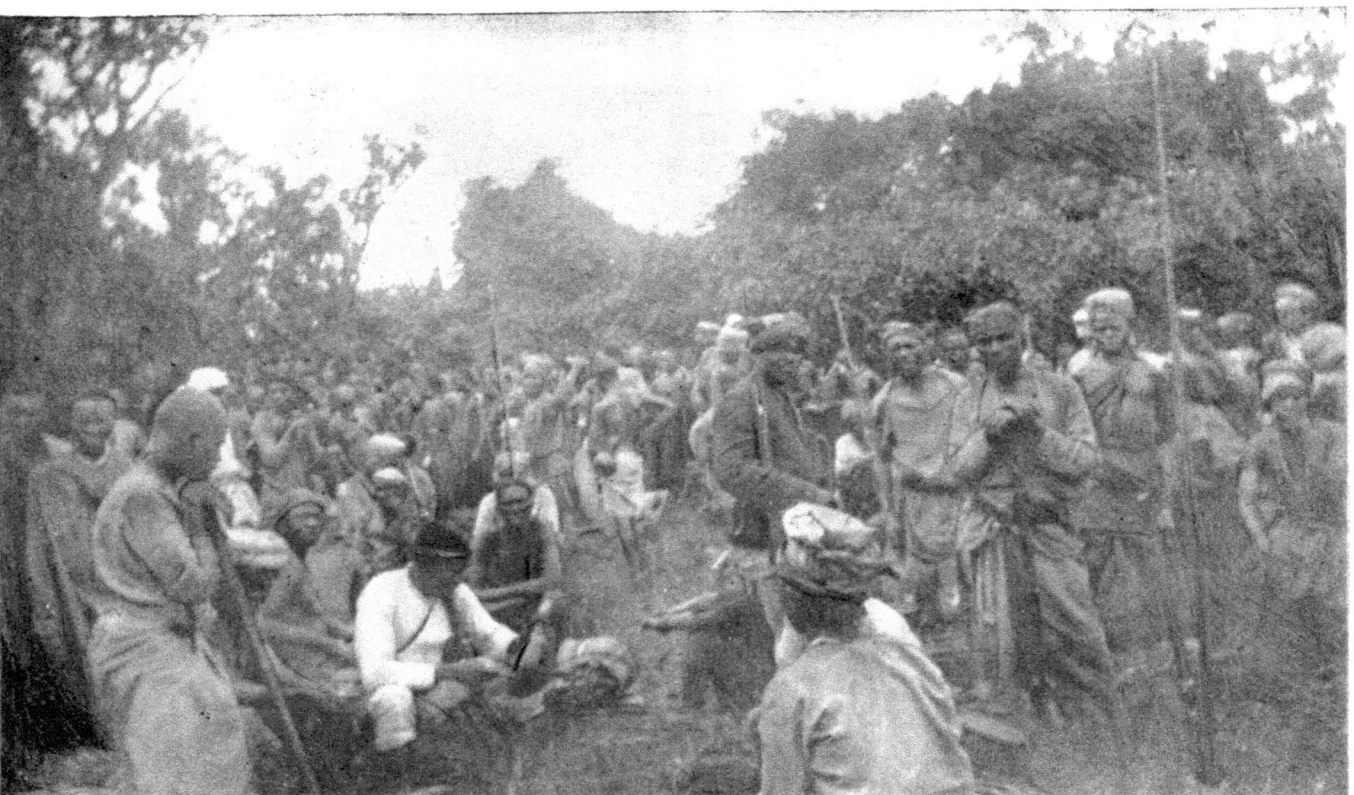

HAMIDI, CARAVAN AND NATIVES.

him second my orders, and he could distribute these orders as he saw fit to the subordinate headmen and all of the porters.

I had many evidences of his pronounced tact and admirable management of Zanzibaris, and found him most obedient to my slightest wish, until we were in Masai land, when, to my surprise, after saying, "Hamidi, to-morrow we will make such and such a *safari* beyond the frontier," in a measure simply to feel my way and see if he had heeded certain rumors bruited about respecting the turbulent state in which the Masai then were, he turned and said, "Bébé Bwana, I will not conduct you thither; the danger is too great."

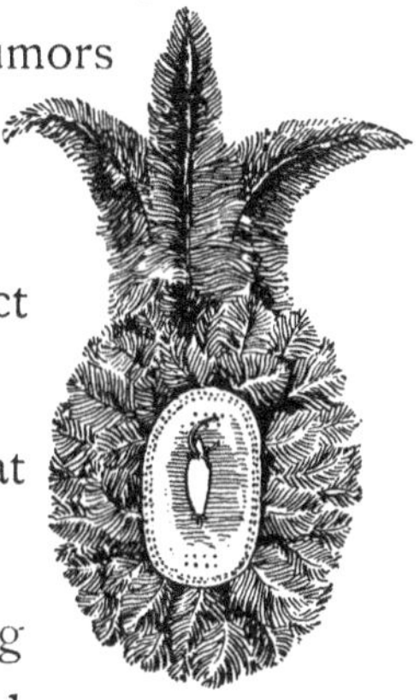

MASAI MASK.

"Then, Hamidi, do you mean to say that you disobey my orders?"

He turned round and faced me, looking square into my eyes without hesitation, and replied, "Bébé Bwana, I swore to the Sultan of Zanzibar and to Bwana Mackenzie to protect you as far as I could from all danger, and to give you my life rather than harm should come to you. Bébé Bwana, take these pistols," and he drew his revolvers from his belt; "kill me, but I will not go."

There was a heroic majesty about the man; I took the proffered pistols, and whether he misinterpreted my movement I know not; he opened his *kansu* without demur, and stood stoically with his breast bared before me.

"I am ready, Bébé Bwana."

"Hamidi, go, or I shall be tempted to do something rash.

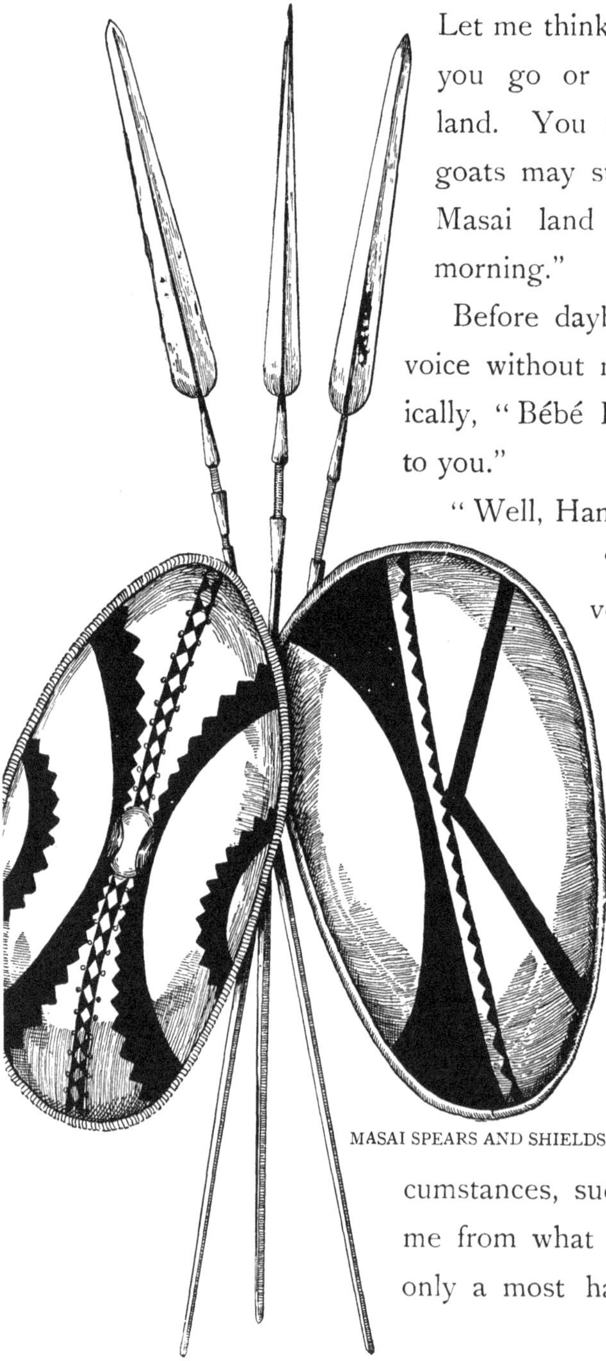

Let me think it over, and whether you go or not I go into Masai land. You and the rest of your goats may stay behind. I go into Masai land at sun-up to-morrow morning."

Before daybreak I heard Hamidi's voice without my tent, saying pathetically, "Bébé Bwana, I must speak to you."

"Well, Hamidi, what is it?"

"I am sorry to have vexed you, Bébé Bwana; if you go into Masai land, I will go too. I might as well be killed one place as another." And this fine man, as heroic and chivalrous and loyal as any white defender of a leader could possibly have been under the circumstances, succeeded in dissuading me from what would have been not only a most hazardous undertaking,

MASAI SPEARS AND SHIELDS.

but would doubtless have resulted in the entire looting of my caravan and annihilation of the Zanzibaris, no matter what might have happened to me.

Another word about this noble fellow. When I would have the men ranged in line and file, assorted in groups, such and such men with ulcers, those with stomachic difficulties, those affected with sunstroke, etc., in making my daily round to administer to their maladies, Hamidi would walk beside me, and when he came to a man who carelessly extended a dirty foot covered with mud, he would seize him by the neck and exclaim, "You toad! go to the water; don't you know better than to put a foot like that before Bébé Bwana?" He always evinced the desire to compel, when necessary, certain respectful homage from the porters, which proved most grateful to me.

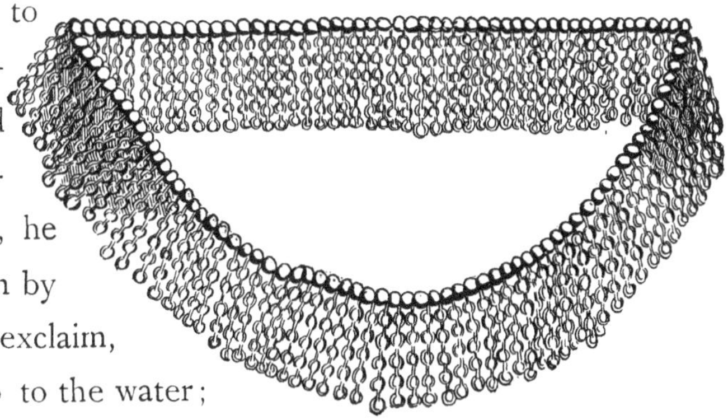

CHAGA METAL CHAIN GIRDLE.

Hamidi called my attention to the fact that many of the married women of Chaga and Taveta wear a leather loincloth which covers the hips and falls half-way to the knees, with a long, sash-like pendant at the side, embroidered and loaded down with glass and metal beads and chains, the leather colored with yellow clays, avowing he could not procure one. There is a certain superstition connected with these leather cloths which has a very strange import as revealing an innate idea of faithfulness, if not of tenderness, according to their conception of such a quality on the part of the women for the men with whom they are associated by marriage. They have never been known to sell, give, or barter one of these cloths after having worn it, until I procured the one in my possession. The reason for this is very rational from their standpoint, considering the people from whom it emanates; the idea that if they should give to any *mzunga* such a cloth, or he should obtain it in any way, the woman would be under some sexual subjection to this man; that he could throw over her a spell at any time, wherever she might be, however unwilling the woman should feel; he could take her from her husband and tribe to the ends of the earth.

When I argued with the women that I was a woman, a *bébé* like themselves, that I could not possibly work such magic over them, and that it would be a graceful thing for one woman to give to another woman such an evidence of her friendship, they argued and protested at first, always refusing to comply with my request; then as I made firmer friendship with them, bestowing gifts and kindnesses upon them, possibly administering to them medically if they chanced to be overtaken with illness, the heart of one woman softened towards me and she professed that she was willing to give me her cloth if her husband would only consent, for which favor I avowed my willingness to give her sufficient material and beads to make two others. Yet she kept settling back in wonderment over the peculiarity of my request, and that I, a woman, and the master of a great caravan, could possess her cloth and yet not care to possess her. However, after the lapse of many days and recurrent consultations with her husband, and all manner of blandishments on my part, she followed my *safari* over fifty miles,

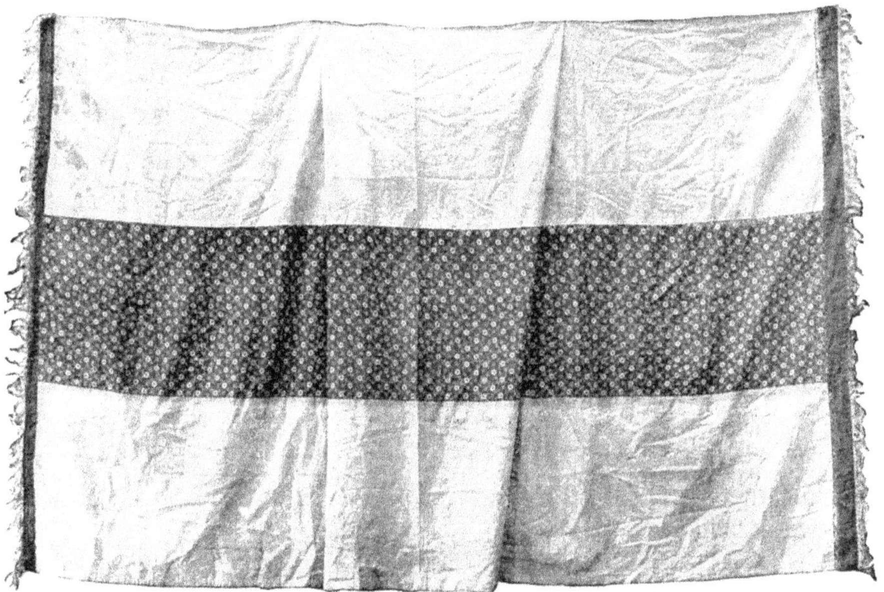

LARGE MASAI NEBARA.

and finally came and tossed it into my tent, exclaiming, "Bébé Bwana, take it, take it; you are my sister, take it!" This episode goes far to evidence how much superior in some ways is the position of a woman going among this tribe over that of any man, however crafty and *savant* he might be, and it is only illustrative of many other occurrences during my *safari*, revealing to me the habits and customs and the family life and relationships of the natives. These leather cloths once worn never change ownership, even among women of the same tribe, but are burned or buried with the wearer upon death. As have other travellers, so have I two or more perfectly new samples of these cloths.

The Wa-Kahé cling with great fidelity to a marvellous superstition quite Egyptian in its doctrine of transmigration in connection with the Colobus monkey which inhabits their forests, to which, however, no other tribe gives credence. They believe that the spirits of their ancestors transmigrate and possess the bodies of these white and sable creatures, hence, under no circumstances whatever, will a native of Kahé kill or consciously permit one of these beautiful simians to be killed, and on approaching the forest where they abide in great numbers, the Wa-Kahé observe an ominous silence and cast furtive glances as they pick their steps with precaution and hesitation that would seem to indicate veritable belief in their superstition.

Leaping from branch to branch of the tall trees the Colobus monkey presents a beautiful apparition; their bodies when fully grown are two feet long from muzzle to root of tail, and covered with a very thick, long growth of soft silky hair, jet black on the back and belly, and silvery white on the sides. Their tails are from two and a half to three and a half feet long, and perfect plumes from root to tip of spotless white hair. The Masai and other tribes, to the horror of the Wa-Kahé, hunt these monkeys, considering their beautiful pelts as great trophies, and desirable trophies and effective accessories for personal adornment.

Wa-Kahé use bows and arrows and spears when they can procure them. They cultivate fine plantations and possess vast bee ranges, which incite maurauders; they hunt and engage in minor blacksmith work. Various furs, the principal being the Hyrax, are used to protect them from the icy breath of Kibo, and their huts were rather on a better order and of more artistic shape than those previously seen by me. Granaries are placed on stilt-like supports, and resemble huge modern beehives, made of heavy braided or roped grasses. Many tribes hang up their produce and harvest inside the slanting roofs of their huts, and the appearance is much the same as a farmer's barn or garret in civilized countries, prompted measurably by the same necessities. Tree granaries differ in no way from similar granaries in other lands, excepting the use of the raphia palm leaves, which frequently attain a growth of thirty feet in length, and constitute an admirable thatching which sheds the water over the garnered harvest when once

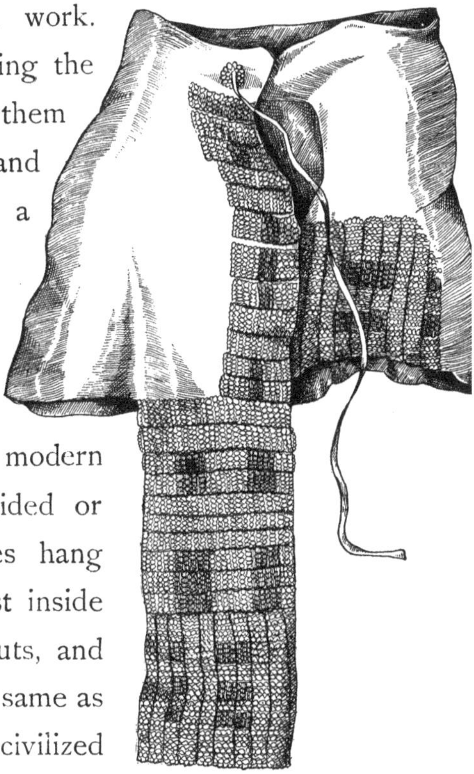

LEATHER BEADED LOIN-CLOTH.

suspended from the branches of the selected trees. Utility is marked on all sides. Many strange and multicolored mosses bearded the trees, presenting the guise of the be-mossed trees of a Florida swamp. There were gray parrots, but not in any great numbers. The ornaments of the Wa-Kahé very much resemble those of the Wa-Taveta, varied with an occasional string of Masai beads or trinkets, and beads from other tribes.

By tying together the ends of a large waterproof sheet, and suspending it between trees or poles, I had instituted the habit of catching rain water. Natives witnessing this would always examine the fabric in wonderment, and would essay to do the same thing with pieces of cotton cloth they procured from the porters, going through with similar arrangements; but, in consequence of the thinness of the cloth, the result was generally unsatisfactory. In passing, these trifling circumstances are mentioned in evidence of the natives' susceptibility in appropriation of useful ideas, and it shows that their brains have the same receptiveness one looks for in children. Failing, they naturally concluded that there was a peculiar charm about the "imperia" of Bébé Bwana, and one covetous sultan was incited to command a youth to steal the waterproof sheet of my Palanquin. He was discovered in the act and captured, and brought by Hamidi as a prisoner one long day's march after me. His family had sent, as ransom for the boy, after returning the stolen cloth, a cow, two goats, four sheep, and a quantity of fruit. Unfortunately, I was pro-

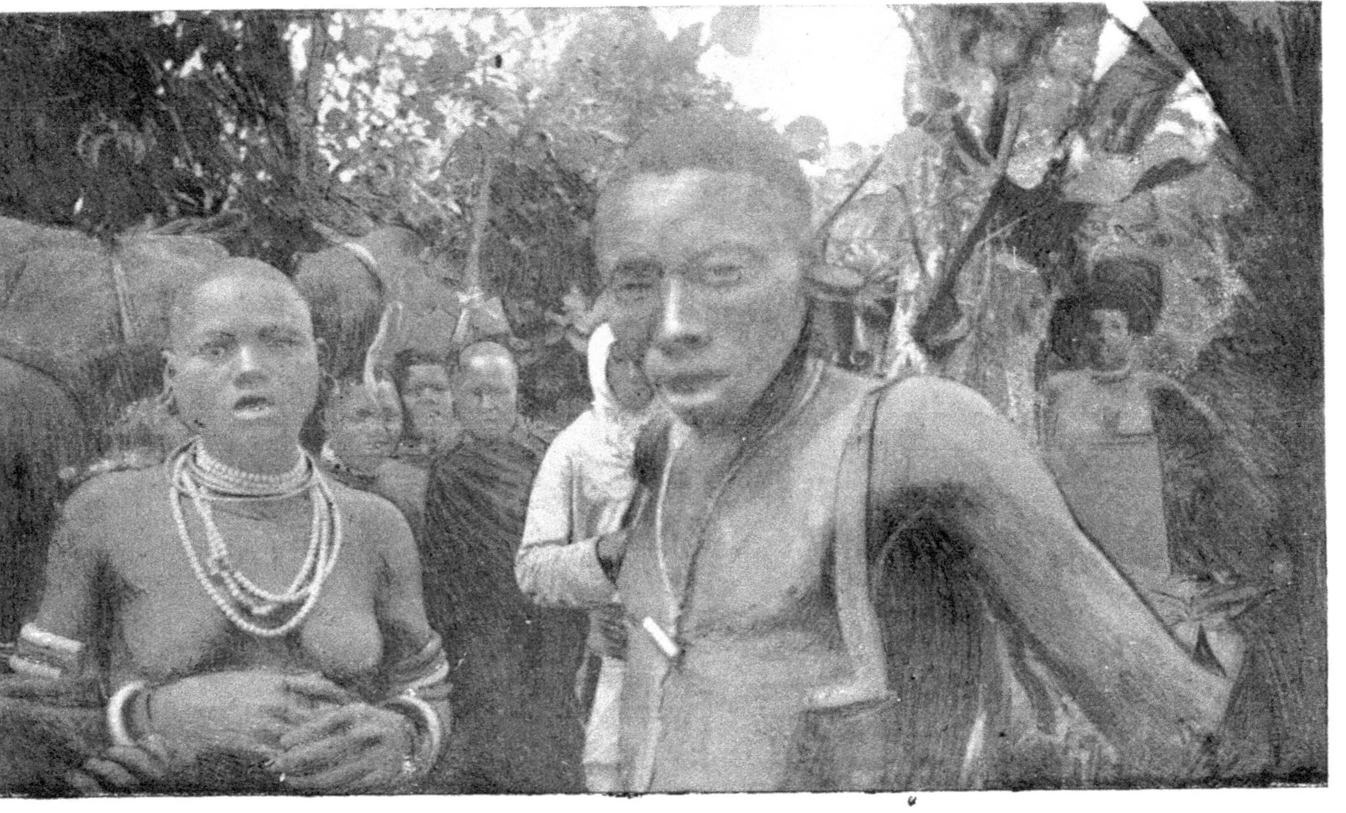

POOR BÉBÉ, NO RINGS.

hibited from acting in accordance with the dictates of my own feelings, being in German territory; hence there was nothing left for me but to hand the boy over to the resident officers at the first station, and enter a plea for leniency and mercy. I was prompted to make a personal affair of it by the touching display of anguish of the boy's aged mother, fearful that her son would be consigned to death, as well as by the boy's own contrition. He was freed after a day's make-believe incarceration and five sticks, and his promises for good deportment in the future. He came rushing to me full of gratitude, prostrated himself flat on the ground, spat upon my toes, arose and tossed at me armfuls of grass furnished by his mother, and quite voluntarily offered to carry a load for a day or more. I cite this to show that these natives are capable of feelings of contrition, as well as of gratitude.

In attestation on the side of their sentimental nature, a little Kilema maiden, seeing that I had no rings upon my hands, murmured very deploringly, "Poor Bébé Bwana! no rings!" Then, with a sudden and spontaneous accession of generosity, she slipped from her own fingers her numerous metal rings, exclaimed as she proffered them to me and as I was about to place them on my fingers, "Bébé m'zuria sana!"—lady very beautiful!—and settled back upon her heels, admiringly gazing at me with her own denuded hands clasped across her equally nude abdomen. Luckily I succeeded in taking a photograph of her at this juncture, which is expressive of the situation.

One day, when we had just started out, I said to Hamidi, "Look you, man. I cannot talk to these black fellows in this way; they crowd too close to me. I must have something to stand on." He immediately issued an order that every porter who desires henceforth to speak to Bébé Bwana must first put down his *sauduki* (box) for Bébé Bwana to stand upon, and

FOUR HEADMEN.

this was maintained throughout the entire journey. When I saw a porter during camp hours coming towards me bearing one box or two, according to his height, upon his head, I knew he had some complaint or request to pour into my ears; and he would put down one box, and say, "There!" and put down another and repeat, "There!" and wait until I had mounted on the extemporized dais. Then he would begin his complaint. It was the source of a great deal of amusement to the officers of various stations, as I passed through sections where the Germans or English were established, to witness this little by-play.

Presently the natives were likewise inoculated with the idea that I must not be spoken to unless I occupied some point of eminence; so they would indicate with their tongues or with their spears a stone or a hummock, and say, "There!" and when I would mount upon it, they would make a salaam and proceed with their business. One day, standing upon a stone, while the men were taking their noonday smoke and rest, surrounded by fifty or sixty young warriors and young girls, in Kilemi, I tried to engage the attention of the natives; and to a young girl, whose eyes were riveted in amazement upon me, and who nervously kept pursing up her mouth, I said, "Do this," and I whistled. With the greatest glee and merriment all the girls commenced to whistle, and one buxom fellow who stood well to the fore among the group, otherwise he would never have taken the liberty, commenced to whistle. The girl turned round and gave him a smart slap on the face and said, "You are not a girl," thenceforth he was the butt of so much merriment that he was obliged to retire to a remote spot for refuge.

To return to Hamidi. If there was any curious thing that he chanced to discover, article of wearing apparel or ornament, or a fine spear, he at once managed to have its possessor come to me, and whilst standing apart, unseen by the native, with a significant glance at the article and at me he would quietly say, "Ha-penda, hi?" (do you like it?) If I would nod or say, "Yes," he would reply, "Very well, you shall have it," and in due course, whether as a gift from the individual, or whether it was paid for by me or by him, the coveted article became mine.

I was surprised one day to have Hamidi enter my tent, saying, "Bébé Bwana, that thing must be left." What "*that thing*" was my looks revealed I felt in some doubt. He touched a chameleon, which I had carried because the little thing seemed to have attached itself to me in the course of my march, and upon inquiry, "Why?" he said, "The men think that it pertains to witchcraft." I found my porters throughout the caravan full of abhorrence of all crawling things, and reluctant to have such tolerated by me; so my little pet was abandoned, and I was tormented by swarms of flies and mosquitoes it had protected me against.

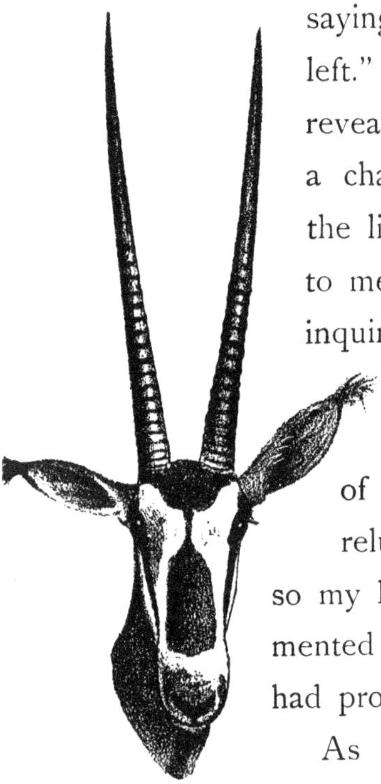

ORYX BEISA BULL.

As my readers have discovered, another character in the caravan was Josefe, my head interpreter. He was the wag and life of the camp. He spoke twenty-seven dialects, English particularly well, and had been employed so constantly upon war-ships going to different ports, that he had all the mannerisms of a laddie of the sea; and when I would call, "Josefe!" he would immediately straighten himself up, pull his coat together, touch his head with his hand and say, "Aye, aye, sir." I announced to my Zanzibaris, "When Josefe tells you what I say, it is as if I spoke"; he was afterwards dubbed "the trumpet of Bébé," not before me or in my supposed hearing; but time out of number I heard merriment ring throughout the encampment when Josefe would circulate about giving utterance to an order. He was personally full of curiosity and interest to see and hear everything concerning the natives whom we visited, as it was his first *commission*, as he called it, in these parts, and was ever on the alert to keep me informed as to what was going on, and from time to time narrated to me many of the stories which were current, many only of topical interest, requiring their own setting to carry any wit or meaning. He seemed very much pleased with his position of *gentleman in attendance.* His vanities I humored as best I could by giving him white and blue yachting coats to wear, and by having extra gold-band decorations sewn on his cap to identify him from others, and was next to Hamidi in importance. I confess I rather revelled in his swaggering manner and braggadocio speech and assumption of dignity, but found him a capital elbow man.

The habit of regarding me as a man, and not being quite able to reconcile my office with that of a woman, was shown throughout my *safari* by the men who were my personal *attachés.* I would open my tent-flap and say, "Boy!" Back would come the answer, "Sabe!" (sir); and they never got over it. If I addressed a porter he would respond, "Dio, Bwana" (yes, master).

My body servant, gun-bearer, and cook had been with some of the most distinguished travellers on extensive *safaris*,

COLOBUS MONKEY-SKINS.

and were experienced and inured to caravan life and hardships, and knew the country fairly well from actual knowledge or through hearsay. Their *raconter* of the different characteristics of the *mzunga* whom they had served, revealed too often the old saying that a man is never a hero to his valet, nor above the scrutiny or criticism of those whom he commands. They are very close observers of actions and words, and make some very astute deductions. When they are favored by the *bwana* of a caravan, they become jealous of any one who invades their legitimate or self-imposed duties, and are guilty of many little spiteful acts to regain their lost empire, and lose no chance to depreciate the invader. For example: my boy, Ramezan, could not endure the thought that I would allow any one to make my bed or brush my clothes but he; and my other boy, Baraka, who assisted in serving my meals, was equally jealous of his function as butler. But these two lads throughout my *safari* served me with as great and efficient attention and cleanliness as if they had been trained under the most exacting teachers in a European household. I have previously written I never sat down in the open on a box, using the top of its duplicate for a table to eat from, but they put a dainty little tablecloth over it, and laid the cover with a certain amount of style and pomp, serving my meagre meals in courses. I think travellers who are deprived of these refined evidences of civilization in making long *safaris* are likewise deprived of an intimate knowledge of the capabilities and adaptabilities of the blacks about them. Besides, it all tends towards maintaining self-respect, and accentuates personal prestige, which is so significant in the eyes of the African, whether he is a porter or a free and independent native.

When we were in camp for a day there would be a general washing of all of the clothing of the caravan, which would be taken by them to a stream or pool and washed, and their tent covers cleansed, and all of my soiled clothing, although it never was allowed to accumulate, washed by the women. The little tricks resorted to in order to obtain soap from me were certainly amusing. Although my stores suffered in consequence of these inroads upon them, I feigned indifference, knowing I had plenty. The Swahali, as a rule, are very clean about their persons and clothing, and never lose an opportunity of taking a bath (or washing) on *safari*. They usually carry one or two changes of clothing. Ramezan, my boy, said one day, speaking of some natives who were not cleanly, "Bébé Bwana no likee; smellee badly; Ramezan cleanee; Ramezan sweetee. Bébé, give Ramezan some soapee. Ramezan washee, makee sweetee." I gave him a piece of soap, going through the formula of requesting him to return the remnant, which he seldom did. As it was his duty to wash the napkins and tablecloths, I had great difficulty in supervising economy on this score, for I had charged him never to serve a meal with soiled linen. Soap, in Ramezan's hands, seemed to melt into nothingness in a moment, the secret of which, of course, was that he used it for his personal bathing purposes, and to whiten his own clothes. He was fastidiously neat and clean. This fact conduced largely to my comfort.

Although I had been strongly advised to take women porters and women to wash and for other duties, I found the few I had a perpetual nuisance. They were always inciting

STREAM FORDED BY CARAVAN.

disputes among the porters, and resorted to all sorts of measures to win from them portions of food and other things which they coveted. One little woman, who happened to be an admirable cook, would volunteer her services to groups of porters who messed together, was like a fatted pig at the end of the *safari*, having received in payment for her services as cook the pick of their rations. This little woman, who carried her full load daily, frequently was in danger of being swept down the torrential streams, which we had to ford or swim, and I found it necessary to detail a strong, tall porter as life preserver to get her safely across. However, I have this to say of the women porters, they compared admirably with the men both in staying qualities and strength, doing their day's march with no more complaining, besides having superficial duties either incumbent upon them or volunteered, which the men had not. Certainly I was personally deprived of their aid in consequence of the desperate and helpless illness of one I took to serve me, to whom I had to relegate every woman to nurse, besides detail a dozen or more porters to carry and guard when encamped against the intrusion of natives.

AN OLD MASAI WARNING ME.

It was a constant source of amazement to see what the porters would from time to time produce from their mats in the way of varieties of beads and other trifles, and the way in which they converted their ration-cloth into garments or transformed a turban into tents. Needles were always in demand. They sewed with thread drawn from the woof of cotton cloth when that they had brought on reels was used. Not only do they sew neatly but with rapidity; and upon occasions where needles were given out to string my trade beads, which were counted before distribution and again on their return, out of one hundred possibly ten might be returned, the missing number were always lost. Then I would say to the porters, "Let me examine your hair"; and often I have found ten or twelve needles secreted in the thick woolly pad surmounting their heads. I discovered that they put for safe keeping all of their little treasures under this clump of wool until they were needed or could be bartered to each other or to the natives. After a stated time, when the heat became oppressive, and their wool too long and burdened with vermin, every head in the caravan was shaved smooth. Several men among the porters who were good barbers were employed by the others at a nominal fee to perform this office. This naturally ended the needle pilfering, and simplified the characteristic search for vermin, which seems indigenous to Africa, and meets the eye on all sides. The few rupees they carried from the coast, and the beads received for *posho*, would be tied in the corner of their cloths, or deposited with one of the headmen, until required by them.

The headmen, *askari*, and interpreters never carry loads excepting during times of emergency; and when there are any sick who must be carried, if the caravan is small and porters scarce because of desertion or illness, the *askari* and others are detailed as carriers.

The manner in which a turban, worn by a porter to ease the weight of the load from his head, will be whipped off in a moment when a camping ground is reached, is interesting. Then, with two or three forked sticks cut from the immediate bushes or trees, he makes a dainty little tent, and carefully sweeps the ground within with a bush besom, and lays down clean grass, puts his belongings inside, and joins a group of porters with whom he messes. Then the cooking commences, and he rushes off — if he is not personally attending the pot — to gather more wood or, perhaps, in answer to my call, to fetch fuel for my fires. He changes his body-cloths, puts on a little white cap, which he has perhaps not yet finished, and the threads may be hanging loose, and takes up his position to sing or talk in a loud voice, telling — if he has visited the place before — what happened when Bwana So-and-so was encamped here last year, or ten years before. Their minds seem to have marvellous retentive powers. Things may be exaggerated somewhat by their imagination, but, on the whole, I found that many of their stories were quite accurate, and had been vividly impressed upon their minds by certain incidents known to more than one porter in the caravan, and would fairly coincide and corroborate each other.

Their trifling manifestations of vanity amused me immensely. Every porter carried a mirror. When in camp he would seek out a quiet corner and pull out his mirror, take his tooth-sticks, and, while admiringly gazing at himself, would polish his teeth and make some little arrangement of toilet, comb his hair, or polish his scalp, and cant his cap in a coquettish way a little over one ear, and then, with great satisfaction, pull himself together and meander up and down through the passages between the tents, assuming the air of a dandy who was thoroughly satisfied with himself.

The picking of the mimosa thorns from their cloths, which would sometimes form a perfect nap over the entire face of the cloth, and the jabbing out of their flesh thorns, which they do in an almost merciless manner, occupied much attention. These thorns, and also bits of flint which had become imbedded in their feet during a day's march, are usually gouged out—in a three-cornered piece of flesh embodying the thorn or flint—either by their own hands or the kind offices of a friend, and they never flinch or seem to mind the operation. But when I got a thorn in my foot, they made delicate arrangements for its removal. Two or three boxes were laid down, with rugs upon them; then I was ceremoniously requested to be seated, and to bare my foot. The porter who had assumed the duty of removing it, having washed his mouth and polished his teeth, asked me for "sweetee water" — which was cologne — and copiously bathed his face all over with it, rinsed out his mouth, and then put on his clean *kansu*. He then lay flat on his stomach on the ground at the end of the box on which my foot rested, with his hands stretched on each side so as to avoid touching me, and saying, "Inshallah, Bébé," which is equivalent to "With your permission, lady," with his lips parted and his teeth thrust forward as far as possible, and pressing steadily and forcibly about the thorn until he had it well clinched between them, he pulled it slowly but firmly out and held it in his teeth, and came and dropped it by my side for my inspection. As a master of surgery, he asked for a piece of cotton wool, and after dipping this in grease, he daintily bandaged my foot. This important ministration ended, he would start on a dead run to his tent to tell with boast and flourish to his comrades the service he had rendered Bébé Bwana.

With great ceremony Josefe informed me that a *boute-sale* was to take place among the porters. This affair was a general auction of all superfluous articles, bottles, and curios. The fun they provoked by the bidding was irresistibly contagious.

CHAPTER XVII.

SULTAN MIREALI.

AS we approached Marungu, Sultan Mireali's province, had crossed the last ravine, and were ascending the last hill to his *boma*, a very stony, difficult pull for my weary porters, there could be heard the buzz and hum of distant voices, occasionally a strident tone would override the others, and on searching for a solution of the hubbub, I descried at the crest of the hill, roughly estimated, two or three thousand people, making a spectacular sight decidedly intensified by the bright red that seemed to prevail in their flashing, ample vestments, as they moved and circled about with considerable agitation, like swarming bees, at one time converging, then spreading out and scattering, only to crowd again together and return; and, as we neared, I discovered that the pivot of attraction consisted in a personage standing upon a huge bowlder, a native, tall and distinguished, who appeared a perfect guy, tricked out in a pair of German military trousers, with side stripes, a white knitted shirt with a brilliant pin on the

KILME NATIVES BRINGING TO ME AS PEACE-OFFERING A WHITE GOAT-SKIN. SULTAN MIRIAME CENTRAL FIGURE.

bosom, a celluloid high collar, a cravat of the most flaming color, a striped woollen Scotch shooting-coat, a flamboyant pocket-handkerchief, and a pair of Russia-leather shoes, exposing blue silk clocked socks. His fine head was disfigured by wearing a black silk pot hat, which was canted backwards, bonnet fashion, by the long porcupine quill ear ornaments thrust through the rims of his ears. He carried an English walking-stick with a huge silver knob, and held in his hands a pair of kid gloves. This clown then was Mireali, conceded to be the handsomest native man in East Africa, the most noble and most majestic sultan if not the most powerful. This chivalrous sultan, notified by his couriers at last, after his weeks of expectancy, I was coming, had summoned all of his subjects — several thousand — to bid me welcome, and add lustre to the honor he desired to pay Bébé Bwana, and to Italicize the function had ridiculously bedecked himself in this cast-off finery of various persons of different nationality, who had but recently left his province.

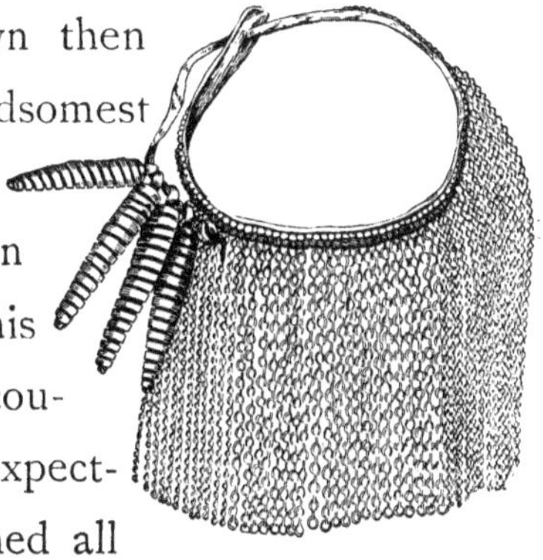

DELICATE CHAIN NECKLACE, WITH SPIRAL BRASS PENDANTS.

Remembering that he had been told to uncover in the presence of a guest, Mireali found himself in a sad dilemma as to how to do it; however, one of his many subjects stepped up behind him and tilted the hat over backwards, and scraped it off from the embarrassed potentate's head. It is a shame a man like Mireali should be so imposed upon by those who should have known better.

When all the salaams and *jambos* had been effusively uttered, and Mireali had welcomed me with great ceremony himself, he conducted me, followed by my caravan, to his old *boma*, which presented rather a ghastly appearance, for his father-in-law, brother-in-law, rival, and enemy, Sultan Mandara of Moschi, had first looted, then burnt his house to the ground, and the charred beams and other *débris* were the only remnants to be seen of his first advance in civilization, for his house had been built by Swahali labor and in just such style as one might find in Zanzibar.

His present *boma* is separated from this site by a rubbled dry stone fence, about ten feet high and three and a half in thickness, upon which usually disported two or three pet goats, and frequently all his wives and the women of his wives would loom up over this fence to see Bébé Bwana. As soon as I had an opportunity of ex-

SULTAN MIREALI IN NATIVE ATTIRE.

changing a few words with Mireali, when he asked for all the white men who had visited him, I ventured to say: "Mireali, why do you wear these clothes? They make you look like a goat. I want to see you in your own native cloth, and see you as Mireali, the great African sultan that you are." He hung his head contemplatively for a few moments, then gazed at me with his fine eyes, said, "Bébé Bwana, yes, yes, to-morrow." The next morning he presented himself with an enormous cloth, as large as four table-cloths sewn together, wound around him, and thrown over his shoulders in the most graceful and artistic manner, trailing regally behind him, carrying a long spear, and backed up by his picturesque coterie of wives and followers, all in native costumes. The wives all wear ample pieces of Americana, which is somewhat superior to the trade gumpty, and quantities of beaded and metal ornaments. He looked truly majestic as he advanced with his picturesque cortege, and I could not help recalling some of the old pictures of Roman senators. His mien was full of composure, yet not restrained to such a pass as to conceal

PRESENTATION JEWELLED BELT, DAGGER, AND ORNAMENTS.

his gracious desire to be hospitable, and there was a lurking anxiety withal, which manifested itself in his furtive glances, as if he sought to divine what would most please me. In the course of the day he brought me sheep, with fat tails dragging on the ground, one or two of which he had been

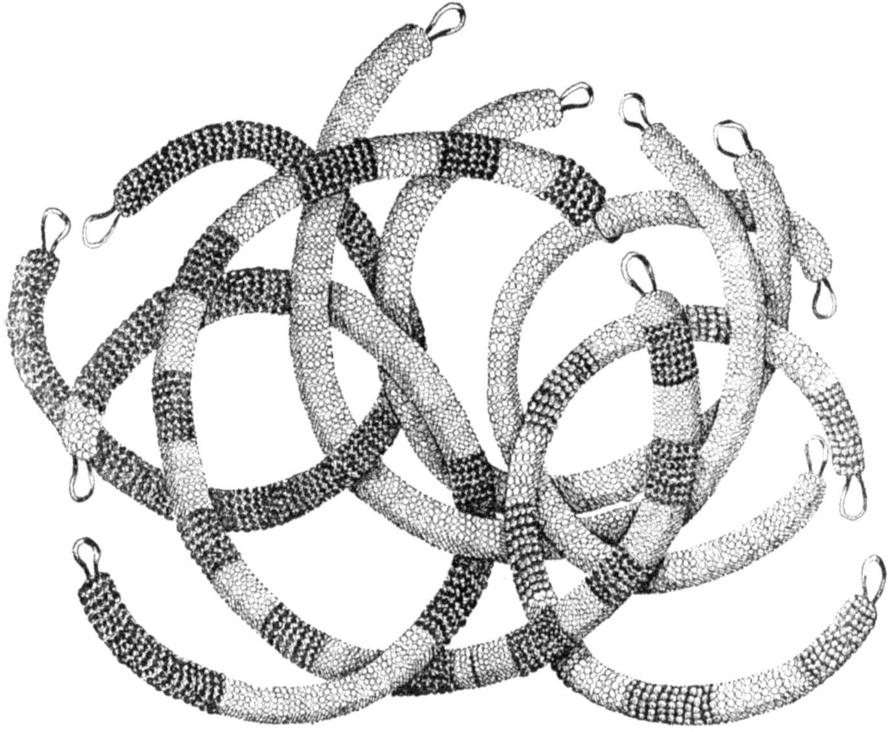

BEAD GIRDLES WORN SOLELY BY MIREALI'S SURIAS (WOMEN).

fattening especially for me, and the creatures could scarcely move, burdened with so much superfluous flesh; also numerous goats, and sent me one cow after another until the number reached ten. This was a thing unparalleled in East African native generosity, for it is conceded that one or two cows are considered a right royal offering; but Mireali, in his eagerness to know more of me, and make me feel he was my friend, and to secure my friendship for himself, had nothing in his province he would not have bestowed upon me, had I expressed the desire to possess it. We had many talks, and I found him intelligent, his brain alert and susceptible of impressions, and with a general discontent with his condition, and a restless craving to become more as the white men. My finest music box he coveted without any disposition to dissemble, and was never happier than when watching the wheels go round, and marking the intonations of the carols.

Finally, in a spasm of desire which overcame him to possess this box, he came and planted before me his own personal spear, his sceptre as it were, and said, "Bébé Bwana, take this and let me have your music box." I gave him the music box, and a jewelled belt and dagger, happy to possess the spear.

I queried, "How will you keep this box from being stolen, as your other treasures have been stolen, by Mandara?"

He led me to an excavation in a secluded spot under the shade of banana-trees in the middle of his plantation, which was lined with stone slabs and completely covered inside with Hyrax and Colobus monkey-skins, and here he placed his treasure with a jewelled sword I had brought to him from England, and after covering it up with a heavy slab and replacing the sod, he said, "Mandara can never find that." This habit of burying treasures, especially ivory, is universally resorted to by all African tribes.

The women, or *surias*, of his wives are totally nude, wearing decorative beaded ropes, six to twenty-four in number, around their waists, arms, and legs, with no other attempt at clothing. They are more beautifully formed than their mistresses, although darker in color, but their features are absolutely pretty, their teeth glittering white, and they seem to give a great deal of attention to the decoration of their bodies with their beads, which are usually white and pale or dark blue, or solid dark colors, and dainty in the extreme. They also wear cloth and leather pendants, which may be denominated as African fig leaves. These articles are likewise affected by many of the men and children, and are profusely ornamented with beads and delicate metal chain fringes. The grace of these women in moving about is the grace which affixes to all people who are in the habit of carrying loads over mountainous countries on their heads with their bodies erect, and they have the movement almost of a gazelle in climbing and descending the mountains. This imparts to them a somewhat haughty mien and swinging motion as they approach you without loads. Although we are in the habit of considering Africans as being simply progressive monkeys, a species of rudimental human beings, with their arms awkwardly pendent, hands and feet large and ungainly, and a certain cattish movement when not shuffling,

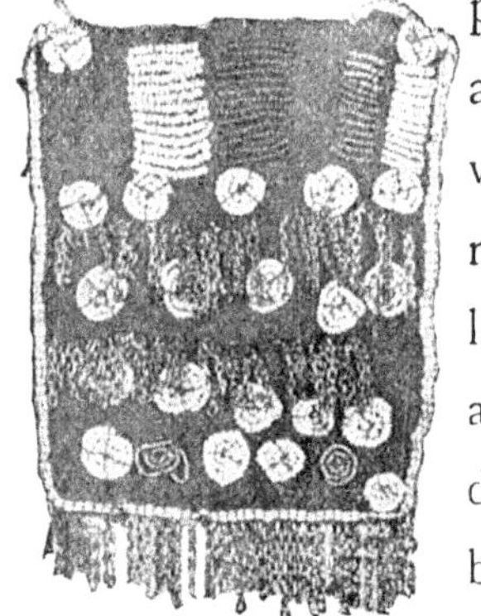

BEADED FIG LEAF.

and flat footed, I am free to say it is not the case with these Chaga people. They are great posers when they are on view, if they hold or have an audience with other tribes, or the white man is present. Their self-consciousness and egotistic vanity transcend concealment.

I asked Mireali, "Do you not love one wife better than another?"

"Oh, I like them all, but the new one is the best for to-day; in a week I shall go back to the old, the big wife, because she knows me better than the others," he quaintly responded.

"But these children, how about them? There are a number."

"Well, yes, they are good little goats, but only the first son of the big wife is worthy of my virility."

This expression rather perplexed me, but later on I learned the true significance of his phrase and thought, "Ah me, what exponents of simple honesty and truth these aboriginals are."

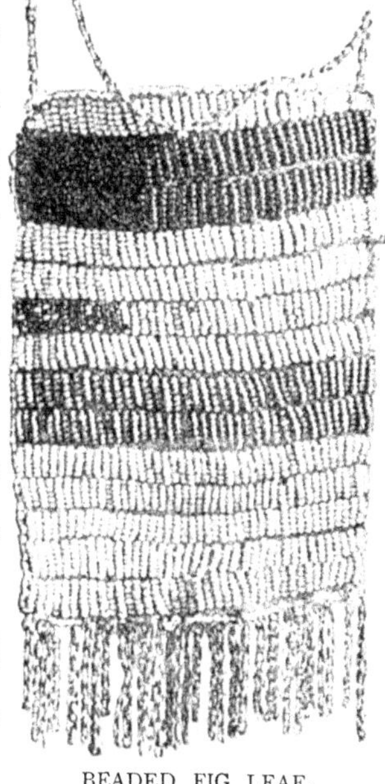

BEADED FIG LEAF.

Complimenting Mireali about the neatness and taste displayed by the natives in packing loads, he turned around and acquainted me with a subtle reason I had overlooked.

"A spray of grass, a few seeds, a chewed bit of sugarcane may betray any one to his enemy. Watch us; we never go exactly by the same path. Look you, Bébé Bwana, see there, that woman bounding through the grass. She is the wife of a well-known Masai, and she is trying to lose her footprints. By and by she will wade across the water, then, on the other bank, later on, cross back."

There was so much suggestion in Mireali's remarks, that from that hour I never ceased watching the natives we chanced to meet, or those who were pursuing the same direction, and discovered that they were more or less erratic in the course of their journey, habitually "losing their footprints." A bevy of native women carrying provisions from sultan to sultan, or merely in the hope of capturing trade from my caravan when we would halt, at one moment would be in plain sight, and later on, when we would have crossed a stream or ascended a craggy steep, they would have vanished, subsequently to emerge away beyond to the right or left of our path from a dense thicket, or were far in advance awaiting our approach, having cut across country.

It was a fine sight to see these women, almost nude but glittering with their barbaric metal ornaments and bright beads, fleet-footed, indifferent to hardships or physical hurt, race up or down the mountain-sides, ford rivers, step upon cruel thorns and sharp blade-like flints, or slide along over the slippery mud with the fleetness and agility of gazelles, balancing on their heads heavy loads of fruit or what not, and never fall. Ordinarily they will cover thirty miles in a day.

One of Mireali's sisters has been the cause of a war with

Mandara. She has been euphoniously named the Venus of the Mountains, and accounted to be a professional Chaga beauty. Mireali's demand of forty cows for his sister, Mandara would not accede to. So he stormed Mireali's *boma*, but did not capture the prize, although he drove Mireali away from his province temporarily.

Mireali was under a cloud and not in very great favor with his subjects because of this defeat. When one of these sultans are defeated, they evacuate their sultanate and retreat into the fastness of the mountains until things have calmed down. The Germans had given their protection to Mireali, so he returned in hopes some day to lay his despotic enemy and relation low.

Mireali has not been free from the crime of raiding lesser tribes, but he aims to improve himself, and seeks to imitate the more enlightened ways of the *mzungu*.

Mireali represents all that is superior and intelligent among these tribes. As rival in intelligence he has the youngest sultan in East Africa, Miriami, who has possessions in Kilema; and this young prince, who had performed in my behalf several acts of real services, for which I strove to give substantial evidence of appreciation, and had bestowed upon him all manner of presents, I discovered that he looked somewhat downcast, when I asked, "Is there anything else you would like? Are my gifts not to your pleasure?"

He replied, "Ah, dio Bébé Bwana; but I want an English saw and an English hammer."

I asked, "What do you want these for?"

He answered, "Ah, Bébé Bwana, I want to build an English house and live like a white man." I promised to send him the saw.

He said doubtfully, "Ah, yes, white men all promise, but they all forget; the *mzungu* always lies."

I interrupted him sharply, "Stop, Miriami, you must not speak to Bébé Bwana in that way. I never lie. I will send you the saw."

And upon my return, while the delirium was raging during my illness, this thing haunted me with other promises I had made these poor trusting natives, and I never rested, day or night, until every one had met a fulfilment, through the consideration of the scrupulous guardian of my honor, and Miriami has his saw.

AGARY BEADS AND DAWA CHAINS, RARE.

So it is, I think, if people when visiting the country of natives, instead of taking useless, showy trumpery, would give them implements useful and simple to understand, and take a little trouble to teach them the uses thereof, they would be found ready and appreciative people, evincing gratitude and no mean amount of aptitude.

The natives' sufferings from the cold in these districts, where the bleak wind rises at four in the afternoon, and the thermometer falls down to fifty-four degrees and even lower, is very pitiful; and although they have quantities of furs, they are constantly asking for cloths and blankets to keep them warm. Various fibres, papyrus, bamboo, *m'whala*, and others, and grasses which abound throughout East Africa, are susceptible of being converted into frabrics, exactly as such have been utilized by the people of Madagascar and Peru; therefore, if simple looms, without any mechanical intricacies, were introduced, the natives could very soon supply their own requirements, as well as produce a commercial commodity. I found a variety of wild cotton, if not cotton certainly a delicate silky, sepia color product, covering vast areas, which might be cultivated.

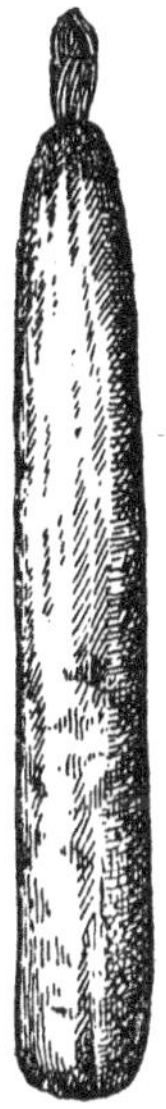

CANDLE MADE BY MIREALI.

The only native-made fabrics I found were sacks varying from a tiny size only large enough to hold an egg or two, graduating to those large enough to hold a huge bunch of bananas, on up to dimensions sufficient to entirely cover a hut. One in my possession is three feet deep and five feet in circumference, and took a woman one year steady work to plait. The twine or cord out of which it is plaited is made by twisting into very hard strands *m'whala*, or bamboo, fibre; the women laboriously punch the cord through the foundation braid with a fish-bone or an iron wire prod. So closely knit are these sacks that they hold water after having been soaked. As usual, the article is colored with yellow clay, variegated with an occasional bright red strand dyed with the juice of the dracæna-bush.

SULTAN MIREALI AND COURTIERS.

It does not demand a stress of credulity to believe that the jewellers who are capable of executing the tedious processes required to produce the delicate chain work, of which I saw so many varieties, and the vulcans of Chaga land who can forge such beautiful spears, and also those who make hide shields, decorate gourds, tan leather, with as great natural skill as they indisputably do now, are capable of much better things, if only trained.

Mireali has made some very fair examples of candles out of the beeswax, and he craves light, and no more welcome gift did I bestow upon him than candles, oil, and soap. He was ambitious to get window glass for a new Swahali house he was about to erect. They could also, by the introduction of such simple sugar presses as are used to-day in Madagascar, express the juice from the sugar-cane, which grows in great abundance, and provide for themselves this appetizing condiment, preserving it for such times as there were no crops, and secure to themselves the benefit of its nourishment when the harvests failed. Apart from and in addition to the usefulness of such, they would regard every new avocation in which they might become skilled as an amusement; they delight in the novelties which the white man brings; and Mireali showed me, with great pride, twelve folding wooden chairs, like steamer chairs, and a table of his own manufacture, before which he sat while eating, and he was pleased as a child when I gave him a tablecloth, some napkins, knives and forks, and a set of little china teacups and saucers, and some tea; and the most notable afternoon tea—"a small and early"—I had during my African season was sitting in his *boma* on a four-legged stool, surrounded by his wives and *surias*, served by Mireali himself with a cup of tea of his own brewing, some sugar-cane, bananas, and an attempt at bread made from banana flour, a tomato salad which he concocted himself, with the flourish of a gormand, and various other knickknacks from his own kitchen. I had taken some boxes of bonbons, but these people did not care for them. The boys took the sugar-plums and used them for marbles, and shot them out of their fingers at targets.

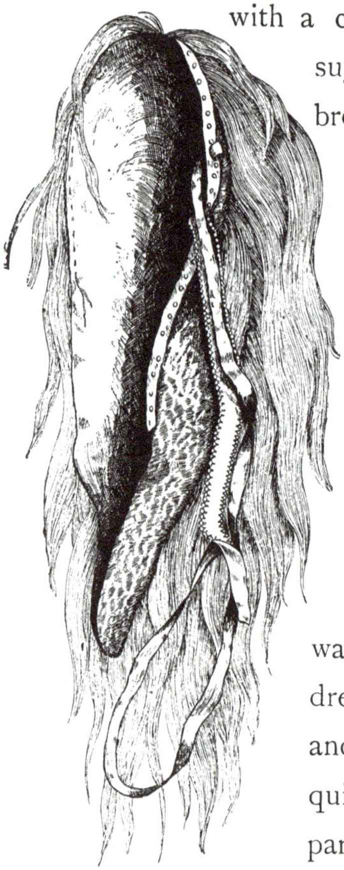

DANCING WIG, FRONT VIEW.

Mireali used to sit by the hour watching me write. When I held a full-dress reception, he fell upon the ground and spat upon the hem of my gown, quite lost in admiration. My blonde wig particularly interested him, and he brought me one of the native's dancing wigs, made of the white hair of the Colobus monkey-skin, shaped to fit the head. My court gown was a source of endless admiration, not only with Mireali, but other sultans and natives. Mireali wanted to know the kind of cloth it was made of. Josefe put my nationality in pawn by quickly informing him that the silk and silver netting covering it were fabrics never worn only by white queens, like Bébé Bwana.

"Aie!" ejaculated Mireali, "it is then queens' cloth"; and so the name maintained from that on, in answer to other questioners.

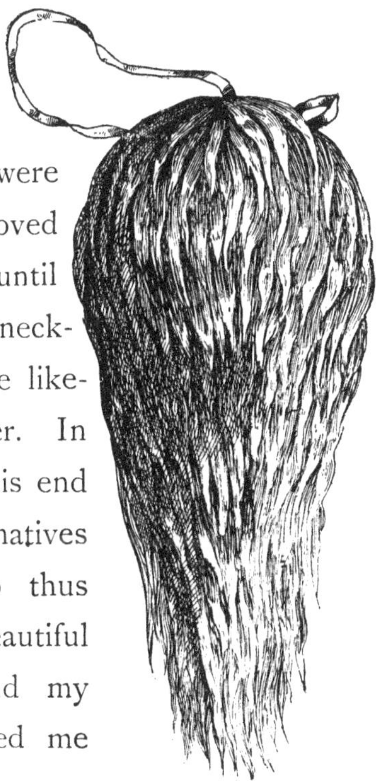

The large crystal multicolored stage jewels covering the gown were from time to time, one by one, removed to bestow upon the covetous natives, until not one remained. My bracelets, necklets and rings and shoe buckles were likewise relinquished in the same manner. In truth, the bawbles were taken with this end in view, notwithstanding the simple natives deemed my apparent willingness to thus lavishly bestow upon them my beautiful jewels as a personal distinction, and my generosity, in their estimation, ranked me in the light of a millionnaire.

DANCING WIG MADE OF COLOBUS MONKEY WHITE FUR.

Whatever is the reason I could not ascertain, but whenever a native presented me with an article, if possible, he or she would keep a bead or two or an ornament or a little bit of chain, no matter what, only some bit of the present they always were desirous to withhold.

Mireali was highly delighted with a powerful sunglass I presented to him, after showing him how the sun's rays could be focused to set fire to dried leaves, tow, or paper. He evinced great excitement, exclaimed in glee, "Bébé Bwana, now I can stand on one mountain and burn Mandara's *boma* and plantations on the other mountain."

In evidence of homage, Mireali danced for me the *rua*, in which he is a past master. This dance consists in floating out in the air a long piece of cotton cloth, eight or ten yards long, one end attached to the body, and whilst the dancer prances and leaps about he keeps his arms swinging and casting out in a loop the cloth, striving to have it describe a circle, and when this is achieved the dance is at an end. He was so graceful, agile, and skilful, he put his competitors to shame. Upon this occasion the moon shone with its fullest radiance, and the atmosphere seemed to palpitate with ineffable effulgence, clear dazzling white, as the white of burnished silver; and as Mireali danced, his shadow fell and flitted in a weird, spectral way. It has no parallel in my memory.

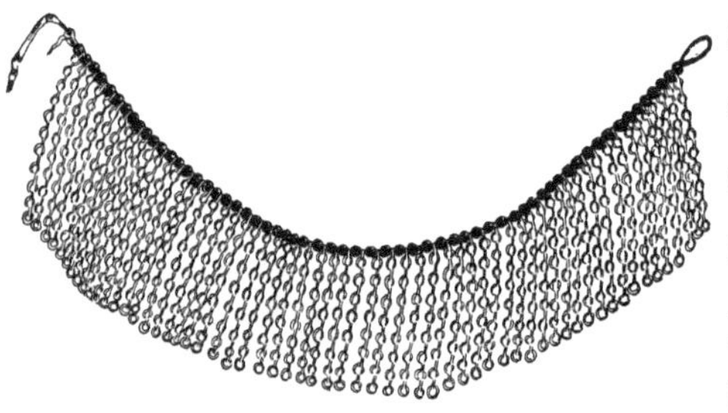

DELICATE CHAIN NECKLACE.

Before departing from Marungu it was my good fortune to take a photograph of a very large group of Mireali's court. The simple, hospitable folk had gathered about my tent to implore me to remain, urging, "Stay, Bébé Bwana, stay; you shall be more powerful even than all the sultans; you shall have all the plantations, all the cows, and sheep, and goats. Stay, Bébé Bwana, stay." They never knew they were thereafter to be my photographic subjects.

Mireali dolorously came to me the morning I made my adieus, with the frame of a large compact English umbrella, with a conspicuous silver handle, but lacking every vestige of cover,—the remains of a gift from an American sportsman, and which had, in its normal condition, served during two years to constantly shelter Mireali from the sun and much-detested rain. He deplored the loss ceaselessly and in pitiful tones of yearning queried, "Can Bébé Bwana make it new?"

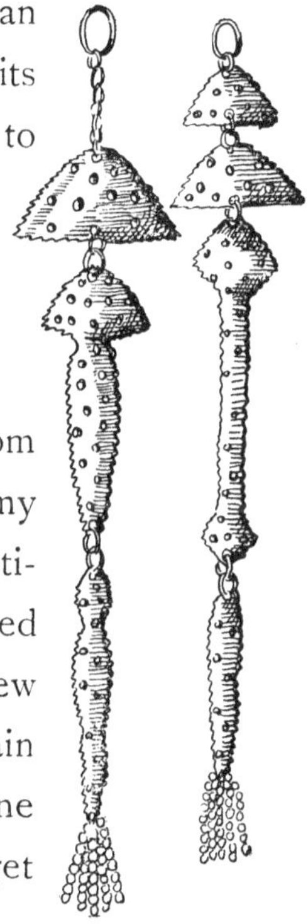

"No, Mireali, but I will send you one from London; meanwhile you shall have one of my red sunshades." He promptly took the substitute, evidently liked it very much, pronounced it "*m'zuri sana*" (very beautiful); after a few circumspect minutes, half ashamed, he again approached me and hesitatingly asked, so none might hear but me, "Bébé Bwana, don't forget the other *mwavuli* (umbrella)."

USERI BONE EAR-RINGS.

After leaving the boundaries of his province, one of his runners came breathlessly into my encampment and delivered a message from Mireali; the import of it was, "that Bébé Bwana must not forget the promise given to her friend Mireali about the *mwavuli*." They are so child-like in their dread of disappointment. Even this superior man could not permit me to get beyond the reach of his voice without this parting admonition.

Whilst at Marungu, a Wa-Kiboso messenger, attended by several load-bearers, came to me from Sultan Sina, carrying a leaf, bearing the imprint of a blood-dripped hand, and bringing as tribute a white goat and a sheep, the latter so fat it could scarcely waddle, and its clumpy tail dragging on the ground, akin to the sheep Herodotus describes, and a superb spear and shield. He was dramatic in gesture and almost classical in figure, with an impressiveness in diction. Although his language was undoubtedly circumscribed, he transcended the limits of mediocre when he announced, "I am as Sultan Sina, who sent me, who bade me show you this leaf, and bring you this goat and this sheep and this spear and this shield, to let Bébé Bwana know Sina, who sent me, is the friend of Bébé Bwana." An emissary, sent by a chief, by a sultan, or merely by a master, has no individuality for the time being save that which identifies him with his master, until acquitted of his task; and in indicating such an emissary, it is customary to

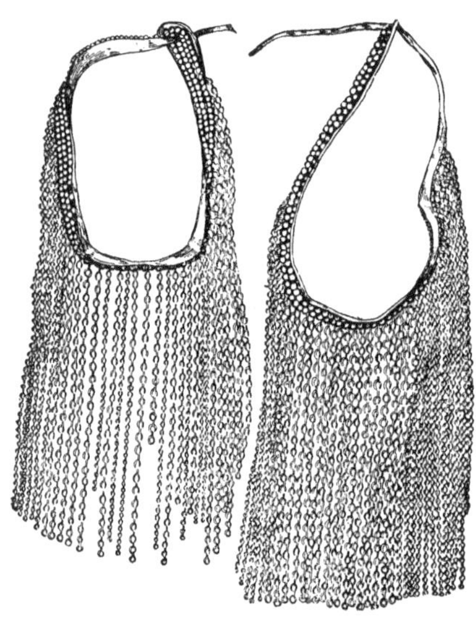

LONG CHAIN NECKLACES.

say, "Mireali, the man," or "Fumba, the man," which is equivalent to saying, he is the messenger of the Sultan Mireali, the Sultan Fumba, or whoever may have despatched him. These messengers have the most marvellous gift of transmitting not only the import of the message, but literally word for word, as it has been imparted to them by those who have sent them; they are perfectly imbued with the sender's thought before starting as an envoy by being obliged to repeat the message until they have proficiently committed its letter and significance.

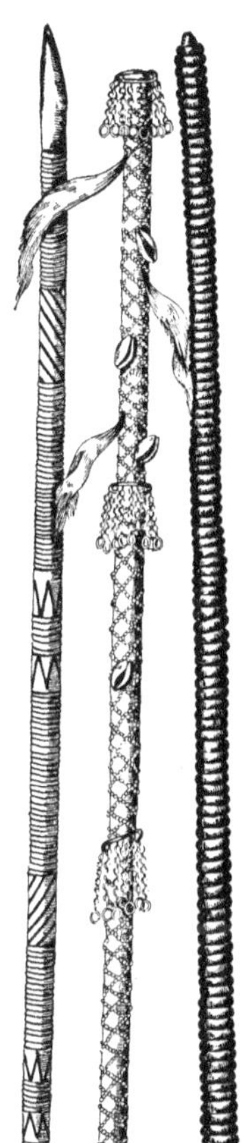
MOSCHI CARVED WOODEN STAFF. MASAI DANCING WAND. STAFF COVERED WITH IRON RINGS.

I found it an admirable thing, when instructing an interpreter respecting any important message, which was to be conveyed in my presence to the natives, to have two interpreters present, and never heed the one who was interpreting, but watch the play of expression over the countenance of the one who was listening, and at the slightest intimation that the spokesman had deviated from my instructions, surprise would involuntarily play over his countenance, and I would check the man and refer the matter to the telltale listener, when he would take up the thread of discourse. In turn I would watch the other man, who would, in a similar manner, reveal his comrade's errors in discoursing, who would likewise be checked and the task recommitted to the first man. In this way I avoided many misunderstandings, and found it an infallible process of discovering carelessness or trickery. When anything was lost on the road, and it was necessary to send back for its recovery, three men were usually selected who were not chums, and full of distrust for each other, in order to make sure that the article would ever be returned, if found.

In my caravan were a certain number of fleet runners who were allotted places near the van and rear, in order that I could communicate with Hamidi, who always brought up the rear, and *vice versa* he could communicate with me. It was a pretty sight to watch these runners disencumbered, with only a gun and a staff, leap and bound through the grass and over the rocks, covering the distance like a whirlwind, and return without seemingly having stirred their pulses a particle; and like all human beings in any sphere of life who excel in any one thing, they were proud of the renown they receive from their comrades for their practised skill.

CHAPTER XVIII.

CHARACTERS.

LONGING for music, I was surprised to hear a dainty little twanging, like that which ensues from thridding a harp-string. It was produced by tightening a bow-string made of sinew and striking it with the arrow, which would rebound and strike rapidly the string before a new blow was given. The tones were harmonious. Most of the native guides have the trick of music-making. In passing through Sultan Fumba's sultanate, I procured a pan pipe, sweetly played by a native, and these two musical instruments were the only native ones I saw or heard, yet the natives accepted with delight mouth music boxes I gave them.

Sultan Fumba is considered the most avaricious sultan in East Africa. However, before leaving this quaint character, I was able to persuade him to give me every article of clothing he wore ; even his crown or cap, which was the same as receiving the crown of a European king without his powers. He has for a prime minister the most crafty creature, who is capable of doing anything that is sneaking and mean, but certainly incapable of doing aught that is manly. I secured an admirable portrait of him, his prime minister, and his courtiers. Although he offered every inducement to get me to tarry in his *boma*, I felt safer and happier to place a long distance between his *boma* and my camp, and so were my men, one of whom advanced the following:—

"Bébé Bwana, natives no goodee, no cleanee, smell very bad, no washee; Bébé Bwana, me no likee, no, no, no!" Ramezan accentuated this protest by significant gestures, clutching his nose between his thumb and forefinger, in order to more fully acquit himself of the meaning which his limited English vocabulary would otherwise fail to reveal. Cunningly, after watching the effect upon me, he insinuatingly added, "Bébé Bwana, Ramezan cleanee, very much cleanee, aie? Bébé Bwana, give me soap, me go river, me wash table-cloth, me wash self and cloths. Bébé Bwana, me take *bunduki* (gun), aie?" All this roundabout method was his naïve way of getting a favor from me.

In truth this boy was scrupulously cleanly, not only in his person, but in his service to me; away out on the plains or in the jungle or in the mountain fastnesses, it mattered not when or where, daily he served my meals with as much precision and ceremony as though in civilized lands. Even when I was compelled to eat from the top of boxes piled

SULTAN MIREALI'S SUBJECTS ATTEND MY FULL-DRESS RECEPTION.

upon one another, and sat upon one, the dainty cloth was spread, the napkin placed, and the usual array of knives, forks, and spoons, and the enamelled dishes changed for each course. Ramezan had for an assistant a young fellow of most general accomplishments as a body servant and steward, called Baraka. These two attended to my personal requirements, and were pretentiously dubbed stewards, looked after my tent when once set, and, in fact, Baraka assisted the headmen and *askari* in putting it up and taking it down, as well as in arranging and collecting small luggage and all articles appertaining to my personal household. Neither of these servants were expected to carry loads, and were ever close upon my heels ready to serve me. Ramezan carried my gun and cartridge belt, and a bottle of coffee to quench my thirst, his own umbrella, and sandals and calabash. Baraka carried one of my cameras, a small medicine case, my rain cloak, a silk gown, extra wraps, and my umbrella when not in use.

RAMEZAN, GUN BEARER.

BARAKA, MY STEWARD.

Certainly my gun bearer had something of a load with the gun, and thirty rounds of cartridges in his belt, besides his own personal effects, which he would string about him. They always dressed in pure white, with little white caps, and did not carry their own mats.

Put my head outside of my tent flap any hour of the day or night and call "Boy!" instantly back would come the answer, "Sabe!" (sir); and to the very last of my *safari* not one of my men ever learned to answer me other than "Sir." Even my intelligent interpreter Josefe would reply from the distance when I would signal to him by sounding my whistle, "Aye, aye, sir!" and he never approached me without touching his hand to his head and presenting arms, extemporizing for a weapon his walking staff.

The natives and general porters had encompassed the bizarre situation by calling me Bébé Bwana. My fine head-

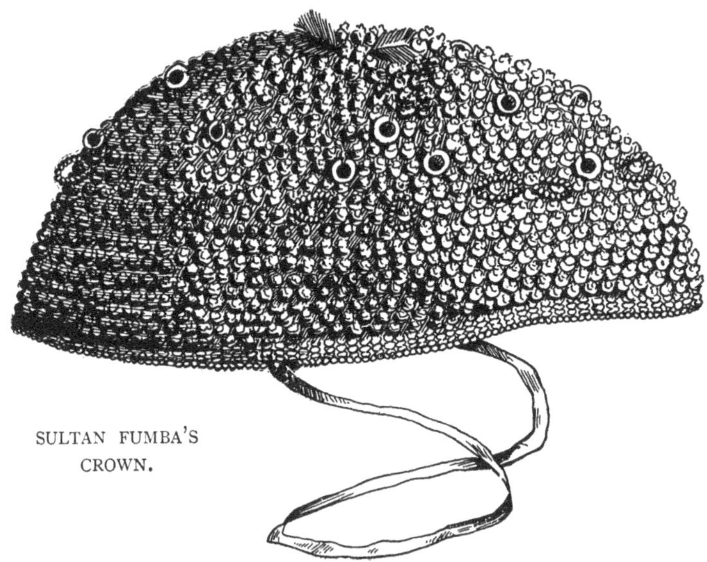

SULTAN FUMBA'S CROWN.

men, with an assumption to show their superiority upon occasions, would struggle to say "Bébé Bwana Sheldune." They never could seem to reconcile my sex with my post, which, in their eyes, indubitably belonged to a man, and I was at first abashed to realize that their natural protest kept inadvertently cropping out in one way or another, despite their obvious effort to conceal their preconceived idea of common propriety according to the only usage they knew. It is, therefore, with a sense of personal pride during my trying expedition, surrounded constantly by these black porters, the majority of them culled from the roughest specimens of natives, deficient in intellect, devoid of any certain knowledge as to the proper attitude that men should assume to a white woman, and many of them full of brutish instincts, that they universally treated me with deference and obedience. Never during my *safari* did I see an indecent action on the part of my porters, who were, of course, more or less subservient to my commands, but on the part of the natives, who were unrestrained and free to do as they listed. All this I firmly hold was due to a certain *régime* I adopted, based upon the combined experience of many wise explorers, and an innate conviction that individual prestige, consisting in personal dignity and self-respect on the part of a leader, must be maintained wherever you may be, if you expect to inspire those whom you aim to guide and command with your personal importance and might. Nothing careless is admissible; no slur of words; no meaningless threat; no hesitancy; no shirking; above all, a certain amount of silence which the natives and the ignorant regard as reserve force. A leader is a target of observation and unmeasured criticism from the lowest to the highest in the caravan; and unless on guard at all times, striving to consistently bear out the ideas porters, *askari*, headmen, and body servants adhere to as becoming a master, in some guileless moment a single heedless action may cause the leader the chagrin of witnessing throughout the caravan a state of demoralizing insubordination. Insubordination in East Africa means a very hazardous thing — possible dissolution of the entire caravan, and ruination to one's plans,

SULTAN FUMBA AND SUITE.

if not much bloodshed. Inflexible strength of will is requisite. Courage, knowledge, dignity, directness of purpose, resolution, justice, and that most trying of all qualities, patience, and consideration for the condition of minds of those whose training and capacity are in contradistinction to your own.

Although allowing yourself to be swayed by reason, you must never vacillate or flinch when a difficult thing should be done. Scout hardships by sharing them, however; show appreciation when irksome service is rendered. Never brow-beat and sneer at shortcomings, but encourage and stimulate your men to their best, even if it is done by inciting a spirit of rivalry. When punishment is deserved, calmly order it quickly administered, however, not without premeditation, then afterwards do not persist in holding the culprit under the yoke of ignominy if he evinces a disposition to redeem his fault by good behavior. Zanzibaris hate to be kicked and cuffed about, any time preferring to stand up and take ten "sticks" to one kick or blow with the fist.

When hardships and utter fatigue pressed heavily upon all, yet it was necessary to proceed to some known spot where water could be had, I have said, "Where are the faithful men in my caravan, where are the brave, strong men who serve me day and night, among my tired, my thirsty, my hungry, my sick men, who will march all night to find water and rest to-morrow?"

Every man able to stand would push forward to the front and signify his willingness to continue the march.

For a long time I was unable to comprehend, when a long day's march was at an end, according to my judgment, if there chanced to be a stream fronting us or a hill just ahead, the men invariably manifested a disposition to cross the stream or ascend the hill. It proved to be from some notion of theirs to start fair in the morning, and in case of streams to avoid the discomfort of marching after an early soaking, for, as they quaintly say, "Better a stone for a pillow than for a burden next sun-up." The philosophy of this was beyond question soon, as the rains came tumbling down during the night, making the streams swollen, and torrential and difficult to ford or swim. The hill-tops were chosen simply to give to the entire caravan a vantage ground from whence to reconnoitre the country from all points, enabling them to descry attempted invasion of wild beasts, or frustrate the stealthy surprises of hostile natives.

Francez, a porter, who spoke English admirably, a fact I did not discover for a long time, used to eye me constantly and ever sought to pitch his little tent near mine. Notwithstanding his lips might be swollen and cracking and his throat burning with thirst, when we would reach a stream he never quenched his own thirst until he had proffered to me a gourd full of the sparkling water. So unremitting was his scrutiny of me and my every move, that, I confess, it at times became most embarrassing. Through his vigilance, one of my *askari* was discovered in the very act of stealing from my tent while he was on duty. Through his lynx eyes I was saved being assassinated, one night, when a thief crept into my tent to steal my gun, and was about to stab me, when he found I was awake and saw him. Francez was in my tent, like a flash, and almost strangled the poor wretch. He called my attention to various things, and brought me two prismatic caterpillars; their bodies were five inches long, white, and the nodules were prismatic, but the colors not very vivid. Unfortunately, I had no means of preserving them, nor, in truth, any other specimens. Another day he brought me a bird's-nest, like a tailor bird, and anon pointed out a lot of brilliant red crabs. He was also quite as much of a dabster in making fire with fire sticks as the natives. A native chanced to pass, the lobes of whose ears had been torn out by weighty ear-rings, and had been mended by cutting off from the ragged fracture a tiny slice of the flesh and joined with porcupine quills, and bidding fair to heal by "first intention"; this poor native was lured by Francez into my presence, and wheedled to taking out the quills and separate the broken parts to show "Bébé Bwana how it was done." He quaintly called my attention to some native women inebriated, and said, "They are black women; the white women never forget themselves any more than the black sultans."

It is a singular thing that the native women, when intoxicated, reveal a certain lack of dignity and helpless inebriation that the men escape. They seem thoroughly brutalized and helpless to maintain anything like personal dignity or self-respect; whereas a chief drunk is always a chief, he never loses the consciousness of his own greatness. I have seen a man, who appeared almost an imbecile under the influence of liquor, shake himself out of it all, roused into a sudden consciousness by some one exclaiming that another chief he was unfriendly to had greater powers than himself, and, with his returned rationality, condign the promulgator of such an idea to some great task, or exact a tribute of cows as punishment for his indiscretion. This peculiarity may be accounted for from the fact that the women let themselves go when they commence to drink, having no prestige to maintain, with no desire to overcome the intoxication, but rather to assist its progress. However, the next morning, after a nightly bout, they appear as fresh and sober as if they had never tasted their *pombe* cups.

However, drunk or sober, profanity is unknown, although they have a qualified equivalent in "you goat," "you cow," "you son of no man's virility." This, however, is the same among all peoples without a God, or a settled idol, or any idea of his Satanic highness. It is the privileged vice of those who know Christianity. Strange to relate, the natives never kiss, moved by tender sentiment. In lieu of kissing, they may be observed to clasp the palms of their hands spasmodically, and impetuously unclasp and press them wide open over the shoulders, across the knees, or upon the breast of the person they yearn to manifest their affection for.

Francez brought me, sewed up in a bit of snake-skin, a perfumed charm to hang on a tree facing my tent, to ward off an impending storm, and circled my tent several times, mumbling some invocation, scattering grass as he walked. This struck me as being very like the Japanese custom of hanging little paper messages, variously addressed, upon trees.

My regular caravan numbered one hundred and fifty-three persons, all told. The official roll call and pay list may not be entirely uninteresting to my readers; the names are phonetically spelled.

SULTAN MIREALI'S BOMA SURROUNDED BY SOME OF HIS WIVES AND SURIAS.

ROLL CALL.

PORTERS.

1 Hassan Hamis.
2 Tunda Yadi.
3 Oomara Mzuana.
4 Demas.
5 Hamis bin Afman.
6 Ali bin Hamad.
7 Semba bin Seligman.
8 Sadi bin Seligman.
9 Yabon Lelli.
10 Sadi Wadyuma.
11 Meni Youma Kebanda.
12 Suadi bin Youma.
13 Soda Wadiherie.
14 Hamis Wadi Suroro.
15 Baraka Montonana.
16 Hanna Amore Kombo.
17 Sadi Wadi Farodi.
18 Dosere Wampere.
19 Marico.
20 Unledi.
21 Munombe bin Kombo.
22 Hamid Unquezilla.
23 Selligman Mamwiina.
24 Baraka bin Seligman.
25 Furiozo Wadehaha.
26 Abdallah bin Selim.
27 Mabruka Imperia.
28 Kara (Samson of caravan).
29 Franczes bin Sadi.
30 Munisa bin Mufta.
31 Mari Marabo.
32 Zied bin Yuma.
33 Songoro Maneyega.
34 Sali bin Massib.
35 Usofo bin Umari.
36 Hassand Ballonza.
37 Fernza Mardaneff.
38 Sali Mhezila.
39 Wadzuna.
40 Farnza bin Sorora.
41 Ebosie.
42 Sali M'gazilia.
43 Manboy Wah! Shehongo.
44 Sadi bin Hamid.
45 Hamid bin Hamid.
46 Hamis Wadzied.
47 Francez (spoke English well).
48 Uled bin Yuma.
49 Hanamoura.

50 James.
51 Bryan bin Mousa.
52 Hassan bin Mufta.
53 Seru.
54 Sud Balleous.
55 Dahoma bin Sellim.
56 Munynamyezia.
57 Yana Hairy.
58 Yuma Wad La Edie.
59 M'Guya.
60 Marbruka Wadzie.
61 Magaza.
62 Hamis Sali.
63 Sadalla bin Seligman.
64 Yacont Samacie.
65 Yuma.
66 Fernza bin Muguro Mari.
67 Hamis Kombo.
68 Umari bin Abdallah.
69 Usinga bin Sali.
70 Usinga.
71 Winecomdo.
72 Feruse Ballons.
73 Min bin Gainie.
74 M'Selliam.
75 Uman bif Tuffick.
76 Sehaba.
77 Abad.
78 Umanie Wad Suboro.
79 Adie bin Hamis.
80 Hamad.
81 Abdallah bin Yuma.
82 Songoro (prey of lions).
83 Hamis Impera.
84 Wadyuma.
85 Kamonice bin Unsa.
86 Yuma Wad Sadi.
87 Nasib bin Ulali.
88 Mabruka Nufta.
89 Allamao Muongc.
90 Muntozo.
91 Kerv Voto.
92 Menahadi.
93 Sodie.
94 Menahazy.
95 Sali Mohozo.
96 Mugumbo Murarba.
97 Munya Shumarie.
98 Hassand bin Abdalla.
99 Hamis bin Adie.
100 Ferusa Surmari.
101 Alrnass.
102 Umari.
103 Simba Madmamba.

104 Abdallah bin Abdad.
105 Minw Hat-tib.
106 Mabruka Wad Hat-tib.
107 Ali bin Hassan.
108 Kermut (Clement, cook's boy).
109 Abdallah (cook).
110 Baraka (steward).
111 Ramezan (steward).
112 Lidia (woman).
113 Beda (woman).
114 Suzzan (woman).
115 Burt Hamis (woman).
116 Burt Hamis Mzuria (woman).
117 Abdallah.
118 Hamis bin Barcada.
119 Nedia Hamis.
120 Hamadia.
121 Songora bin Hamis.
122 Wadeyuma.
123 Demodio Sadi.
124 Almass.
125 Morboro du Kombo.
126 Sali bin Yongo.
127 Winum Shumaro.
128 Sani bin Abdulla.
129 Marbruki Wadi Haftu.
130 Hamis bin Adie.
131 Fenesa de Sumara.
132 Ali bin Hassand.
133 Simba Vidi Mombo.
134 Darfurf Wad Ballouse.
135 Gomorez.
136 Wadicu bin Huma.
137 Abdalla bin Hamis.
138 Winy Hastibu.

ASKARI.

Hamis bin Abdallah.
Hassan.
Adie.
Winikondo.
Safe.
Sumallie.

ASKARI (*continued*).

Maza bin Kombo.

Hamidi.

Hamis bin Baraca (Pagaiza).

(Took the place of the thief.)

NEPARA.

Hamidi bin Ali (headman of headmen).

Mabruka Keseysah.

Bin Allah.

Ali.

Josefe (chief interpreter).

Umbi Bwana (Masai interpreter).

In addition to these men there were usually forty others, comprised of volunteers and guides, and porters' slaves.

CHAPTER XIX.

SULTAN MANDARA OF MOSCHI.

IT would be impossible to narrate half of the rumors current as to the extremely crafty and atrocious deeds of the ambitious, brutish, and abominable Sultan Mandara; but without doubt he is much feared for his cleverness and duplicity. He is a keen, intelligent observer, and a deep student in his way, despite his marked deficiency in uprightness, justice, mercy, or morality. Proficiency in crafts and general knowledge in many diverse avenues have been and ever will be during his life the keynote of his power among the Chaga tribes. In the old feudal days of his tyrannical sway he was a treasonable disturber of all covenants between these tribes, carrying whatever he listed by force of arms, united with chicanery, and was seldom defeated. When he wanted warriors he levied on some minor tribe, who dare not refuse his mandates as they valued their freedom or their lives. He exercised his rights as potentate of Moschi with an imperious, overbearing despotism which has about come to an end. During my sojourn at Moschi he set a trap into which he himself untowardly fell, in order to possess a quantity of ivory he had received information of, through the good offices of some of his spies, certain minor sultan possessed and had buried, as is the African custom when treasure is to be safe guarded, awaiting an opportunity to dispose of it to a coast-bound caravan, and

MANDARA, SULTAN OF MOSCHI.

who had injudiciously discovered its hiding-place to prying eyes in his eagerness to sell it to one of my headmen.

Mandara's avarice set him to intriguing in a hazardous fashion. He sent his prime minister and other important headmen of his court to the unfortunate betrayed sultan to inform him that the Germans were now, as he knew, the rulers of Chaga land, and that he must pay a tribute of forty-five tusks

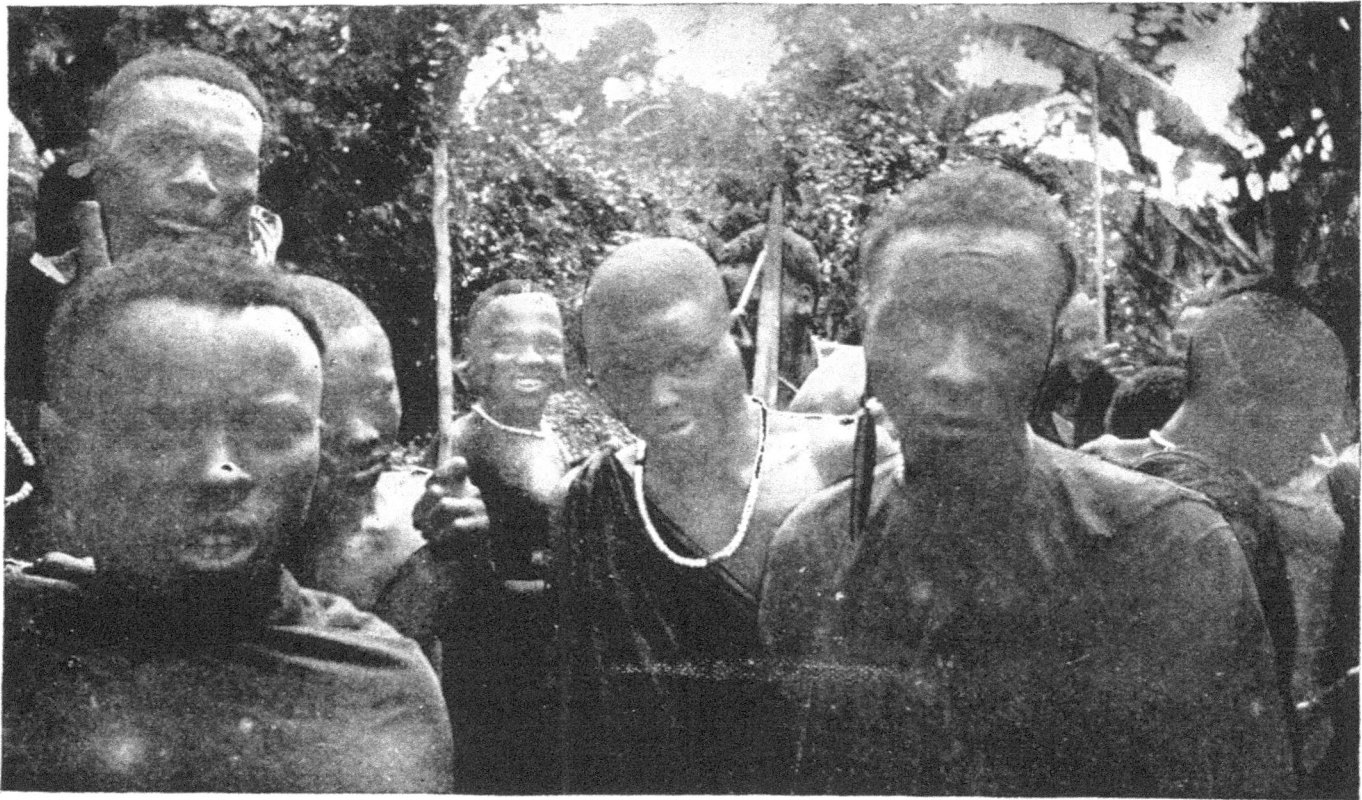

CONTEMPLATIVE NATIVES.

of *pemba* (elephant ivory) not under two *fasilla* (seventy pounds) in weight each and every tusk. However, as he, Mandara, was *well* with the Germans, he would graciously undertake to oblige the sultan, who was his blood-brother as well as his old friend, by conveying the ivory by his *safari* to the Germans. In a purely confidential way the prime minister was charged to convey to the sultan further information of the Germans' dealing with their tyranny, and that they were about to descend upon him and his tribe without mercy, because he had been tardy in sending this tribute, exactly as they had descended upon the Masai, "with their big guns that killed a thousand men at one boom." It sufficed. The ivory was immediately committed to Mandara's caravan, and the terrorized sultan entreated the prime minister to enjoin upon the great and powerful Mandara the necessity of using his influence to stave off the wrath of the Germans in his behalf, and he would send as a reward four fine milch cows. A few days after this occurrence, Mandara sent to the German station, saying such a sultan had sent through him a tribute to them of *twenty* tusks of fine ivory. They were received, but in a brief time the officer in command, Baron von Witzslaben, learned the true inwardness of the transaction through hearing of a document written by Mandara, — who is one of the few natives who write, — and demanded the instant disgorgement of his ill-gotten plunder. Seeing that he had overreached himself, Mandara feigned a severe attack of fever, — fever is always an excuse in Africa for disinclination, disability, and failure,—and pretended he could not then attend to the demand. Four German *askari* were sent with the officer's compliments, and the kind consolation that if his Highness was so ill and did not see his way to make speedy recovery before sundown, if the balance of the *pemba* was not forthcoming, it would not matter much, gunpowder tea would be served; and the German batteries were, with much parade, conspicuously turned in readiness upon Mandara's *boma* during the passage of the official message. Of course, his life would be worthless to him if he was so prostrated; death would be a relief to him. An answer came speedily back to the station from Mandara:—

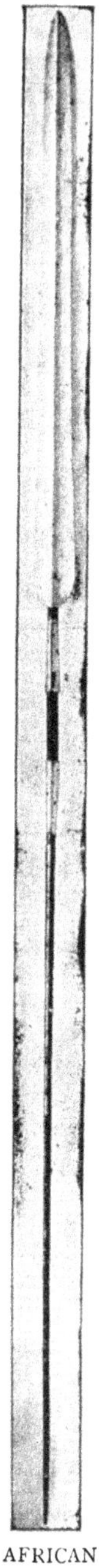

"Bwana Deitch, wait till noon, soon the *pemba* will be sent, and two cows as well."

Meanwhile Mandara's eldest son living—he is reputed to have murdered several of his sons, fearful that in order to gain accession to his possessions and sultanate they might be tempted to kill him—was enticed into the German *boma* and genteelly held as hostage for another offence committed by his tricky father, that the officer in charge likewise determined should be adjusted without evasion or delay.

Intrigue seems one of Mandara's fundamental traits of character, and if not already will very soon attain a climax the Germans will not tolerate. Either Sina of Kiboso, or Mireali of Murungu, are destined in the

AFRICAN SPEAR.

course of events to depose this arrant knave, if forsooth the inexorable Germans do not annihilate him and his tribe. Presumably he thinks, with his civilized brothers, "The king can do no wrong." However, the man is not totally bad, and should be judged in accordance with his environments morally and physically, and in a manner from his own standpoint, and the ethics of the code of the natives as they seem to be, and not from the remote standpoint of European enlightenment or by European sentiment or conventions.

Mandara had been exceedingly curious to see a white woman, and he had offered a gratuity of forty, eighty, and even one hundred cows if some Arab caravan would fetch him a white wife. This fact, which was patent to everybody in East Africa who knew aught of Mandara, had filled the white men whom I met with considerable apprehension lest I should be detained by him at Moschi or waylaid by his orders. I was very glad to be forewarned, and determined, in my own mind, to exercise every possible precaution and be more than guarded when I visited this sultan.

At Moschi I was the guest of the German commander, and he was very averse to my crossing the ravine separating his station from Mandara's *boma*, unless I went under the protection of the German soldiers. As my policy had been to go *solus* to visit sultans of importance, without the protection of any outside power, without government headmen or soldiers, I declined this proposition; and after much solicitation and many presents from Mandara, consisting of cows, goats, sheep, beautiful furs, I determined to visit him, and did so, attended by twelve soldiers and an interpreter of my own caravan. Baron Von Witzslaben said before I left the encampment, "Mark you, I have my cannon set; if you do not return within the two hours, I shall send a squad of soldiers to demand your delivery, and will throw Mandara in chains. If he refuses, I shall forcibly liberate you, bombard his *boma*, annihilate him and his iniquitous subjects. I consider it at best most rash that you are going with your paltry corps of *askari* and few attendants, but do not have any fear. I will protect you if occasion arises."

HELD IN BONDAGE.

I thought, as I was struggling down the mountain-side picking my way over the stream at the bottom of the ravine, and struggling up the path leading to Mandara's *boma*, with the natives of his tribe flanking the pathway in droves, that perhaps it *was* rash, and after a few words of caution given to headman and interpreter as to what I expected them to do in case we were debarred return, we had attained the gateway of Mandara's *boma* and found a hearty welcome awaiting us. All the important men of his tribe were arrayed in state finery, and they conducted me, with considerable pomp and many salaams, to Mandara, who was prostrate by paralysis, unable to move his body below his waist, excepting through the assistance of his attendants, in a dark, gruesome hut,—his Swahali house had been destroyed by Sultan Sina, of Kiboso,—stuffy and malodorous, as are all native habitations; he was lying on a long Arab *kitanda* (bed), covered with animal hides for warmth, and a smoky fire in the centre of the room. In his helplessness and emaciation, one could scarcely believe this man possessed the power to terrorize all the lesser chiefs of the Kilimanjaro district, and from recent accounts cause the Germans a large expenditure of gunpowder. He has lost one eye, but the other is so bright and alert, with such a strange furtive glance in it, whilst a sinister smile always discloses his teeth, with an amount of nervous energy and crafty look about his mouth, that one cannot help but feel that he is in the presence of a man of prowess and full of trickery and cunning, and capable of cruel subterfuges and brutal treachery.

He was fairly jubilant on seeing me, extended his hand, but in a piteous voice said, "Ah, now I have lived to see a white woman, and here I am so helpless." He immediately asked me to take off my gloves. He examined my fingers, and a singular coincidence occurred in the fact that I wore an old-fashioned seal ring surrounded with diamonds, which seemed on a casual glance to be a counterpart of the signet ring presented to him by Emperor William; and he said at once, "Ah, you are the friend of the king." I said, "Certainly, I am the friend of many kings, and I trust I may call Mandara my friend." And, a thing most peculiar, he seized both my hands and spat upon them. The blood flushed to my cheek, and in a moment of anger I rose to my feet and took my pistol from my belt, when my headman said, "Be content, Bébé Bwana: Mandara never was known to spit on any one's hands before in that manner; it is an evidence of homage; do not be angry." I will have more to say of this custom later on, but it was deemed the greatest evidence of humiliation and homage that this chief could have possibly paid me, loathsome as it seemed to me.

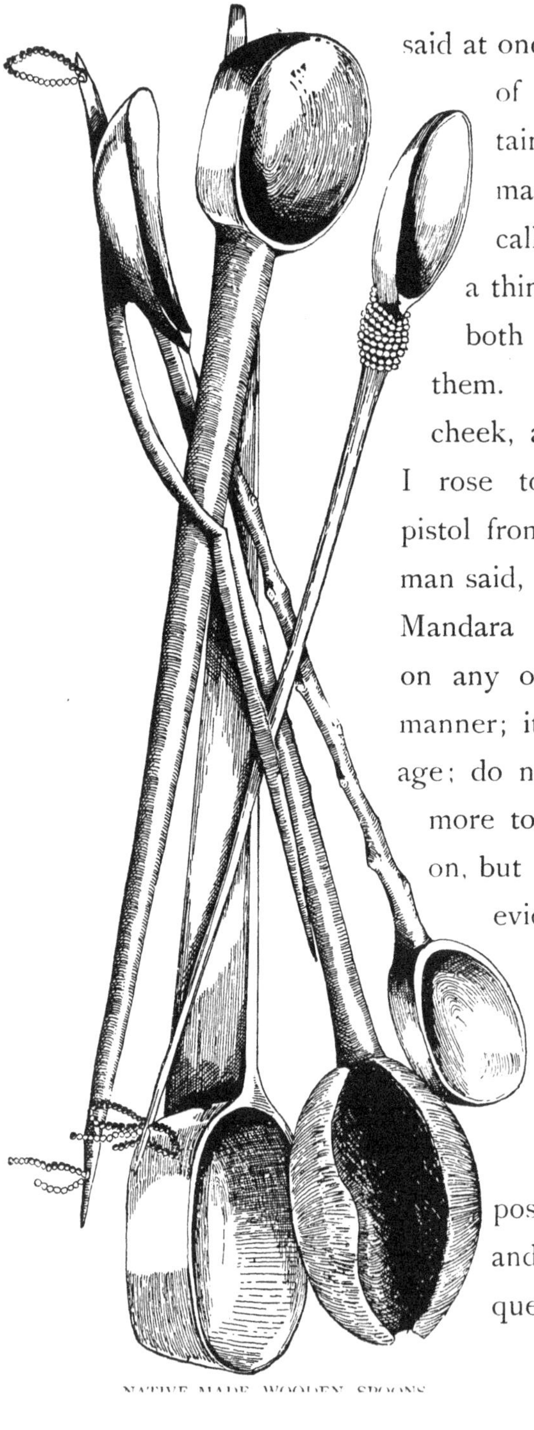

After resuming my self-possession, he turned to me and said, would the white queen let him see her hair.

NATIVE MADE WOODEN SPOONS.

I let it down and pulled it well about me, and he said, "Ngăi, Ngăi! it is the threads of the sun's light"; and he said, "May I touch it?" And waiving for once my rule of *noli me tangere*, I answered, "Certainly." He stroked it in a strange, caressing way, and called out to summon his wives to come and look at the white woman's tresses. When I gathered them loosely up and replaced the pins, he indulged in an undertone conversation with these women, who, overcome by curiosity, ventured to ask why I did not shave off my hair, as they did theirs; and Mandara sneeringly retorted, "It is too *mzuria sana* (it is too beautiful); why should she cut it off?" And then he continued in an incisive tone, "She is a white queen, and you are all slaves and black." He quaintly drew himself up in a helpless way on his elbows, turned towards me, and said, "I have expected you for many moons. The last moon, when it kissed Kibo, brought a message to me and said, 'The white queen is coming.'" I stopped him and queried, "Mandara, was the message not brought by one of your runners?"

And he laughed and said, "Perhaps, perhaps. But the message came, Bébé Bwana; I knew that you were to pay me a visit." To this I protested that, had he not been disabled, I should never have condescended to take the trouble to visit him. It was his place to have paid me a state visit, with pomp and ceremony, and I should have received him in court dress, such as white queens wear.

"Ah, ah," he dolorously replied, "to show you how much I,

Mandara, the greatest sultan of Chaga, care for this honor, I will give you the last piece of work I shall ever execute." It was a bracelet cut into diagonal strands on the surface, made of an amalgam of silver and pewter, which he placed himself upon my arm, and, assisted by one of his attendants, bent with long, slender pincers so that it clasped close, and said, "Wear this until Mandara follows the sun home, and nobody in his province will ever dare to do you harm."

He possessed many strange jewels, contained in a little casket he fingered over, that had been given to him by European officers, hunters, Arabs, and from various other sources, including the princely gifts sent by the Emperor William. After presenting Mandara with a jewelled sword and a ring he coveted, and I was on the eve of leaving, he requested me to give him my picture to put with a collection of prints he possessed of white women. "Yes, you shall have my photograph if you let me take yours." In a tone of injured vanity, he said, "But see, Bébé Bwana, I cannot stand, I cannot hold my spear, I cannot aim my *bunduki*" (gun); and he signed one of his wives to cast aside the large Hyrax fur robes that covered him, exposing his mere skeletons of legs. "Once I was the deer of the mountain; animal nor bird could go where I could not. I have stood on one mountain and killed my enemy who stood opposing me on another mountain. I, Mandara, am the greatest *fundi* living! I, Mandara, am the greatest warrior and fear not Sina, and fear not Masai! I, Mandara, am the greatest sultan."

He tried to get me to consent to take a photograph of his eldest son, the scion of his Highness, protesting that he had looked like the crown prince when he was his age. After much parley, I procured a sketch which is a very good counterpart of Mandara, the egotistical invalid, stripped of the glory of his own opinion. I sent him my promised photograph, accompanied by five hundred grains of quinine, and tea, sugar, and blankets and cloths he coveted very much, and received in return many additional beautiful presents, among which was his own personal fine spear, many goats, sheep, and tusks of ivory. Mandara is very boastful of a number of connecting natural caves beneath the hill he occupies. I was not permitted to pass the entrance of the first. The story runs that during an attack by his enemies, he has had them allured into these caves where a large posse of his warriors, there lying in ambush, charged upon them and killed several hundred. These caves recall the following circumstance: Mandara is the most dissolute sultan I met. He respects nobody's rights, and does whatever he lists; frequently has raided adjacent tribes, and captured the young girls and women, driving them into his harem like cattle, and when he has wearied of his captives he would magnanimously bestow them upon his favorites, who are debased enough to consider it a great favor and a decidedly economical plan in comparison to procuring wives by purchase.

ARAB FLAGS OF WELCOME.

The women were not fine, and looked dejected. The beads and other gifts I bestowed upon them were accepted with avidity. I was able to procure a woman's ample *kaniki* (blue cotton), beautifully embroidered with multicolored beads in Turkish designs. In consequence of the sudden cold winds that sweep over this district, men and women wear furs or hides as do the Masai, quantities of Chaga chains, and lustre beads, pewter and brass ornaments. Their burial customs are the same as all through Chaga land.

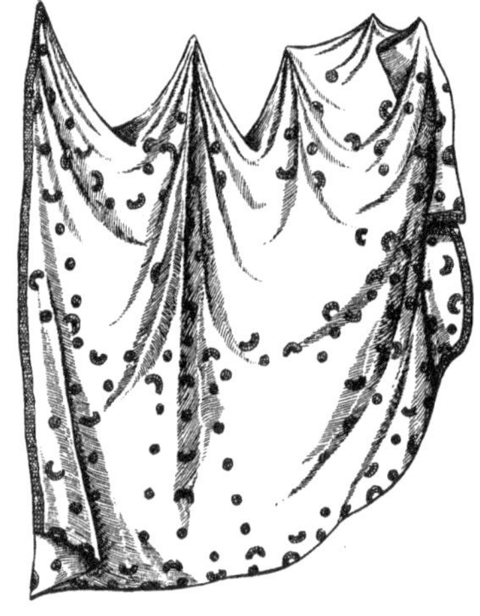
BLUE COTTON BEAD AND CHAIN EMBROIDERED WOMAN'S CLOTH.

They all seemed uneasy and dubious what attitude the Germans would take towards them; and well they might. I was able to procure a pair of native-made goat-skin bellows from Mandara's chief *fundi*, some fine bows and arrows, and several Colobus white and sable monkey-skins. I made blood-brotherhood with Mandara's son, which was the same as though the ceremony had been between the sultan and myself.

The invalid of my caravan was much terrified by a native woman's constant apparition before her tent during the night marches. This poor soul had lost her reason during a tragic encounter with lions in the jungles, whilst she and her son were in flight from slave raiders, I believe, and they were picked up by an English caravan and turned over to the

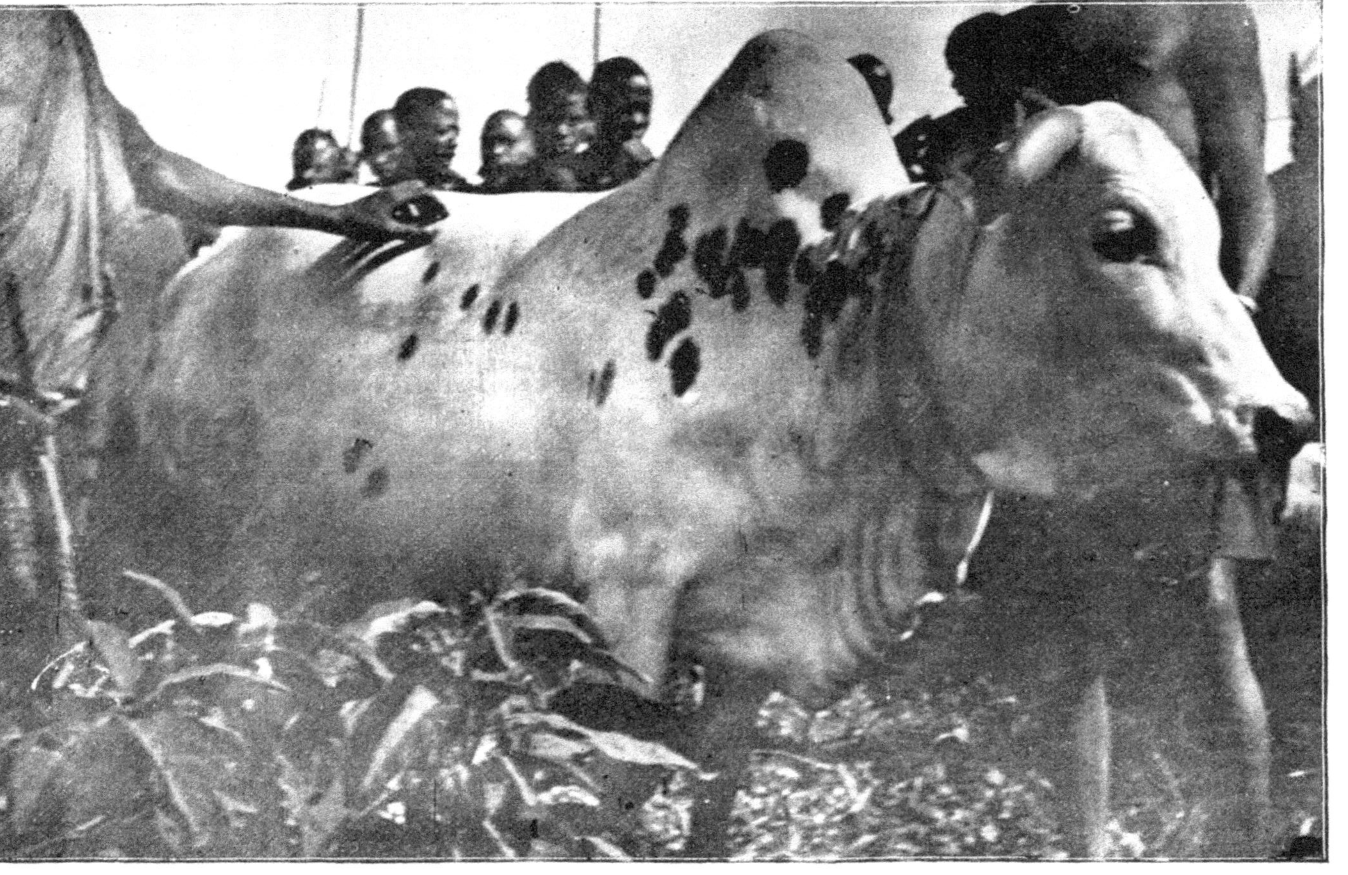

COW SENT BY MIREALI.

Germans. This mad woman, although harmless, had some vague idea coursing through her disordered brain to carry off the invalid to some sequestered place. Indeed several attempts were made during my *safari*, by natives, to kidnap this same fever-stricken one; augmenting my vigilance as well as my apprehensions and cares. Dr. Baxter had assisted me by medical attendance from Taveta to Moschi when the case had reached its crisis; however, the necessities of ambulance care could not be relinquished in this case until Pangani was reached when homeward bound.

One of the most touching incidents came under my personal observation whilst at Moschi, respecting a little native child, who had been captured by a slave-raider with other unfortunates, and freed by the German government. The missionaries are generally made custodians of the freed slaves, and receive from the government a pittance of not over five dollars (one pound), I believe, to take, educate, rear, clothe, and feed them. In this way it happened that the celebrated mission doctor, Wm. Baxter, who has spent the best part of his adult life in Africa, during a professional visit to the station where the little child, not over six years of age, had been placed, noticed him, and the child was immediately drawn by the doctor's kindliness and evinced love for children, and became deeply attached to him.

When the doctor had finished the duties of his professional visit, and returned to his own post, distant from the place where he met the child something like twelve or fifteen miles, and over a very difficult range of rugged steep foot-hills of Kilimanjaro, intersected by deep ravines, gulleys, and water courses, as well as being infested by wild animals, a day or so elapsed when one night he was aroused by his attendants, who brought a little native waif utterly worn

OUT OF THE FOREST.

out by fatigue and hunger. It was his little friend, who, unattended, had braved the terrors of night and prowling animals, and the hardships of a perilous journey, as he followed the tracks of the good doctor, guided only by his child's affection and innate instinct of trapper.

Touched as the doctor was by compassion for the devoted brave little soul, after the child had recuperated it was necessary that he should return him to his legitimate protectors. With much grief and disappointment to the child, and reluctance on the part of the doctor, this was done.

Before a fortnight had elapsed, again during the blackest hours of night the child put in an appearance at Moschi, the doctor's station,* having eluded the vigilance of his warders, and ignoring the terrors he had encountered during his former escapade. Heroic little chap! The doctor could no longer resist his pleading words of love and desire to be his *m'toto* (little boy), and took measures to secure the right of guardianship.

When I saw this child he was trudging up a steep hill, bearing on his staff just like a little old man, his face radiant with a welcome for the doctor, who had been on a long journey. What will the future of this child be, I wonder!

*Since this went to press the Germans have expelled the English missionaries from the German Kilimanjaro district.

CHAPTER XX.

FLEETING SIGHTS.

MARCHING over the southeastern foothill of Kilimanjaro, after leaving Moschi, towards evening, there was an ominous rustle of the leaves and movement of the branches in a shady bosk, which seemed to indicate the presence of a skulking animal or serpent. Investigation revealed three albinos who, in terror, were striving to gain concealment. Their hair was not the yellow-white discoloration found throughout Africa, prompted by individual fancy, although not tribal, produced by bleaching with lime, but it was pure dazzling white, soft and flossy; and their eyes were a very pale pink, the iris dilating and contracting with quick, nervous snap, resembling the action of those of white rabbits; eyelashes white and coarse like spun silver, and in striking contrast to the sickly unprepossessing ashy black of their complexions, which has no given place in the scale of colors. They looked dejected and debased, were quite deficient in the allure and elasticity presented by most of the East Africans. They were shy, and refused to hold communication with any of my interpreters or personally with me. I proffered to them tempting gifts, which they would not accept; finally, as they became over-embarrassed by our friendly overtures, they ran away and again hid in the adjacent bushes. Their teeth were filed in points and stained brown with nut-juice. Low of stature, and craniums sloping from the forehead to the apex, thick protruding lips and jaws, they resembled Aztecs; and certainly, from all physical indices as well as their deportment, seemed to rank as the lowest intellectually, if not the most degraded Africans met. What their tribe could not be ascertained; and from information subsequently gleaned, naturally leads to the conclusion that albinos are simply freaks of nature liable to occur in any tribe, yet tabooed by their own families and tribes, and by all other tribes. Per force of circumstances, based upon the stigma of nature, they become the denizens of sequestered places, pursuing a migratory and precarious existence.

Marvels trooped on all sides calling for attention and too often provoking alarm. It had, up to this period, been a keen disappointment that we had not seen, even at a distance, elephants. Struggling down the deep dip of the hills into a ravine, when the van of my little army was in the bottom, which made the crotch between the hills, and the line of men extended over a mile behind, so that the last man's head had not been seen over the brow of the hill, elephants' fresh tracks were before me. My first thought was to get a photograph, if they should put in an appearance; then with a sportswoman's pride my heart swelled with the idea I could possibly get a shot at them; this was absurd, with only rifles of small calibre. A crush and crash and heavy thud of the ground put my Zanzibaris' hearts and mine too in pawn. The quadrupedal earthquakes were emerging from the trees and about to cross our path. In wild dismay I cast a hasty backward glance to see how the Zanzibaris were going to behave, and there was not one single human creature in sight; it seemed as though the earth had swallowed the entire caravan, not even a human sound. I stood alone in my glory! My knees relaxed, my spine gave way, and down I sank amid the tall grasses, terror-stricken. Elephant number one came in full view and beat about to the right and left, with his trunk in close proximity to me, evidently aware of the presence of aliens, but never paused, when snivelling and puffing hot breaths of infantile complaints came trotting after a baby elephant reluctantly following its sire, then came the ungainly mother, lashing the youngster into a quicker trot by slapping it on one side of its haunches, then on the other, with her trunk. They all three sniffed about and tossed their trunks into the air, and the male returned to round his small family up, but trotted off without desire to molest us. After a few minutes had elapsed, soot-balls began to blossom amid the foliage, and presently my loyal, leal, brave fellows emerged

AFRICAN STREAM SWUM BY CARAVAN.

smiling, chattering at the top of their voices about the *tembo* (elephants). A wandering band of hunters, evidently on the trail of these elephants, passed us during the day; they carried loaded spears with huge barbed poisoned arrowheads, which they throw at the elephants, but always strive to get back the loaded shafts when the elephants are brought low, as they are difficult to make and invaluable.

The keen sight of the natives is astounding as exemplified by native guides. A guide would say, pointing, "Bébé Bwana, very soon comes such or such a mountain, or vine, or plain, or village." And I would strain my eyes striving to penetrate the limitless spaces, unable to descry the slightest indication of the aforesaid, or the slightest premonition of the appearance of a caravan he might aver was coming; neither could I with my field glasses espy a single object to verify his assertion. However, in due course of a day or two's march we would be in full view of the announced object, or within shouting range of the caravan. There is just one cogent objection to offer on this point: may the natives not be so well posted as to the physical aspect of the country, and familiarized with such by constantly traversing it; and may they possibly not have learned from experience that the *mzungu's* caravans march at a certain rate of speed and are most likely in a given time to reach a point they know as a fixed fact, or that a caravan, rumor has bruited is *en route*, will be met? or can it be that these naturals actually have that same keenness of vision peculiar to birds and some wild animals, and in some marked individual cases extremely acute? Another remarkable trait, or gift, which it would seem is an attribute possessed by all native peoples, is their acute faculty of hearing. The native guides, like the North American Indians, would sprawl flat on the ground and press their ears close upon it, then announce with a degree of accuracy certain discoveries: "a herd of buffalo," "simba," "zebra," "elephants," "a *safari*," "natives," "water."

At Lake Jipo, and, in fact, on the banks of various streams, personally I distinctly heard men talking in a low voice over the water from the opposite bank, by sending the voice close to the water's surface, and even heard them speak across ravines from the edge of one precipice to the other. The latter denotes some peculiar vibrant qualities of the atmosphere, whatever may be the secret of the former. On all sides could be heard the laughter of merry girls and *léon* (lads), and the voices of men and women from distances which would prove a rarity or peculiarity in the carrying properties of the atmosphere.

Water seemed to be my African ordeal. Shouts and yells are always in order with Zanzibaris on *safari*, and only when particularly vociferous does a leader heed them, although there is usually an intonation that is significant when prompted through peril.

A great shout of warning from my followers rang up from the valley to me, as I was cautiously picking my steps along a customary goat-path on the mountain-side. Although not easily flustered, their repeated yells and wild, significant gestures, I must confess, slightly alarmed me. The thought flashed through my brain that possibly I might be on the eve of stepping into some gorge or trap unseen by me but discernible to my followers from below. As their yells continued, I deemed it wise to pause and ascertain the cause of the augmenting commotion, so I wheeled around, and planted my back against the craggy mountain-side. At this act their yells redoubled. I demanded an explanation. No answer came, none was needed. The rains of the night before had gorged the usual water courses and, as an overflow, rushed in a perfect deluge down upon me where unwittingly I stood. It was only by crouching upon the ground and clutching the scant shrubbery that I kept from being swept over the steep side to the bottom of the ravine in the belching waters. It was over in a moment. My sense of the ridiculous, together with thankfulness for my escape, put me in such good humor that even the terrified porters seemed to catch the contagion of my merry mood, and were never so light-hearted as during the remainder of the day after this incident which threatened danger to their leader. Although drenched to the skin, an hour's march in the sun made my clothing as dry as usual. Each day every garment became saturated with perspiration, the heat was so intense, and great caution was required to avoid sudden chill. When we halted I always put on an additional garment, a long silk gown which was carried by Baraka or Ramezan. Another thing I must confess, that I was just feminine enough to feel more comfortable to have my short travel-stained frock well covered down to my feet when standing about among my porters. My woman's costume was never a hindrance to my progress, and I cannot conceive how masculine attire would have in any way been an advantage to me.

This brings me to state that there is a certain recognized distinction in the native women's costumes, which has as subtle and significant an import as the sleeves of the Japanese women's *kimonas*. A Taveta or Chaga woman who is dissolute with Swahali caravans usually wears the cloths of the coast tribes, and is more or less stigmatized by the more conventional of her own tribe. This, too, from no high sense of virtue, but from tribal prejudice, based on the fact that the woman has bartered her favors to porters or to aliens; hence therein resides the secret of her disgrace.

Ideas of hospitality among natives are of a very singular strain. If one sultan visits another sultan, or a man of importance another, or even friend visits friend, the host puts at his guest's disposal one or more of his own wives, and allows him general freedom throughout his home. These civilities are commonly interchanged throughout Chaga land as well as at Taveta.

A quaint sight presented itself during a little call upon a chief's family. A she-goat with her kids bleating about her as she stood over a native baby who was laid comfortably upon a sheaf of grass suckling it, letting her own young await their turn, when the adopted baby should be satisfied; presently the child slept, and the goat cautiously picked up her feet and backed away without disturbing its slumbers. This goat returned at regular intervals to see if all was well with her charge, and was ready to answer its demands when hunger's cry called to her.

A native promenaded before me, shaking his head in order to display his elaborately dressed hair, plastered with grease and red clay. He expressed entire willingness to dispose of it for a stipulated amount of beads, wire, and cloth. Whilst awaiting the tonsorial preparations, it occurred to me to inspect the man's head; the revelation of its animated condition compelled me with regret to refuse to carry out the bargain.

The difficulties of photography in a tropical country like Africa, during the rainy season, when I visited it, are obviously great. Negatives become affected by the heat and the moisture, and a fungus growth will develop upon them which, if not entirely effacing the picture, certainly produces regretable blemishes. However, there is nothing which puts a traveller's narration so much in evidence, or constitutes so admirable a syllabus to refresh the memory of passing events, as photography, good or bad. The place one visits for the first time, for example, my circumnavigation of Lake Chala, and the photographs taken, cannot be discounted by any contradictory statement prompted by jealousy or incredulity. It is to be regretted that the glowing colors of the foliage, which is so multifold, and the gorgeous floral effects, as well as atmospheric effects, cannot be reproduced; and then, too, the lack of artistic focus, unavoidable in instantaneous pictures, deprives the view of perspective, and when a representation of grass over ten feet high is in the foreground, looking across a plain fifty to one hundred miles wide, with a mountain several thousand feet high as a far-away background, or rather the central point, the effect is somewhat distorted and disappointing. Nevertheless, it serves a purpose far transcending the force of mere description.

The natives' horror of being photographed makes it most difficult to obtain satisfactory portraits of them. Once, and only once, with their knowledge I held up my camera before a group of natives, employing the photographer's fiction to attract their attention, "Look here and you will see a bird fly out." The result justified the deception. Their good-natured, laughing phsiognomies depict anything but brutality or savagery.

Glass negatives are constantly in peril of damage, gelatine is liable to melt or mildew, and the necessary chemicals to develop at once the negatives are too frequently utterly spoiled by the atmospheric conditions. There is much to be accomplished in perfecting photographic paraphernalia for tropical use.

It had fully been my intention to take a phonograph, despite its unwieldiness, but at that time there was no guaranteed surety that the wax cylinders would withstand the climate, and the project was wisely abandoned on the

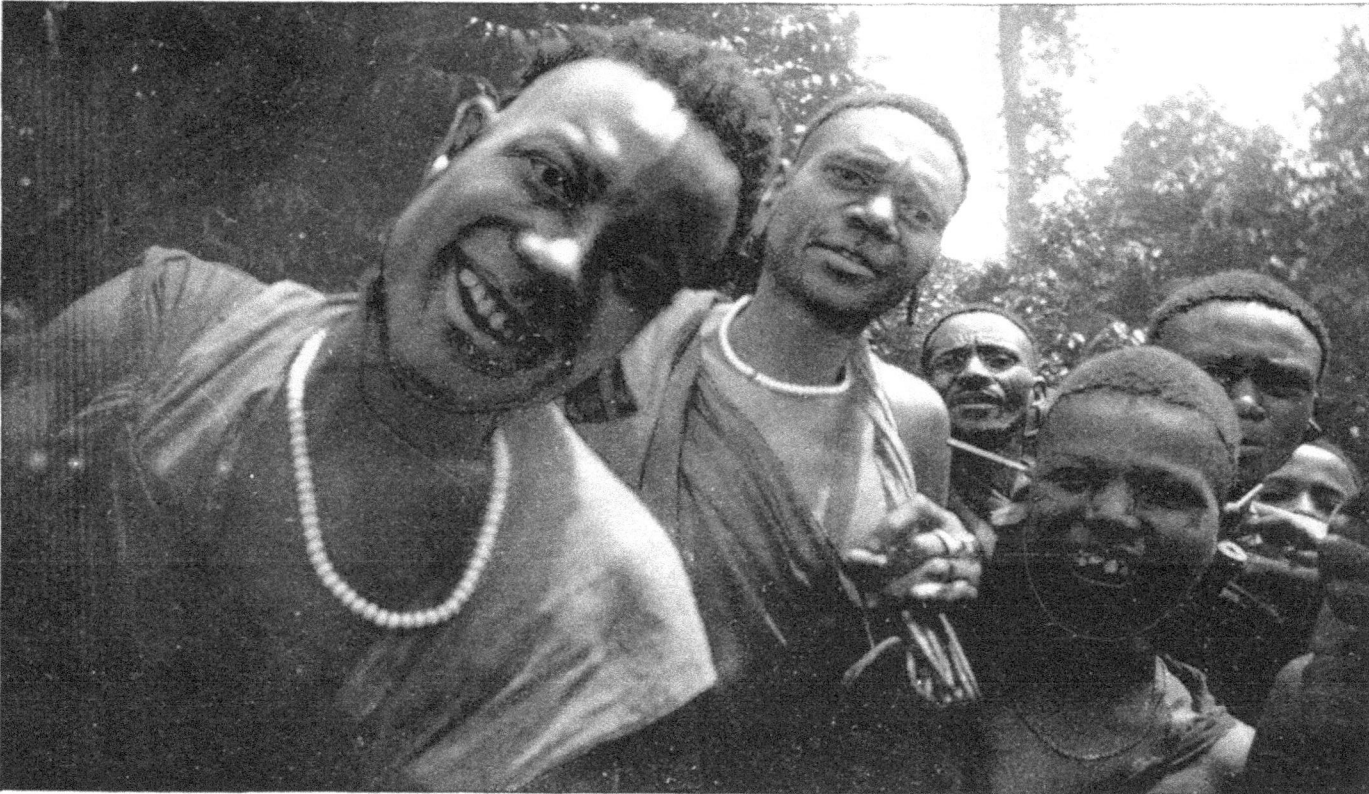

PHOTOGRAPHIC FICTION.

advice of skilled electricians. The Sultan of Zanzibar was the possessor of a phonograph which he kindly proffered for my use, but this instrument was not in working order; moreover, I naturally declined the responsibility entailed, fearful it should be damaged. Now I am quite convinced it would have been worse than useless, terrifying the natives to such an extent they would have stigmatized me as a mistress of *black art.*

CHAPTER XXI.

HOMEWARD BOUND.

OUT of the German fort at Pangani, the moment the first gun was fired and the reveille beat, I ordered my porters to carry me, only too glad that the night of dread and suffering had at last ended, and eager to outdistance the commander's limit of power before he could prohibit my egress.

The mosquitoes had martyred me; my entire body was mottled and burning from their merciless stings. In my utter helplessness, for the first time I relinquished a thought or a care as to my personal effects; in consequence, for the first time, articles disappeared.

Alack! when within a few days' march of Pangani, I met with the unfortunate accident which so nearly cost me my life. At the time there were nothing but German swamps and unpicturesque stretches of valley country elongated between distant mountains, and, as I experienced a slight degree of fatigue and natural reaction, deemed it a sensible thing to husband my strength, betook myself to my Palanquin, and allowed myself to be carried.

Bent upon accomplishing some detailed work and arranging botanical specimens, I paid too little heed to the construction of an extemporized tree bridge. As it was the rainy season, the sap was well up in the trees; those

PORTERS TESTING THE BRIDGE.

selected on both brinks, and felled for our purpose, looked fair and sturdy; and when duly strapped together in the middle, and all was ready, a number of porters were sent ahead to test the structure; they crossed safely. I should have walked across, however, without a thought of danger. I allowed myself to be carried in my Palanquin; the bark proved to be unsound and slippery; my bearers maintained their footing with difficulty; when in the middle of the bridge, over the swollen torrent which noisily tumbled in its stony bed twenty or more feet below us, the bark peeled off from the logs, and the usually sure-footed porters were hurled with me down into the rushing waters, whereas they at their peril were dashed headlong into the dubious channel, and compelled to struggle for their lives. For a hazardous moment, only a moment, although time and space are so immeasurably elongated into eternities during like terrors, I was whirled about, protected from injury by my Palanquin, but with my head down and completely submerged in thick yellow water, in jeopardy of drowning. Several additional porters—for my bearers, poor fellows, had all they could do to save themselves—precipitously descended the bank and plunged into the seething waters and extricated me with great difficulty from the Palanquin in which I was helplessly buried beneath a confused mass of cushions, besides being under water.

Poor, affrighted fellows, in their wild efforts to carry me out of the water, up the steep rugged bank, hopelessly slipped and dropped me a second time, with serious injury to my spine, where I had struck the rocks. A second rescue, and I was carried, limp and helpless, as I thought permanently disabled, up the bank. When I had somewhat recovered from the shock, I realized that my life depended upon reaching the coast at the earliest possible moment.

Meeting the German officer at Massindi, where he had preceded me, I did not mention the fact of the disaster to him, although my helplessness was not possible to conceal.

THE COURT DRESS.

He took it for granted I had the fever, a very natural conclusion, as he was then stricken with the malady, yet proposed to extend his official journey back to a mountain village where the natives were rebellious; hence it did not excite his suspicion to know, notwithstanding illness, that I would, that I must, proceed on my journey.

To this point coin had been useless to me, and the remainder of my rupees seemed too small to meet the demands for the balance of the journey. I was given an order on the officer-in-chief at Pangani to refund me for the surplus loads I had gladly transferred to the officer then at Moschi, at coast rates, deducting the fifteen rupees a load for transportation, when I found coin would be required at the fag end of the journey. That claim has never been settled. However, another officer at a station later on answered my request sent by a messenger at night for one hundred rupees, which have been refunded.

By instituting frequent relays of sturdy carriers, — for many of my porters were without loads, who were induced by promises of extra reward to carry me in a light hammock, marching day and night, — one day they made the extraordinary distance of forty miles through the swampy country of Rufa. The German surgeons at the various stations were horrified that I should proceed in the dying condition they deemed me to be in. However, after using every effort short of force, and having exhausted all arguments to induce me to tarry and recuperate at Bomo and Lewa, the gentlemen were more than hospitable, and went so far as to compassionately tender to me personal care, cooking with their own hands delicacies, proffering and even loading me down with the choicest articles they had in store when I would depart. Some few of these German stations were comfortable habitations, though not quite finished, and the saw and hammer of the carpenters could be heard. It must be remembered that I was utterly powerless, and had to lie just where placed, dying, it seemed, by degrees, my poor brain half delirious; but the rule of my camp life had become so indelibly stamped that I knew enough to be silent unless sure of the words I was to utter.

Nervous dysentery had several times assailed me after leaving Chaga land, and now it caused serious havoc, and it was impossible to eat a bit of solid food, or taste beef tea or beef extract. Every day my distress and emaciation grew more apparent, and Hamidi and Josefe were constantly by my side, if, indeed, not assisting my carriers. They would lift me tenderly in and out of the hammock, fan me, carry an umbrella over me, try in every possible way to tempt me to eat, and encourage me when my vitality was about to ebb out. The tenderness and delicacy of these two men, as well as that of Ramezan and Baraka, I can never praise too highly. In fact, every man in the caravan developed unexpected traits of devotion and gentleness. My big man Kara was ever eager to serve, when a single-handed aid was required in carrying me through the swamps; and others, too numerous to mention, expressed in deeds their solicitude, and were fired with the desire to bring me alive back to the coast.

The vague remembrance of the salutes fired in my honor by the Germans still affects me in a strange manner—the country, the natives, the intermingling of so much military display, primitives and rattle of guns, my desperate condition, the deed accomplished, the narrowing down of my soul's desire only to return alive and receive the adulation of *the one* whose mortal lips are now silenced by a journey to that bourne where one goes, but nevermore returns to terrestrial haunts.

A CLANDESTINE MEETING.

To the officers and even to the good doctor I was so very uncivil. When proffered courtesies and medical attention, I was at once apprehensive that if I became either their guest or patient they could exercise in the name of humanity a warrantable edict based upon the fact that my condition was altogether too precarious to admit of my being removed from their hospital or fort. One thought possessed me, namely, to catch the steamer at Zanzibar and start home; the one boon I yearned for was to live at least until I should once more see my husband and reach my home.

All the chances seemed against me; the doom of death seemed upon me. Having hired *dhows* to transport us to the anchored ship off Zanzibar, although there was little wind, by employing sixty oarsmen the *dhow* I had embarked upon with about fifty selected porters, headmen, interpreters, arrived at the steamer in the unusual time during monsoons of twenty-eight hours; the rest of my caravan and implements followed a day later. With difficulty I was carried on board of the "Madura." Capt. Avern and all on board were shocked at my ghastly apparition. I was laid upon the skylight; all sorts of arrangements had been made to secure for me every comfort, and contribute to my well-being. Friends came to see me; doctors were consulted; and the late Capt. W. E. Stairs, who was just forming his caravan, full of compassion for his own expedition, which proved fatal to him, implored me to execute certain documents as he ventured to whisper to me his solemn conviction, shared by all, that I would die on the voyage. Upon my emaciated upper arms he slipped a pair of silver bracelets which only measured six inches in circumference. He exclaimed, "I never beheld such an object of physical ravages at Nelson's starvation camp!" In truth, I seemed to be surely dying from the sequences of the injury to my spine, starvation, and dysentery. After having escaped African fever — no, not actually escaped, for I find that I too have become a victim to that insidious African complaint — fever, what you will — from which seldom, if ever, any traveller in Africa escapes —

the craving to return. Africa is a hard but irresistibly fascinating mistress, holding fast with magnetic sway her votaries.

After a safe, although thrilling, venture among hostile and peaceful tribes, and a safe march through a difficult country, with only one dead and one thief left behind me, my heart

REPAST OF ARAB FAMILY.

bounding with delight born of success, it seemed a cruel fate to be thus disabled.

Despite my serious illness, so exhausted I could not articulate an audible sound, suffering excruciating agony, I feel a glow of pardonable pride, in which my friends and my sex must join me, in the fact that I personally discharged all of my men, and saw them disband, and that I made full settlement of every payable obligation connected with my caravan, as completely as though in the possession of my normal health. My misfortunes were not to end when embarked on the dear old "Madura," although every professional care and personal consideration were extended to me, and the after deck of the ship fitted up for my occupancy like a private yacht; reposing, in order to breathe, on the skylight day after day, semidelirious, one day a sudden gust of the monsoon lifted my mattresses with me upon them and hurled me against the iron stanchions of the ship's railings, and, but for the canvas sides, would have carried me into the ocean. My skull was fractured. The captain, surgeon, and officers at first thought it must result seriously, but the captain had personally provided for my use a couple of tons of ice, and its constant applications to my head kept down inflammation. Strange fact, I shall always regard this calamity in the light of a benefit, for it aroused me from a subtle comatose condition, which was gradually enshrouding my sentient being and chaining my will. Day and night through my distracted brain passed in review all of the incidents and the solicitudes of camp life. A little concert-hall song one of the porters used to drone out in broken English, in which the refrain was "Lady Locket lost her pocket," would come mumbling from my lips; anon some order would be cried out, and the personages haunting my delirium were the phantoms of those who had served me with such marked patience and loyalty during my *safari* of over a thousand miles. Various gifts and prayer symbols were brought to me by the headmen and principals of my caravan from their wives or from themselves. A curious incident, revealing the chance and odd juggling of life's course, occurred: awaiting my arrival was a Zanzibaris servant, known to many as Saala bin Osman, who desired to accompany me back to England, although he had but just returned to Zanzibar. He narrated with considerable pathos that he had become a Christian boy, and that his father and brother were dead, and that his Mohammedan friends would no longer tolerate him; in fact, that his life was in danger. Whilst his story was in progress, Hamidi, my headman, dressed like a satrap, in spotless white and crimson velvet and gold-lace, came with a troup of magnificent personages, who proved to be my working porters, transformed into Zanzibaris gentlemen of color. Saala and Hamidi exchanged glances, surprise broke over both faces, and they exclaimed

ARAB MUSICIANS.

in concert, "This is my brother!" And so it proved Saala's supposed dead brother was my trusted Hamidi. Had I ever dreamed I should have lived to reach England, I should cer-

WOMAN WATER-CARRIER.

tainly have brought Hamidi with me. Suffice it my voyage of horrors progressed; once more we were at Aden, then Port Said, and the local color changed; the sights and scenes assumed the guise of familiarity, and my condition was even more deplorable, and we sighted Naples.

With all the reserve force I could command I gathered myself together for the shocking ordeal of meeting my husband. A voice, that set my heart thumping, tremulously asked, "Does she live?" Ah, yes, she did live, and felt that from henceforth protected and safe, she would surely recover, proud and happy in the thought to be at last in sheltering, loving arms; and, more than all, success was imbued with a new glamour, for he smiled and in well-measured adulation approved.

"DOES SHE LIVE?"

Friends and the dear faithful Jacques overwhelmed me with such a welcome. The little town, the loved home, was redolent with a greeting, and brilliant with flags, among which conspicuously floated my own American flag, which had acted as a talisman throughout my *safari*. Weeks of suspense and agony, then my constitutional vitality asserted itself under the auspices of skilled medical care and unabated nursing of devoted friends and faithful servants, and once more I was well and strong. The rest has no place here in this volume, save in the few words in the dedication.

CHAPTER XXII.

AFTERMATH.

QUERYING was it worth while? After serious retrospection over the pros and cons, the expenditure of time, money, personal force, hazards, loss and gain, and finally facing as best I may the irrefutable sorrow which is upon me, requiring more courage to bear up under than all else which has befallen me, or can befall me, I am prepared to answer the query provisionally, without a tinge of cant.

Yes, it was worth while, if it lies in my feeble power after the quest I ventured to make to contribute something substantial towards the betterment and enlightenment of the natives, as well as to be instrumental in convincing their future rulers and teachers that more humanity and practical common-sense will be more fruitful. If the time, money, personal force, hardships, and ethnological researches result in putting into my hands useful productive work to do in behalf of the primitives, if in my future work I may develop those rare attributes of nobility and meritorious character which shall make me a worthy exponent of the philosophy and example of him whose name I proudly bear, then, I reiterate, it was worth while.

Jacques Sheldon

www.ingramcontent.com/pod-product-compliance
Lightning Source LLC
Chambersburg PA
CBHW031457270326
41930CB00006B/124

9781906393137